Managing Change

The ability to manage change successfully is an essential part of business. It is a skill that is much valued by employers, and it is therefore one of the most commonly delivered courses. This book helps you to understand three key activities for managing change: diagnosing, explaining and enacting. Both practical and action-oriented, it gives students and managers the tools they need to deal with the messy reality of change. It combines theory and diagnostic tools with practical examples that focus on actions and outcomes. It also includes short vignettes and longer cases, from a range of international contexts, for classroom study or for use on distance learning courses. *Managing Change* is written for advanced undergraduates and graduate students taking modules on change management, strategy and organizations. Its class-tested approach has been successfully delivered in a wide variety of settings, including over fifty executive short courses with FTSE-listed businesses.

Nic Beech is Dean of the Faculty of Arts and Professor of Management at the University of St Andrews, Vice Chair of the British Academy of Management and Lead Fellow of the UK Advanced Institute of Management. He has undertaken significant projects funded by the Economic and Social Research Council, European Union and industry partners, and his five previous books include *Human Resource Management: A Concise Analysis* (with E. McKenna, 2008) and *Managing Creativity* (with B. Townley, Cambridge University Press, 2010). He presents regularly to professional and business executives and teaches at undergraduate and graduate levels.

Robert MacIntosh is Chair in Strategic Management at the University of Glasgow Business School. He has worked with a range of FTSE-listed businesses, large public organizations and many small to medium-sized firms. In recent years he has co-chaired the Action Research SWG of the European Group for Organization Studies and been a Council member for the British Academy of Management, and he holds visiting appointments at Edinburgh Business School and the Universities of St Andrews and Strathclyde. Originally trained as an engineer, he has over twenty years' experience teaching and researching change management.

MANAGING CHANGE

ENQUIRY AND ACTION

Nic Beech and Robert MacIntosh

CAMBRIDGE
UNIVERSITY PRESS

CAMBRIDGE UNIVERSITY PRESS
Cambridge, New York, Melbourne, Madrid, Cape Town,
Singapore, São Paulo, New Delhi, Mexico City

Cambridge University Press
The Edinburgh Building, Cambridge CB2 8RU, UK

Published in the United States of America by Cambridge University Press, New York

www.cambridge.org
Information on this title: www.cambridge.org/9780521184854

First published 2012

Printed in the United Kingdom at the University Press, Cambridge

A catalogue record for this publication is available from the British Library

Library of Congress Cataloguing in Publication data
Beech, Nic.
Managing change : enquiry and action / Nic Beech and Robert MacIntosh.
    p.   cm.
Includes index.
ISBN 978-0-521-18485-4
1. Organizational change. 2. Organizational change – Management.   I. MacIntosh, Robert.   II. Title.
HD58.8.B432   2012
658.4′06–dc23   2011053272

ISBN 978-1-107-00605-8 Hardback
ISBN 978-0-521-18485-4 Paperback

For Linda and Rosie

NIC BEECH

For my beautiful wife, Anne, and our magnificent children, Euan, Eilidh and Eva. You are the source of all that is good in life, and I am at my happiest when at home and in your company. Thank you for your patience whilst I worked late, early and in between the things we were supposed to be doing.

ROBERT MACINTOSH

CONTENTS

PART D
EXPLAINING

PART E
EXTENDED CASES

FIGURES

TABLES

CASES

ACKNOWLEDGEMENTS

We would like to acknowledge the valuable contributions of those who have taken part in the development of the materials in this book. Across taught courses, workshops and various executive development programmes in a number of institutions, we have been lucky enough to receive help and guidance on what works well and how best to package what might otherwise be messy messages. In addition, we would like to offer our sincere gratitude to our colleagues at Cambridge University Press, particularly Paula Parish for her patience during the early stages of developing this book; Philip Good, Raihanah Begum and Charles Howell also helped with those parts of the publishing process in which we needed expert guidance. Finally, Mike Richardson helped to copy-edit the text, and any remaining errors are undoubtedly our own.

Nic Beech would like to acknowledge the support of the Economic and Social Research Council, grant number RES-331-27-0065, during the writing of this book.

PART A
Foundations

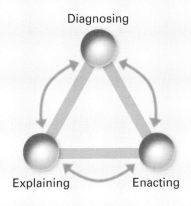

Change is ever-present in organizations. We are sympathetic to the argument that, rather than talking about organizations as nouns, with the implication that they are 'finished objects', it is more helpful to focus on the processes of organizing, with the implication that we are always engaged in the practices that constitute a current state of affairs that will shortly become different (Chia, 1995; Tsoukas and Chia, 2002). In this view, the practices of organizing are always unfinished and 'in process'. Indeed, these processes of organizing are not generally simple and singular but, instead, are open to multiple interpretations. Different people involved in the same set of organizational practices may have quite different stories of what are ostensibly the same set of events (Buchanan and Dawson, 2007). This makes the job of managing change intensely complicated. Actions are open to interpretation and reinterpretation and good intentions can go awry. What started out as a clear communication can become translated so many times that it takes on new meanings (Oswick *et al.*, 2010) and ambiguity can pervade the field of change.

However, this complexity may not necessarily be negative. Constant change, ambiguity and multiplicity of meaning can be problematic if the aim of management is to control everything that happens. However, if the purpose is not to control but to facilitate and lead (Currie and Lockett, 2007) in such a way that creative action can be recognized and built upon, the ongoing flow of activities can present an opportunity to enable change. This entails neither control nor anarchy but a form of engaged dialogue (Beech, MacIntosh and MacLean, 2010) in which those engaged in organizing practices recognize differences and agreements, and develop practical steps that move things along (MacIntosh, Beech and Martin, 2012) even when the 'perfect answer' cannot be found. The spirit of this book is one of dialogue. Our aim is to be practical and realistic about the complexity of organizational contexts and to be informed by serious engagement with theories of organization, so as to enable a thoughtful-action-oriented approach.

The purposes of the book are to:

- assist people who will be managing change in making practical judgements in an informed way;
- facilitate students in developing an understanding of the multifaceted nature of change in a way that encourages rather than stifles action;
- provide access to theoretical thinking, in order to demystify it and to give an appreciation of its necessary detail and complexity;
- mobilize learning from cases and primary research in order to help readers build up a picture of what has worked (and failed to work) elsewhere, so that they can make decisions about their own approach; and
- provide students with the foundations of knowledge that will enable them to succeed in studying and being employable in jobs that entail change.

The aim of Part A, Foundations, is to orient readers towards developing their judgement in managing change. In order to make informed judgements, it helps to be able to differentiate different types of change and to be able to articulate which practices would be appropriate for those types. In Chapter 1 we introduce an overview of the enquiry–action framework on which the book is based, and in Chapter 2 we review a range of contributions to the change literature in order to enable readers to develop their approach on the basis of insight into the rich traditions of change-related research.

REFERENCES

Beech, N., MacIntosh, R., and MacLean, D. (2010) Dialogues between academics and practitioners: the role of generative dialogic encounters. *Organization Studies*, 31(9): 1341–67.

Buchanan, D., and Dawson, P. M. (2007) Discourse and audience: organizational change as multi-story process. *Journal of Management Studies*, 44(5): 669–86.

Chia, R. (1995) From modern to postmodern organizational analysis. *Organization Studies*, 16(4): 579–604.

Currie, G., and Lockett, A. (2007) A critique of transformational leadership. *Human Relations*, 60(2): 341–70.

MacIntosh, R., Beech, N., and Martin, G. (2012) Dialogues and dialetics: limits to clinician–manager interaction in healthcare organizations. *Social Science and Medicine*, 74(3): 332–9.

Oswick, C., Grant, D., Marshak, R., and Wolfram-Cox, J. (2010) Organizational discourse and change: positions, perspectives, progress and prospects. *Journal of Applied Behavioral Science*, 46(1): 8–15.

Tsoukas, H., and Chia, R. (2002) On organizational becoming: rethinking organizational change. *Organization Science*, 13(5): 567–82.

1 Practising change management

Our argument in this book is that much of the time in organizations we are managing change through the deliberate selection of practices that we hope will produce particular results. The triggers for such **change work** may emanate from within the organization or from shifts in the external environment. They may be optional or unavoidable, and they may be rapid and radical or slow and evolutionary. There are many tools and techniques that pertain to change situations, but choosing what to do, and how to do it, is not straightforward. In this book we elaborate a framework that does not dictate a prescribed path to managing change but treats the process as one of enquiry and action. This entails being skilled at asking searching questions so that the circumstances and purpose can be understood and matched to action. Action in this field is normally somewhat experimental, as even the most popular 'tried and tested' practices can fail in new situations. Therefore, the approach adopted here is to build up a repertoire of options and to be active both in the selection of which action option (or combination of options) to take and in the adaptation and development of change practices. Hence, change management is regarded as being based on skills of judging situations, selecting and adapting from prior practices in order to develop new ones and subsequently being able to understand and evaluate how these actions are working and thus make appropriate adjustments. In short, the change manager is an active learner, engaged in a continuous cycle of enquiry and action.

We refer to the activities relating to planning, executing and responding to organizational change as 'change work'.

Managing change is very likely to entail some degree of disruption. Often the situations that managers encounter are difficult, perhaps even intractable. It is not that all change is inherently problematic but, rather, that when things are simple and doable there is less call for management intervention. As a result, it is normal that change managers find themselves in the midst of so-called 'sticky' or 'wicked' problems that it is not easy to resolve. Such problems are composed of divergent perspectives and tensions. The perspectives come from those directly involved in the situation, such as staff, managers and internal experts, and from people in the social context of the change. The social context includes as stake-holders a wide community of people with some interest in the way that the change works out. These can include customers, service users, suppliers and competitors, amongst other groups.

Our view is that change is hardly ever an objective thing – that is, it is hardly ever the case that one can say unequivocally 'This is the right and only thing to do' and be correct in such an assertion. Different stakeholders normally have perspectives that result in there being more than one view of what the right thing is. Even when a change has been conducted we are unlikely to be able to say with certainty that it was the right or wrong thing. Most claims of success are disputable. For example, making efficiency gains through process improvement and headcount reduction might be seen as exactly what was needed by some stakeholders, but perhaps not by those who lose jobs or those who hold on to jobs but were friends with those who did not (Extended Case 6, Power Provision plc, provides an example of this). Similarly, developing a more sustainable way of working might not be applauded by those who believe that their investments may be adversely affected. In addition, the changes we are concerned with do not happen in a laboratory. There are many uncontrollable contextual factors that impact real-world situations. The apparent success of a new strategy may not be solely to do with the actions of the organization but may also be attributable to the behaviour of competitors, the general state of the economy or customers' level of confidence and disposable income. Many of these factors are simply beyond the control of the managers. Therefore, when trying to manage change, one is not dealing with a situation in which best practice can be rolled out across all contexts. There is no guarantee that what appeared to work last time will do so next time, nor that techniques that did not lead to the desired results in one context will fail again if used elsewhere.

The matter of best practice in change management is a contentious one. There have been many efforts to produce best-practice prescriptions or theories of change, and, like change itself, they constitute a disputed territory. What we mean by the word 'theory' is an attempt to explain and generalize from one instance to another. For example, research might be conducted that examines many cases for their strengths and weaknesses and then concludes with a generalized list of things to do (and actions to avoid). However, many people operating in practice also produce their own theories of change. Working on the basis of previous experience, or on received practical wisdom, people develop a preferred way of acting. This is a local theory, in the sense that it generalizes from what has worked (or is perceived to have worked) in the past to what should be done in the future. Our purpose in this book is to help people improve their theorizing such that, as they make judgements about what to do next, they do so on a considered basis and draw from as wide a range of ideas and experiences as is appropriate for the change at hand. We would regard this type of theorizing as being practical at heart. It is not about producing elegant statements or models but esoteric ones. It is about helping to make decisions about how to act when time and other resources are pressing and the context is problematic, with divergent demands, multiple perspectives and no single best way to answer the problems.

Hence, being able to grapple with such situations and make actionable judgements promptly are the first skills that change managers need. Change management entails being able to understand rapidly how things are going (from multiple perspectives), and this relies on the learning abilities of the change manager and those enacting the change. Putting judgements into action with others, experimenting, reviewing, making new decisions and acting as a source and stimulation for learning are the next set of skills. These present a challenge, as they require a style of leadership that is about facilitating others when there is a lack of certainty (because something new is being undertaken) and being able to acknowledge things that are not working, and then seeking to improve them. It is not about knowing the answers, because change is a journey into the unknown. Therefore, it is important to establish relationships and expectations that include the realization that the change leader is not always right and an awareness that the path is not likely to be smooth. Lastly, there is a process of reflective learning by looking back at how things went and extracting personal and organizational lessons for the future. This entails skills of enabling honest (self-)criticism and getting beyond defensive rhetoric and into generative dialogue.

This list of skills is demanding, and it reflects the demanding nature of change management. This book is intended to provide some guidance and insight into working with these skills in order to be able to grapple with difficult change issues. Our starting point is to propose a framework that is intended to help make these judgements.

The enquiry–action framework

The enquiry–action framework sets out three key areas of practice that change managers undertake, and we suggest that there are choices available within each of these three practice areas. The enquiry–action framework focuses on questioning and understanding the context, content and process of change as well as developing a repertoire of alternative ways of enacting change. We are mindful of the dangers of separating enquiry and action, since action is part of our enquiry process and, equally, enquiring is a form of action. Indeed, we would suggest that, although it can be helpful to separate these focal areas analytically, in practice they are integrated as aspects of change management practice. Figure 1.1 represents the relationship between these activities within the framework.

On first reading, there is a natural ordering to the themes in the enquiry–action framework, but we would not regard them as following a strictly linear sequence. Each of the three focal areas (diagnosing, enacting and explaining) incorporates a number of possibilities that provide ways of enacting that aspect of change. For example, activities within the diagnosis could focus on under-standing the current and desired states of the organization. Diagnosis can be

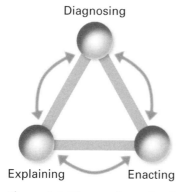

Figure 1.1 The enquiry–action framework

about setting a clear purpose, but on other occasions it can be about under-standing the different interpretations that people make of the purpose and recognizing the consequences (both positive and negative) of such ambiguity. It can concentrate on how far people are (potentially) engaged with a change or the state of play politically and whether stakeholders are aligned or not. Equally, diagnosis may need to uncover the cultural context of change, people's established habits and ways of thinking, in order to recognize where it is possible and desirable to introduce innovations. Each of these areas of diag-nostic activity is discussed in the chapters in Part B. Depending on the require-ments of the change being proposed and the context of the change, diagnosis might need to be an extensive area of activity with several variations being worked through, or it could be a 'light touch' diagnosis in which the aim is to act with speed. This principle holds for each of the three focal areas in the frame-work. We would advise at least some activity in each area, but the actions chosen and the time and effort expended will vary with the nature and impor-tance of the change and its context.

In enacting change it is rarely the case that one form of action will work well for all aspects of the change and all the people who are involved, so it is important to establish a repertoire of options for action. This means embarking on change with a combination of options and enough flexibility to be able to cope with the unexpected events, tensions and paradoxes that arise. Accordingly, the second focal area entails the change agent and other participants making informed choices about a set of interventions that can involve different foci. The choices include: changing the structure or the organization; exploring and engaging with the identity aspects of change – that is, who we are as a group and what we see ourselves doing as a result of who we are; choosing customers and competitors; changing processes; aligning people and their activities; fostering learning and development; and, finally, developing change through dialogue. Of course, the specific circumstances of any change situation may require a blend of more than one set of actions, and the diagnostic work undertaken in the previous focal area may highlight complementary courses of action.

The next focal area involves a switch in emphasis from enactment to explain-ing. Communication is often cited as being central to organizational life in general and to change in particular (one expression of this is John Kotter's observation that we under-communicate 'by a factor of ten' in change situa-tions: Kotter, 1996). Our argument is that communication is too often consid-ered as the monodirectional transfer of instructions or explanation of the change, typically from senior figures to more junior members of the organization. Similarly, the idea of piloting a new process in one area and then 'rolling it out' across the organization can be experienced by those who receive the roll-out as a hierarchical imposition. This style of communication, however well intended, is likely to elicit some degree of resistance, and so alternative styles of communication are generally worth considering. A specific literature explores relationships between different managerial levels (for example, in the context of strategy development, see Floyd and Wooldridge, 2000), and our focus here is on the nature of dialogue within the organization and across its boundaries. Dialogues often incorporate narrative structures as participants, recipients and leaders of the change create stories in which the change process is made meaningful in the lived reality of everyday organizational life. Such dialogues and narratives offer opportunities to understand leadership behaviours, political positioning and cultural norms (Alvesson and Karreman, 2000; Bebbington *et al.*, 2007). As such, we see them as central to attempts to introduce and sustain change.

No change effort – indeed, no managerial or organizational act – can ever be fully understood in isolation (Marshak, 2009). Rather, the ways in which people respond to the intended change have an impact on the future nature of the organization and the actions that become regarded as normal. Our emphasis here is on becoming attuned to reading signals and reactions by developing and interpreting evidence. Although we would contest an overly simplistic sense in which 'evidence' proves that change is working, we believe that reflexivity on the part of those leading and enacting change is significant (Nutley, Walter and Davies, 2006). With all the abundant complexity of organizational life, taking the time and effort to reflect on the ways in which the change process was enacted offers the best hope of developing an attitude of enquiry within the organization.

In some circumstances there is a natural ordering to these three focal areas: from diagnosis, via enactment, to explanation. However, the diagram seeks to indicate that change can start in any of the areas. In some cases enactment is under way, and it is helpful to explain what is going on and then to diagnose, because the change is having unintended consequences. Alternatively, it is possible to start by explaining things and in so doing to recognize the need to analyse the situation and then act in a new way. Equally, the sequence can reverse, and explanation can lead to a realization that a particular line of action is needed.

We introduce the three focal areas in the framework and cover each in a separate section. We use a mixture of cases to illustrate the application of the tools to practical situations. Extended cases are presented in the final section of the book. The nine extended cases are a mix of public domain cases (ABB, Oticon, Admiral Insurance, Nokia, Her Majesty's Revenue and Customs (HMRC) and Apple) and cases drawn from our research that have been anonymized (ITS Canada, Island Opera and Power Provision plc.). A further seven mini-cases are embedded in the chapters, and, again, these are a mix of well-known organizations and anonymized illustrations. The frequent referral to examples is intended to reinforce the practicalities of the various tools used in the book and to offer a way of encouraging critical consideration of models and theoretical constructs. However, the mini- and extended cases serve a second purpose, which is to provoke a response to two questions. First, what would I do in the situation as described? Second, in what ways is the situation in the case similar to, and different from, the situations that I face in my own organization? Hence, theory is engaged with the purpose of enabling practice.

The three areas of activity should not be thought of as completely separate but, rather, as having permeable boundaries such that the conduct of work in one focal area can be directly influenced by activities within either or both of the other two areas. For example, what is enactment of practice for some might also be treated as part of a diagnostic by others if it is simultaneously a pilot study to uncover practices that might be considered elsewhere in the organization. Equally, the enactment of changing dialogue in an organization could rely on reflexive learning as part of the process.

This approach offers a structure within which managerial judgement can be translated into thoughtful action. When a change within a particular context is considered, the change agent can decide if a focal area is highly significant, and therefore should have time and resources spent on it, thereby exploring several activities within the area in some depth. Alternatively, a theme might be regarded as less important for the change at hand, and so it might be dealt with in a 'light touch' way. The cultural context can also play a role in these decisions. A common issue in change is the need to win the support of senior managers and organizational members who will be affected by the change. In some cultures, showing that there is a careful diagnostic phase in which solid research will be conducted is important, as without this the change will encounter a sceptical response ('What is the basis for this?'). Conversely, in a culture that sees itself as action-oriented, doing too much diagnosis could build up resistance. Therefore, the framework can be regarded as providing resources from which the change manager can choose suitable combinations.

REFERENCES

Alvesson, M., and Karreman, D. (2000) Taking the linguistic turn in organizational research. *Journal of Applied Behavior Science*, 36(2): 136–58.

Bebbington, J., Brown, J., Frame, B., and Thomson, I. (2007) Theorizing engagement: the potential of a critical dialogical approach. *Accounting, Auditing and Accountability Journal*, 20(3): 356–81.

Floyd, S. W., and Wooldridge, B. (2000). *Building Strategy from the Middle: Reconceptualizing Strategy Process.* London: Sage.

Kotter, J. P. (1996) *Leading Change.* Boston: Harvard Business School Press.

Marshak, R. (2009) *Organizational Change: Views from the Edge.* Bethel, ME: Lewin Center.

Nutley, S. M., Walter, I., and Davies, H. T. O. (2006) *Evidence Use: How Research Can Inform Public Services.* Bristol: Polity Press.

2 | Current perspectives and classic ideas

The aims of this chapter are to:

- introduce concepts and frameworks from the literature on change management;
- enable readers to distinguish between different modes of change;
- consider the relationship between change management practices and modes of change;
- encourage reflection on the theories that can support the enquiry–action and other frameworks; and
- help students develop an understanding of classical ideas and contemporary thinking alike about change.

Change has a long history in the organizational and management literatures, and it is prudent to place contemporary developments in context relative to other prior contributions. We therefore review contributions from respected scholars that we have found helpful before discussing their application in the enquiry–action framework. The review in this chapter is necessarily limited, since there is a vast amount of work that could be included. We have selected four approaches to conceptualizing change that have been influential in the literature, so as to offer a partial yet indicative and constructive means of introducing change.

Approach one: foci and modes of change

Change in organizations can be thought of in many different ways, and Andrew Van de Ven and Scott Poole (1995; 2005) have developed a useful framework that helps in systematically arranging the plethora of alternatives. There are two axes to their framework. First is the issue of **change focus**, or what they term the 'unit of change'. Some ways of thinking about change focus relatively closely on a particular company, product or process. For example, someone seeking to champion a new product might be expected to be concerned principally with change in relation to that product, rather than the whole company. Other models focus more broadly on multiple entities interacting together in a system, such as several companies competing in the same market, or several proposals for new products competing with each other for limited investment funding. The second axis is the issue of the **mode of change**, dealing with where the change originates and what influences its direction. Some change is initiated outside the organization, for example by governments or by competitors who introduce a new dominant product. In such cases the change is almost 'prescribed', as the organization has little choice but to change, and often the prescription also extends to which choices of direction are viable. Alternatively, change can be generated inside the organization by pursuing a new strategy or following an innovative idea, and then internal actors can have more say in the direction of travel. Van de Ven and Poole refer to this type of change as 'constructive' (see Figure 2.1).

The change focus is the process, practice, product or person in which change is being developed.

The mode of change relates to the origins and direction of the change.

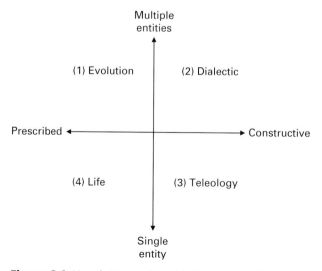

Figure 2.1 Van de Ven and Poole's framework of change

When we combine these axes, the result is a framework that enables us to see clearly how some common models of change relate to each other. There are four prevalent types. Life cycle models (Stark, 2006) are seen as being prescribed (external influence) and having a narrow focus (single entity). Products, project teams and even organizations are often spoken of as having life cycles. This organic metaphor implies that there are phases of initiation, growth, production or 'harvesting' and decline and death. This metaphor assumes that external pressures have a big impact (hence it is relatively 'prescribed') and that, generally, the life cycle impacts on a single entity. There are various implications of adopting this metaphor for the way that we practise change management. It would be assumed when starting a new project or product that its value to the organization will be for a limited period, and so a measured stance is adopted towards investment and exclusive attachment to the product or project. It is unlikely, for instance, that a company that thinks like this would be satisfied if it did not have several replacement products in preparation for the time when the current one begins to decline.

At each stage of the cycle there are somewhat different implications for what managers should do. For example, during initiation it is necessary to help people develop ideas, to challenge old ways of thinking and to be willing to indulge in trial and error. However, as the product or process develops and comes to maturity, the managerial effort is to encourage people away from trial and error and towards efficient performance, in order to reap the benefits before overseeing the withdrawal from this product and the simultaneous build-up of the replacement. At such stages, it is natural for people to feel disappointed and emotionally attached to the old way of doing things, and so managerial practices will tend towards supporting people out of established ways of acting and helping them into new (and less 'secure') areas of performance. Therefore, this way of thinking about change implies a set of practices that are contingent on the stage of the life cycle and relate closely to the experiences and competences of people who are going through the change.

The next type of change maintains an external or prescribed mode, but enlarges the focus from the individual entity to a system containing many entities. This could be, for instance, a market that contains many companies competing with each other, or a single company that has many projects vying with each other to be selected for investment. The type of change envisaged in this way of thinking is evolution. Evolutionary change is dominated by external conditions and the extent to which any particular entity is fit to survive in those conditions. Within a population of companies that are competing, variety will come about as the companies seek to develop new competitive strategies and offer alternative products or services to the market at particular prices. Some will be more successful than others, and a process of 'selection and retention' occurs through which some are profitable and continue and others either fail or have to introduce innovations in order to survive. If these new innovations are successful they, in turn, can produce a threat to the continued existence of other companies. As a result, change in the market (both products and the companies that supply them) occurs through an evolutionary process of those that are most able to win in the environment, becoming leaders in that environment until the next threat impacts upon them. Hence, it can be said that there are 'waves' of change, and effective organizations need to be ready to meet the next wave (Morgan, 1988). The management of change for an organization that perceives itself to be in a multiple entity/prescribed situation will start with an external vision. **Stakeholder mapping** and understanding what competitors and customers are thinking are high priorities, as is the ability to sense changes in the environment and make early adaptations within the company in order to cope. It is an advantage in such circumstances to have a flexible structure, so that people can be deployed at short notice to those activities that are demanded by the changing environment. The rhetoric associated with this style of thinking is often deployed by chief executives and those leading change when they argue that 'there is no choice but to change', or that 'doing nothing is not an option'. If the other members of the organization are convinced by this rhetoric it can greatly assist the speed and ease of change.

Stakeholder mapping is a technique for mapping the parties involved according to the level of interest they have in the change and the amount of power they have either to support or to resist the change (see Chapter 5 for further details).

The next model of change we consider is what Van de Ven and Poole term **teleology**. This style of change is when a single entity is changing in a purposeful and internally driven ('constructive') way. A teleological perspective is often the way in which 'change champions' think. There is an internal drive to improve things or develop a completely new way of doing things, and the inspiration is a great idea or a vision. This is a notable contrast to the evolutionary perspective, in which new ideas are made necessary because the external environment demands them if the company is to survive. The teleological perspective seeks to develop something that it will impose on the environment. Teleological perspectives can entail a cognitive or problem-solving approach. This implies a series of managerial actions that start with some degree of dissatisfaction with the way things are done at the moment. Once a problem or an opportunity has been identified there is a search for possible solutions/actions. Then the best solution is chosen, often by reference to the purpose and values of the organization. Following this, goals for the change are set and implemented. This resembles classic theories of decision making (see, for example, Lindblom, 1959) and seeks to make change an analytical process. Conflict and politicking are regarded as inappropriate in teleological change, and managerial effort is put into building consensus and ensuring that sufficient options are examined and that the chosen path of change is managed towards the expressed goals. Hence, there is an emphasis on clear communication, establishing a set of agreed criteria for decision making and keeping people focused on the goal.

Teleological change is aimed at a specific outcome and is defined by its end point.

The last conceptualization is of change as **dialectic** (Cunha and Da Cunha, 2003). In this view, change occurs when one idea or entity comes into conflictual contact with another. In the classic terminology, this is a thesis, or idea, being met by an alternative or antithesis. The antithesis is not a complement to the thesis but seeks to displace it. Some of the classic theories of dialectical change are concerned with how societies and economies change, for example from an economy based on ownership of land to one based on the ownership of capital for industrial production. The conflict is realized as one seeks to replace the other. Once the conflict is resolved the new state of affairs becomes the thesis, and in time this too is likely to be challenged by a new antithesis. When these ideas are applied to organizations the changes tend to be more modest and shorter-lived. However, there are many instances in which one idea, such as centring activities on a customer focus, is in conflict with and replaces a prior one, such as centring activities on efficient production. In some cases the antithesis replaces the thesis and in others the thesis is displaced but, rather than the antithesis being established, a new synthesis occurs. The synthesis is a new idea but may contain a combination of aspects from the thesis and antithesis, often along with additional novel ideas.

Dialectic change entails a conflict or struggle between two opposing propositions.

When this perspective is adopted, managerial activities will not be about reducing conflict (as they are in managing teleological change) but, conversely, will be concerned with stimulating the right sort of conflict. Some forms of conflict are personalized whilst others remain at the level of ideas (Friedman *et al.*, 2000). In the main, change managers seek to avoid personalized conflict, although some managers believe that some degree of personal competition can inspire higher performance (Jehn, 1997). However, this is a disputed view, and probably relates best to very particular environments; in some sporting teams, for example, it is assumed that having competition for places raises the standard of play by everyone. However, idea-based conflict can be very positive as long as it is managed carefully. It is important to ensure that ideas that will be competing with each other are not seen as belonging to particular individuals. In other words, all participants in the change process should be joint owners of the process and be equally committed to whichever idea wins out. This is a proposition that many people will agree with, but in practice it takes some skill in team management and communication to maintain. There are structural aspects to this. If people believe that rewards or promotion will be connected to their association with the 'winning' idea, then the conflict may move from being about ideas to being more personal. Accordingly, careful attention should be paid to rewarding the team-oriented behaviour that is needed.

Van de Ven and Poole's framework is particularly useful in helping change managers recognize the situation that they are in and identify which activities to prioritize. We illustrate this by reference to a company that we will call Festival Co., which is responsible for the world's largest festival of its type. The festival mainly presents folk music but there are many other events as well, such as art collections, workshops, storytelling and educational concerts. The festival takes place over three weeks, and its 300 concerts take place at a range of venues, some of which are owned by Festival Co. but many of which are not. In addition, Festival Co. runs a number of other, smaller festivals in jazz and classical music and provides the main concert venues in its area. The start-up of the festival that, fifteen years later, is the world leader in its field can be seen as teleological. The first ideas came from enthusiasts within the company and the change was focused on a single entity. The company started the festival within its own main venue and the intentions were both to support a particular form of live music making and to generate profit at a time of year when bookings at the venue were minimal. The festival was very successful, and it grew quickly in its early years.

Fast-forwarding through the story, some years on there were questions over the directions that Festival Co. should take. Many others had copied Festival Co., and in fact Festival Co. had been very supportive of what it regarded as 'sister festivals' in other countries and had helped several to become established. At the same time, the idea of festivals as a primary mode of organizing live music had developed as a significant business model (Paleo and Wijnberg, 2006). As a result, the external environment had changed considerably and there was much greater competition for the spending of festival goers. There was a concern that the festival might be in danger of entering another phase of its life cycle in which the environment would have a greater impact on what it could do, and if there was no renewal then the festival could begin to decline. Festival Co. started to change some of its practices towards those that others in the field had adopted. For the first time they appointed an external artistic director. They sought and recruited a very high-profile performer, who brought a considerable artistic reputation and greater media awareness to the festival. However, this also meant reorganizing internally and putting a professional management team around the artistic director in order to bring the new artistic vision to life. They refocused the festival on marketable 'strands', which are musical themes that concerts and other activities could be clustered under. Strands have included a focus on the music of particular countries and have incorporated bringing international musicians from that country to perform and exploring the influences of that country's music on others. The festival was expanded, more venues were used and a new venue was taken over and restored by Festival Co. This can be thought of as an evolutionary phase, as Festival Co. was responding to external pressures by developing its distinctive offering to the market and bringing about significant change in its size, make-up and activities.

The evolutionary change blurred into more teleological change, because, although they were responding to externalities, as things progressed the decisions about which strands to develop were decided on the basis of internal discussions rather than being market-led. In fact, Festival Co. would be seen as a market leader in its field. Therefore, at different points the ongoing change over fifteen years could be seen as being teleological, then evolutionary/life-cycle, then teleological again. There was no significant evidence of dialectical change, because, internally, change was driven through consensus and, externally, although there was competition, there was still a high degree of respect for and collaboration with other festivals. For example, managers would normally visit and often help out at other sister festivals. As a result, there was a sharing of learning rather than traditional 'fight to survive' market politics (Lampel, Lant and Shamsie, 2000).

As the nature of change altered, so did management practices. During teleological phases there was more of an internal focus, building on people's ideas, developing proposals and working collaboratively across departments. For example, the arts team, which was responsible for programming, and the commercial team, which was responsible for managing income from non-ticket sources such as catering, merchandising and other sales, worked together to find the best blend of concerts that would enable both furthering of the artistic vision and sufficient income to make a profit, which could entail some cross-funding of less popular but aesthetically valuable events. During evolutionary changes there was more of an external focus to management practices. For example, managers conducted a search for, and appointed, a new artistic director in order to lead the festival in a new direction. They placed greater emphasis on learning from other festivals and on managing their stakeholders. Subsequently, the management put a great effort into building up internal cooperation and multifunctional teams as they entered a new teleological phase. Thus, connections can be made between the type of change and the practical approach to managing the change.

However, it is also important to draw attention to the nature of the model when it is in use. It is not an 'absolutist' model, which is used to categorize changes and practices as if they are fixed, solid and unquestionable. Rather, it is an aid to managerial judgement. The point is not to spend large amounts of time debating the exact position of a change in a particular quadrant of the model. The aim is to enable those involved in the change to debate and come to an agreement on the general approach they are adopting and then decide how best to act. In the brief discussion of Festival Co., one quadrant was not used at all (dialectical change). It is not uncommon that one or more quadrant is not used, and the point is not to try and force-fit experience into the model; rather, the intention is to understand and aid practice.

Approach two: speed and scale

Bernard Burnes (2009) offers an alternative framework (see Figure 2.2). This is equally useful, but it helps change managers decide how to act on the basis of a different form of analysis that is more applicable in some situations. Burnes also has two axes in his model, and the first concerns the speed of change. Some change will be relatively slow and take a considerable time to complete; for example, changing an organizational culture can take several years in reality. Conversely, rapid change can take place almost overnight; for example, the structure of an organization can be changed in what Burnes terms a 'bold stroke'. The other axis combines the nature of the environment and the scale of the change. At one extreme, turbulent environments are combined with large-scale organizational change, while, at the other end of the scale, relatively stable environments are associated with smaller-scale changes.

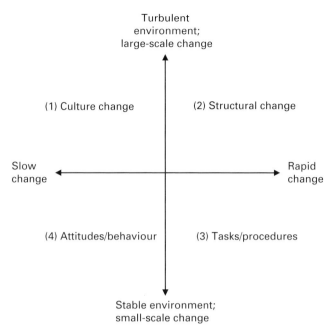

Figure 2.2 Burnes's framework of change

The first type of change is slow and large-scale and is exemplified by culture change programmes. The whole organization, or at least large parts of it, will be involved. The change impacts on everyone and has deep significance, as culture involves the values, beliefs and fundamental assumptions that operate in the organization. Most people are not in the habit of changing their beliefs and basic assumptions overnight, and so such change is often gradual, with backward steps as well as forward ones, and it is typical for several change initiatives to be part of the overall change programme. Because of the length of time involved, it is often the case that this sort of change is emergent (Weick, 2000) – that is, although there may be plans set out at the beginning, it is necessary to learn as things progress and to adapt to the circumstances (Chia and Holt, 2009). Adaptation can entail changing plans, improvising and sometimes taking unforeseen directions. Hence, the necessary management practices include challenging the old culture, engaging people in defining the new culture, setting in place symbols and support processes as people start to change and persevering so as to make sure the change becomes the new normal practice. It is important that all the parts of the system support the change; for example, it is self-defeating to try to change an individualistic culture into a team-oriented one but to keep individual performance-related pay, which discourages team work. Chapter 6 discusses this type of change in more detail, and Case 2, ITS Canada, provides an example.

The second type of change remains at the large-scale or organizational level, but in this case is fairly rapid. It is typified by changes in organizational structures or processes. A restructuring is a major undertaking and is very disruptive for most organizations. Hence, they are typically undertaken only when there is a pressing need. They can occur because of rapid expansion through the acquisition of other companies, or because of a need to produce a radical shift in the way things are done, such as moving from a function-based hierarchy to a dispersed geographical structure. The point about a structure is that it organizes how people operate. In a functional hierarchy, for example, the focus is on groups of people who do the same thing working in close proximity. This has the advantages of enabling skills and expertise to be shared and excellence to be achieved in the function. However, the specialists can become remote from those who receive their services. Change to a dispersed geographic structure is often effected in order to avoid the problems of a functional hierarchy and to put specialists into multifunctional teams located closer to their customers. Hence, the focus is on the customer's needs. However, this structure is less good at developing and sharing expertise across the organization. Once it has been decided to make such a change, the structural part of the change can happen almost overnight. However, there may well be a longer learning period in which people need to adapt to the new working arrangements. The managerial practices associated with this type of change include clear decision making and prioritization. There is a need to communicate the reason for the change and what will happen so that ambiguity is reduced. In addition, coordination is needed so that all the aspects of the change are neatly executed simultaneously. In short, good project management skills come to the fore in this type of change.

The next type of change takes place in a more stable environment and is smaller in scale. The third type is small-scale and rapid. Examples would include changes to technical systems or developments in procedures through a **kaizen** approach. Such changes are not a major disruption to people and would leave most of the normal ways of working in place. Management practices can be a top-down spreading of good practice, in which a new procedure is trialled and then rolled out to others, or there can be a more engaged approach, in which staff in their local environment are encouraged to develop improvements to the systems they operate.

'Kaizen' is a Japanese term meaning 'continuous improvement', and it is often used in the context of total quality management.

The fourth type of change is concerned with small-scale change that is relatively slow. This would include behavioural change, in which people need to develop new skills and activities that can take time to learn. Typically this can be achieved in a developmental and collaborative way, and so the associated managerial practices tend towards an engaged approach, stimulating staff members' understanding of a need to develop new ways of behaving, and supporting any training to develop these skills.

The crisis of digitalization in the music industry (Hesmondhalgh, 2009) provides an illustration of how technological change in an industry provokes a range of changes that Burnes's model is helpful in analysing. The increase in the downloading and file sharing of music is seen as a major threat to established music companies, which have made most of their profits through the production and distribution of CDs and records. These companies grew their market share and profit by controlling contractually the releases of artists, and almost all artists needed such a relationship in order to reach their market. However, significant changes in the marketplace have occurred, and traditional record and CD shops have been early casualties. Currently, major producing companies are struggling with matters of copyright and the ability to generate revenue from the digital availability of recordings (commercially sanctioned versus person-to-person non-profit transactions). Musicians are refocusing from an environment in which live performance promoted a CD release to a situation in which over 80 per cent of CDs released do not make any profit (Frith, Cloonan and Williamson, 2009). As a result, those who can make money effectively from live performance or from other uses of their music, such as in film or advertising, are those who can thrive in the new environment. In some ways, this takes us back to a model of the music industry that pre-dates the prevalence of recorded music, when live performance was the dominant mode of production and of revenue (as has always remained the case in some genres).

These changes in the music industry can be represented as different types of change depending on which focal organization is chosen. In musical retail there is large-scale and turbulent change, such that web-based retailers are likely to increasingly replace record/CD shops in a restructuring of the industry. If the music producers are to survive they will need to invest in large-scale change that revolutionizes their cultures and procedures. Focusing on CD production alone is not likely to be the main plank of profitable survival without modification to take account of the purchasing/sharing practices of consumers in the future

(Snowball, 2005). For some musicians, moving to a focus on live performance may be a relatively major shift, entailing changes in the way they produce music, the number of musicians used and the amount of equipment, adding to the cost of touring. However, for others, it would represent a relatively small-scale change to their practices (Randall, 2010). Hence, when considering one technological change, we can see that different actors in a market may occupy different positions on Burnes's framework and face quite different change challenges. Equally, a single organization might go through several of these types in its history. Like the Van de Ven and Poole model, Burnes's approach can help managers evaluate the situation they are in, define the type of change that they want to engender or have to face and make informed judgements about the change practices they should undertake.

Approach three: metaphors of change

The third approach to understanding change that we outline comes from what is known as the linguistic turn in management (Alvesson and Karreman, 2000). The use of metaphorical analysis has developed strongly in recent decades (Tsoukas, 1991). The way that people incorporate metaphors into their language can reveal insights into the way they conceive reality, both explicitly and (more significantly) implicitly. To those who are living out these metaphors, the fact that they are metaphors and ways of conceiving reality rather than being reality itself can be a surprise. Robert Marshak (2009) argues that metaphors carry with them implications for action because practices are often guided by the way people see the world through their 'dominant metaphors'. However, unintended problems can occur when the metaphors are inappropriate for the change objective or when incongruous metaphors are operating within the organization. Marshak identifies four common metaphors that people use regarding organizational change: 'fix and maintain'; 'build and develop'; 'move and relocate'; and 'liberate and recreate'.

The 'fix and maintain' metaphor sees the organization as a mechanistic system. Change practices are about identifying breakdowns in the system and repairing or replacing them. This type of change is aimed at relatively small-scale alterations that do not make radical changes to the system itself but instead, for instance, improve the efficiency of the functioning of one part of the system.

The 'build and develop' metaphor, like the 'fix and maintain' one, seeks to work from established practices, but is less focused on simply fixing problems and more concerned with managing expansion or developing a new opportunity. This process may be understood as being more 'organic', and hence managers may act as coaches, mentors or trainers who are there to help staff develop their practices. In the 'fix and maintain' metaphor there is typically a clear problem definition and a view of what the solution is. Conversely, in the 'build and develop' way of thinking there may be a more open-ended, and hence somewhat uncertain, prescription of the outcome of the change.

The third metaphor, 'move and relocate', is also known as transitional change. This is a more radical form of change (Huy, 2002), and it entails the organization substantially altering how it operates, for example by decentralizing decision making or by expanding or contracting operations. The management practices in such a change include the exploration and investigation of alternative ways forward, planning for change and acting as a guide for people as they go through the change.

The fourth metaphor is of change as a transformation: 'liberating and recreating'. In this way of thinking about the change it is not only about moving forward but is about changing the 'state of being'. The common image is of the organization as being in a process of 'becoming' (Tsoukas and Chia, 2002) – that is, a consistent dynamism that has deep significance. In other words, the organization is not just changing 'what we do' but 'who we are'. (This topic is discussed in more depth in Chapter 8.) Changing the culture in an organization can be regarded as transformational change as it leads to the alteration of the basic principles as well as the practices and activities (Brown, 1998).

For Marshak, the first use of metaphorical analysis is to diagnose unarticulated assumptions and beliefs on the basis of the imagery that is present in language. In a number of long term-research projects in which we have interviewed change agents, participants and key stakeholders, we have heard talk of 'toolkits', 'not fixing what isn't broken', change as 'modular' or 'putting solutions in place'. In Marshak's model, these signals indicate a 'fix and maintain' metaphor. When a 'build and develop' metaphor is operating, the talk may be of 'building on our strengths', 'developing new features', 'increasing' or 'growing' certain aspects of the organization. In a 'move and relocate' metaphor, change leaders may talk about 'getting from A to B', 'desired end states' or 'being on a journey'. Finally, a 'liberate and recreate' metaphor may be indicated by an expressed desire to undergo 'organizational reinvention', 'thinking outside the box' or 'creating a new vision'. The language used by those involved in and receiving the change is one indicator, but it is also necessary to pay attention to behaviour and the meanings associated with the language. For example, it is possible for a leader to talk about being on a journey when what he or she means is that some people need to develop in order to catch up with everyone else. Thus, the words of 'move and relocate' may actually belie an unspoken 'fix and maintain' or 'build and develop' mindset. In addition, language can deliberately be used to mislead. Hence, in this book we pay particular attention to the diagnostic process of observing both words and actions, since actions are no less a part of the metaphor that people are living out in the change process.

Metaphorical analysis can highlight potential problems in change. For example, having diagnosed the metaphors in play, one might question whether or not they are the most appropriate for the change at hand. To introduce transformational change in a culture in which 'don't fix what isn't broken' is a common attitude will be highly problematic unless careful preparatory steps are taken. Equally, significant problems can occur when there is a misalignment of ways of thinking. For example, in one of the cases discussed later in the book there was a merger of two public health sector organizations that performed broadly the same function in neighbouring areas. The chairman talked about the change as being 'modular' and said that the 'new' area could in effect be 'bolted on'. This was indicative of a 'fix and maintain' way of thinking. However, others experienced the change as being much more radical, as it impacted on their daily practices, the targets that guided their behaviours, the teams that they led, who they reported to and – for some – even the uniforms that they wore. It was not uncommon to find people from the 'new' area (which, of course, did not regard itself as new) who saw the change as both transformational and an unwelcome imposition. They felt that the effective ways of working that they had developed were being 'trampled down' and that, although there were also improvements, the 'merger' was really a 'takeover'. From the chairman's perspective there was less of a problem, because what was happening was simply a roll-out of best practice. Therefore, metaphorical analysis can be used to diagnose how people are conceiving change, to gauge the extent to which there is a fit with the change itself and between different people's conceptions in the organization and to decide what sort of management practices should be prioritized.

Stephen Fineman, David Sims and Yiannis Gabriel (2005) introduce an alternative metaphor, which we find particularly useful when seeking to manage change. Their view is that we should focus not on the 'object' of an organization but on the processes of organizing: not on the noun 'management', but on the verb 'to manage'. In line with this more dynamic way of thinking, they introduce the metaphor of a river. Like a river, the 'raw materials of organizing – people, their beliefs, actions and shared meanings – are in constant motion' (2005: 11).

Depending on where you are, the river can look quite different. From high above it can look like a continuous line; if you are in a boat you are more aware of the currents, the wind and other river users; and if you are swimming you will be even more aware of the movements of the water, the shapes of the banks, underwater plants, and so on. Equally, your reasons for looking at the river will lead to you notice some qualities and ignore others. For example, cartographers will be concerned with the overall size and direction. Conversely, swimmers will be concerned with their immediate context and their own safety in the water. Similarly, with processes of managing change, in order to understand the complexity of what is going on we need to be able to look from the perspective of others who are either closer to or more distant from the change, and who will be there for quite different reasons.

Approach four: complexity and change

Another development in the change literature has been the use of complexity thinking to explain, explore and even prescribe how to manage change in organizations. Complexity theory draws on a diverse range of source literatures, including physical chemistry, biology and computing science. Two broad schools of thought have developed as complexity theory has been applied to organizational settings. One group of researchers adopts a punctuated equilibrium model of change, which describes periods of relative stasis periodically interrupted by episodes of rapid and often radical change (see, for example, Gersick, 1991). Another group suggests that change is continuous, or at least a rapid series of incremental adjustments (see, for example, Brown and Eisenhardt, 1997).

There are some helpful resources that offer an introductory overview of examples applying complexity to organizational settings (MacIntosh *et al.*, 2006), as well as texts that gather together contemporary contributions to organizational complexity (Allen, Maguire and McKelvey, 2011). In essence, complexity thinking tends to be organized around a few key concepts. First is the observation that small signals can be amplified to produce large-scale outcomes. This is the so-called 'butterfly effect' (Lorenz, 1963). Second, significant change tends to occur when the system under consideration is not in equilibrium. This is challenging, since much of our organizational theorizing has historically assumed that equilibrium is the default position, yet Prigogine suggests that systems in highly unstable states become susceptible to tiny signals and random perturbations that would have had little impact were they still in equilibrium.

Processes of positive feedback can turn these tiny changes into 'gigantic structure breaking waves' (Prigogine and Stengers, 1984: xvii). Third, feedback processes are central to the relationship between stability and change, and in particular the balance of negative (i.e. restorative or damping) and positive (i.e. amplifying) feedback influences the extent to which system-wide change occurs. Fourth, order emerges through the repeated enactment or application of simple rules. For instance, Reynolds managed to simulate the flocking behaviour of birds using only three rules.[1] Eisenhardt and Sull (2001) suggest that organizations in high-velocity environments work with simple rules to determine which products to launch, which markets to operate within, etc. Most complexity theorists suggest that self-organization occurs when these concepts are simultaneously present, and the challenge of managing change is transformed when one conceptualizes the organization itself as a self-organizing phenomenon.

The conditioned emergence framework (MacIntosh and MacLean, 1999) offers one way of operationalizing complexity thinking in relation to organizational change. This framework suggests that there are three interacting gateways to change (MacIntosh and MacLean, 2001). The organization must reconfigure its simple rules (sometimes referred to as order-generating rules or deep structure), ensure that the organization experiences sufficient instability and make explicit efforts to encourage positive feedback (since most organizations are dominated by processes that engender negative feedback).

Pascale (1999: 85) notes that 'one cannot direct a living system, only disturb it', and Stacey's extensive work in this area (see, for example, Stacey, 1995) centres on the assertion that, for complex systems, we cannot accurately predict (or control) what happens in the future. Nevertheless, the conditioned emergence framework suggests that managerial influence, if not control, can be exerted by working through the three interacting gateways of rules, feedback and disequilibrium.

Each of the four contributions reviewed above developed separately with its own purposes and set of underlying assumptions in mind. Looking across the four theoretical contributions, it is possible to see that they might offer a useful starting point in forming a judgement about how to deal with a specific change

---

[1] In 1986 Reynolds managed to produce a computer simulation, which he called Boids. In the simulation, each individual boid follows three simple rules: (1) steer to avoid crowding and collision; (2) align towards the average line of flight of other local boids; and (3) head towards the average positional location of other boids in the flock. Using these three rules, a whole flock of boids can emulate the flocking behaviour of real birds. An internet search for the term 'boids' will identify several online versions of the simulation that you can experiment with.

challenge. A first step could be to decide which question, or combination of questions, offers most insight into your change situation.

(1) Are we inclined to think of this specific change situation as episodic/continuous and controllable/emergent (complexity scholars)?
(2) Can we determine the nature of the change we face or are we strongly influenced by external constraints (Van de Ven and Poole)?
(3) Is this an internal change or are we in a situation in which several organizations are changing at the same time, such as a group of competitors (Van de Ven and Poole)?
(4) Is slow and careful change needed or is there a need to move more quickly (Burnes)?
(5) Is this a large-scale change impacting on major processes or a lot of people, or is it more minor (Burnes)?
(6) What are the divergent perspectives at play in this change:
    (i) fix and maintain;
    (ii) build and develop;
    (iii) move and relocate; or
    (iv) liberate and recreate (Marshak)?

Building an understanding of typologies and classification systems, such as those described in this chapter, offers a means of locating your own approach to change. Each of the typologies foregrounds some issues whilst setting others to one side. We are not advocating any one of these three contributions to the literature in isolation, but, as a set, they offer an excellent basis for scholarly and practical analysis alike. There are many more propositions in the literature that we might describe as prescriptive or recipe-oriented, such as Kotter's eight-step framework (Kotter, 1996), which suggests that change involves:

(1) establishing a sense of urgency;
(2) creating a coalition with sufficient power to lead the change;
(3) creating a vision to direct the change;
(4) communicating that vision throughout the organization;
(5) empowering colleagues to act on the vision;
(6) creating and delivering quick wins;
(7) consolidating improvements and reassessing the plan; and
(8) reinforcing the change by linking change activities to outcomes.

Some find structured advice in this form extremely helpful, and prescriptive models such as Kotter's have had significant impact on the practice of change in many organizations. However, we would argue that such prescriptions overlook a prior stage of establishing which kind of change process is appropriate for the challenge at hand. In this sense, the typologies and models developed by Van de Ven and Poole, Burnes and Marshak offer a more situated means of diagnosing change and moving forward to action in ways that are sensitive to the particular circumstances. These models inform the exploration of the enquiry–action framework that follows. Addressing the questions posed above aids diagnosis of the type of change, the actions that are likely to be more appropriate and what should be looked for in evaluation and explanation. In the next chapter we consider four options that can be used in diagnosing why there should be change and how it should be managed.

REFERENCES

Allen, P., Maguire, S., and McKelvey, B. (2011) *The Sage Handbook of Complexity and Management*. London: Sage.

Alvesson, M., and Karreman, D. (2000) Taking the linguistic turn in organizational research. *Journal of Applied Behavioral Science*, 36(2): 136–58.

Brown, A. (1998) *Organisational Culture*, 2nd edn. Harlow: Pearson.

Brown, S. L., and Eisenhardt, K. M. (1997) The art of continuous change: linking complexity theory and time-paced evolution in relentlessly shifting organizations. *Administrative Science Quarterly*, 42(1): 1–34.

Burnes, B. (2009) *Managing Change*, 5th edn. Harlow: Pearson.

Chia, R., and Holt, R. (2009) *Strategy without Design: The Silent Efficacy of Indirect Action*. Cambridge University Press.

Cunha, M. P. E., and Da Cunha, J. V. (2003) Organizational improvisation and change: two syntheses and a filled gap. *Journal of Organizational Change Management*, 16(2): 169–85.

Eisenhardt, K. M., and Sull, D. N. (2001) Strategy as simple rules. *Harvard Business Review*, 79(1): 107–16.

Fineman, S., Sims, D., and Gabriel, Y. (2005) *Organizing and Organizations*, 3rd edn. London: Sage.

Friedman, R. A., Tidd, S. T., Currall, S. C., and Tsai, J. C. (2000) What goes around comes around. *International Journal of Conflict Management*, 11(1): 32–55.

Frith, S., Cloonan, M., and Williamson, J. (2009) On music as a creative industry, in Pratt, A. C., and Jeffcutt, P. (eds.) *Creativity, Innovation and the Cultural Economy*: 74–90. London: Routledge.

Gersick, C. J. G. (2002) Revolutionary change theories: a multilevel exploration of the punctuated equilibrium paradigm. *Academy of Management Review*, 16(1): 10–36.

Hesmondhalgh, D. (2009) The digitalisation of music, in Pratt, A. C., and Jeffcutt, P. (eds.) *Creativity, Innovation and the Cultural Economy*: 57–73. London: Routledge.

Huy, Q. N. (2002) Emotional balancing of organizational continuity and radical change. *Administrative Science Quarterly*, 47(1): 31–69.

Jehn, K. A. (1997) Affective and cognitive conflict in work groups: increasing performance through value-based intragroup conflict, in de Dreu, C. K. W., and Van de Vliert, E. (eds.) *Using Conflict in Organizations*: 87–100. London: Sage.

Kotter, J. P. (1996) *Leading Change*. Boston: Harvard Business School Press.

Lampel, J., Lant, T., and Shamsie, J. (2000) Balancing act: learning from organizational practices in cultural industries. *Organization Science*, 11(3): 263–9.

Lindblom, C. E. (1959) The science of muddling through. *Public Administration Review*, 19(2): 79–88.

Lorenz, E. (1963) Deterministic non-periodic flow. *Journal of Atmospheric Sciences*, 20(2): 130–41.

MacIntosh, R., and MacLean, D. (1999) Conditioned emergence: a dissipative structures approach to transformation. *Strategic Management Journal*, 20(4): 297–316.

MacIntosh, R., and MacLean, D. (2001) Conditioned emergence: researching change and changing research. *International Journal of Operations and Production Management*, 21(10): 1343–57.

MacIntosh, R., MacLean, D., Stacey, R., and Griffin, D. (2006) *Complexity and Organization: Readings and Conversations*. London: Routledge.

Marshak, R. (2009) *Organizational Change: Views from the Edge*. Bethel, ME: Lewin Center.

Morgan, G. (1988) *Riding the Waves of Change: Developing Managerial Competencies for a Turbulent World*. San Francisco: Jossey-Bass.

Paleo, I. O., and Wijnberg, N. M. (2006) Classification of popular music festivals. *International Journal of Arts Management*, 8(2): 50–61.

Pascale, R. T. (1999) Surfing the edge of chaos. *Sloan Management Review*, 40(3): 83–94.

Prigogine, I., and I. Stengers (1984) *Order out of Chaos: Man's New Dialogue with Nature*. New York: Bantam.

Randall, C. (2010) Communication, artists and the audience, in Townley, B., and Beech, N. (eds.) *Managing Creativity: Exploring the Paradox*: 157–76. Cambridge University Press.

Snowball, J. D. (2005) Art for the masses? *Journal of Cultural Economics*, 29(2): 107–25.

Stacey, R. D. (1995) The science of complexity: an alternative perspective for strategic change processes. *Strategic Management Journal*, 16(6): 477–95.

Stark, J. (2006) *Product Lifecycle Management: 21st Century Paradigm for Product Realisation*. London: Springer.

Tsoukas, H. (1991) The missing link: a transformational view of metaphors in organizational science. *Academy of Management Review*, 16(3): 566–85.

Tsoukas, H., and Chia, R. (2002) On organizational becoming: rethinking organizational change. *Organization Science*, 13(5): 567–82.

Van de Ven, A. H., and Poole, M. S. (1995) Explaining development and change in organizations. *Academy of Management Review*, 20(1): 510–40.

Van de Ven, A. H., and Poole, M. S. (2005) Alternative approaches for studying organizational change. *Organization Studies*, 26(9): 1377–404.

Weick, K. E. (2000) Emergent change as a universal in organizations, in Beer, M., and Nohria, N. (eds.) *Breaking the Code of Change*: 223–41. Boston: Harvard Business School Press.

PART B
Diagnosing

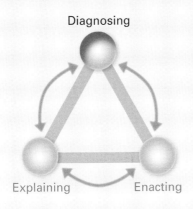

Diagnosing

Explaining   Enacting

When several large public sector organizations were asked to merge, a change forum was instituted in order to allow senior managers to meet regularly and plan what would be a major structural change. A change team was also set up in a UK-based engineering firm to tackle the organizational sources of the firm's gradually declining competitiveness. In both cases, one of the first pieces of activity undertaken in the change process related to establishing a diagnosis of the organization's current position. Within the enquiry–action framework, diagnostics are the first of three areas discussed. Over the next four chapters we discuss four approaches to **diagnosis**. Chapter 3 first considers the extent to which it is possible and appropriate to define the change challenge precisely. In Chapter 4 we present an approach that assesses the level of engagement and vitality within the organization. Most organizations aspire to have staff who are engaged by their work, since it is thought that committed staff produce better results, build better relationships with customers and suppliers, are less likely to leave the organization and help foster an atmosphere that is conducive to both innovation and change. In Chapter 5 we consider the political dynamics of the organization, as any attempt to change the organization is likely to challenge existing power structures, personal empires and allegiances. Working with, rather than against, these political forces is essential in modern-day organizations. Finally, in Chapter 6, we suggest ways of diagnosing the extent to which organizational culture and habitualized routines might inhibit or enable the change process. All organizations develop routines for the execution of complex tasks such as negotiating contracts, developing new services or products, recruiting and training staff, etc. These routines form one part of the organization's culture, but routines can also crystallize to the point at which they unintentionally stifle the ability to learn new solutions to existing problems. The relationship between learning and unlearning is therefore an important one.

'Diagnosis' is a term, often associated with the medical profession, that means to understand the nature and cause of a particular phenomenon.

3 Clarity and ambiguity

Learning objectives

The aims of this chapter are to:

- explore the different ways in which change objectives can be set;
- investigate the consequences for analysis and action of the way that objectives are framed;
- equip the reader with an approach (WXYZ) that can be applied in large-scale strategic change and smaller-scale developments; and
- encourage the reader to be aware of the strengths and limitations of setting clear change targets.

In Chapter 2 we highlighted some of the ways in which scholars have tried to classify change depending on the nature of the change – large- or small-scale, internally or externally driven, proceeding slowly or quickly. However, here we begin to set out ways in which the broad sense that change is needed can be translated into a more particular definition of what needs to be changed and how this might be achieved. Since organizations are complex and multifaceted, the process of specifying the change challenge tends to proceed iteratively. It may be attractive to think of a more logical and linear process whereby treatment follows diagnosis but in organizational change it is not unusual to revisit the specification of the change challenge repeatedly as the change itself unfolds. Of course, this revisiting could be taken to suggest that the change was inaccurately or incompetently specified at the outset. However, in practice it may simply be that new information has come to light as the change proceeds.

Researchers have long been fascinated by the ways in which individuals frame problems and the consequences of that framing. Karl Weick observes that 'problems do not present themselves to practitioners as givens' and that, 'to convert a problematic situation to a problem, a practitioner must do a certain kind of work' (1995: 9). The kind of work to which Weick is referring is one category of change work that involves problem framing or problem setting. This is the conscious or unconscious process by which we define the problem(s) that we will tackle. Donald Schön (1983) suggests that problem setting is what we do when we define the decisions to be made, the ends to be achieved and the means that may be chosen, and there are a number of studies that claim that the framing of decisions has a profound effect on the ways in which people approach those decisions (see, for example, Kahneman and Tversky's classic 1979 study on perceived risks in decision making, which helped establish interest in this area of research).

Some argue that changing the definition of what is being studied can change what is seen, and that 'when different definitions are used to chart the same territory, the results will differ as do topographical, political and demographic maps, each revealing one aspect of reality by virtue of disregarding others' (Martin, 1986: 15). For instance, the introduction of the Dyson as a bagless vacuum cleaner changed the nature of that industry. Many of the incumbent firms began to struggle to compete, losing both market share and money. In interviews we conducted within a well-known vacuum cleaner firm, it was clear that the problem was being defined differently by different groups. Those in marketing and product development felt sure that consumers wanted a more powerful machine, because the power rating of the motor implied greater suction, and greater suction meant higher cleaning efficiency. The design engineers did not see the problem in the same way at all:

[T]hey [the marketing people] keep asking for more power. We're building cleaners with bigger and bigger motors but that just means that the machines get more expensive and heavier. Worse still, my team is now designing systems to dissipate some of the suction produced, because if it was all directed at the carpet the machine would suck so hard you wouldn't be able to push it along.

(Senior design engineer, in interview)

For the engineers, the problem was one of improving product reliability and reducing the costs of production by standardizing components and streamlining assembly processes. However, the senior managers of the firm were thinking at a different level of abstraction and were concerned about the cost base of their operations. This led to a decision to close UK-based factories and move production to eastern Europe, where wage costs were lower. Each group had framed the problem in its own terms. Everyone saw the same symptoms – lower revenues and declining market share – but each group diagnosed different causal mechanisms and therefore arrived at divergent conclusions on how best to move forward.

Organizational issues in general are prone to multiple interpretations, and this is particularly true of issues relating to organizational change. In this sense, they are often referred to as 'wicked problems',[1] and in the aftermath of a change process it may be possible for some stakeholders to argue that they were 'solving the wrong problem when one should have solved the right problem' (Mitroff and Featheringham, 1974). There are relatively few studies that explore the ways in which problems are surfaced and formulated, as noted by Lyles and Mitroff (1980). It is therefore important to consider whether it is possible and/or appropriate to have a precise definition of the change challenge in place at the outset of the change process. Consider the vacuum manufacturer described above. At the outset of a change process, the problem facing the organization could have been described with precision and clarity (see closed problem framing below). Equally, the problem could have deliberately been set with an inherent sense of ambiguity (see open problem framing below). As might be expected, these provide different impetus to the change process.

Filling the vacuum

(1) Closed problem framing: the challenge facing [name of firm] is to reduce operating costs by 35 per cent within two years.
(2) Open problem framing: the challenge facing [name of firm] is to regain our place as the market leader.

Some might be attracted to the clarity and specificity of the closed framing above. It might help galvanize efforts and would be more likely to produce a solution that focused on issues such as product design and manufacturability (as favoured by the engineers) and the overall cost structure, including wage costs, taxation regimes and location (as pursued by senior management). Such precision may be more helpful in some contexts than others. Using Burnes's (2009) schema (see Chapter 1), it may be more appropriate when the change needs to be

---

[1] Horst Rittel and Melvin Webber coined the term 'wicked problem': '[W]e are not calling them wicked in the sense that they are ethically deplorable. We use the term wicked in a meaning akin to that of malignant (in contrast to benign) or vicious (like a circle)' (1973: 160).

made quickly, perhaps driven by external pressures. Similarly, in Marshak's (2009) terms, this may work better in 'build and develop' than in 'liberate and recreate'. The question then is whether the ambiguous nature of the open framing above has any merit. We believe that it might help in at least two ways. First, it might help keep a wider group of stakeholders engaged with the change process. Staff working at a manufacturing site under threat of closure may be inclined to disengage with the change process altogether because they know that the only realistic way to deliver a significant cost reduction rests with low-cost labour. A natural disenchantment with the way the problem is being framed might lead on to a more confrontational change process. Second, the clear focus on costs simply foregrounds one issue whilst relegating other issues to the background. Many scholars have noted the consequences of this selective approach, in which some issues receive attention whilst others are, in relative terms at least, ignored (see Dutton, 1993, for one useful example). In this particular case, we have the benefit of hindsight, which shows that lowering the cost base of the firm did not secure the firm's competitive position. Instead, the firm continued to struggle, because its product offering was perceived as weak in relation to the award-winning Dyson machine. This may be a good example of solving the wrong problem. Perhaps framing the problem in the more ambiguous sense implied by the open framing (2) above would have opened a wider set of possibilities to those involved in the change. The kinds of enquiry we suggest in Chapter 9, relating to new business models, new technologies, new products and new markets, might have been considered alongside any cost-related issues. Hence, in some circumstances it may be helpful and appropriate to be knowingly unclear, as acknowledged by March, who notes that ambiguous purposes are intentions that cannot be clearly specified (1994).

John Shotter argues that there is a gradual and iterative process involved in specifying such issues, and he notes that 'the expression of an intention is, as a process of temporal unfolding, the passage from an indeterminate to a more well articulated state of affairs' (1983: 29). The US scholar William Starbuck's account of being treated for severe breathing difficulties serves to illustrate this iterative approach to diagnosis (see Starbuck, 2006). Starbuck was working in Germany and had been admitted to hospital on several occasions with respiratory problems. He gives a colourful account of meeting a German clinician, who prescribed medication before performing any tests. The professional researcher in Starbuck was somewhat horrified, and he asked the clinician whether this was a safe way to proceed. The clinician argued that beginning to treat the patient was the best way of finding out what was really wrong, because feedback would become available based on whether particular treatment or drugs were working. We believe that the iterative loop of diagnosis and treatment described by Starbuck's clinician applies to the challenge of organizational change.

Specifying change challenges

We suggest that there is a two-stage process involved in attempting to specify the change challenge in a particular situation. The first is to take a position on whether it is possible and appropriate to define the change challenge with any precision at the outset. Thereafter, if precision is desirable, we suggest a particular exercise for setting out a statement or problem framing. This iterative process is described in Figure 3.1.

Open problem framing

When framing a problem in an open-ended way, one invites others to read into the problem from their own experience base and their own particular organizational position. In so doing, open problems invite multiple readings and promote a sense of ambiguity. In the case of the vacuum cleaner firm, the open framing of the problem focuses on a future state that few stakeholders would find objectionable. The suggestion that the issue is to 'regain a position as market leader' is likely to offer a basis for some consensus to emerge over the end game, despite simultaneously creating the space for multiple – perhaps competing or contradictory – solutions to emerge. A second tactic may be to focus on moving away from a set of current circumstances that are uncomfortable. A small player in a larger supply chain might frame a change challenge, which is to stop being

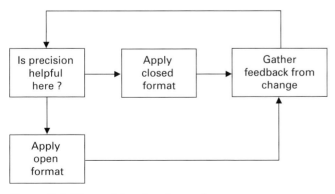

Figure 3.1 The problem-framing cycle

pushed down on price by larger customers elsewhere in the chain. Again, this is likely to be accepted by most, if not all, of those involved.

Hence, framing problems in an open way is not difficult and may in some circumstances be highly appropriate. However, an open framing can be damaging if it occurs by default and inadvertently limits options for action. If the way forward is unclear, it might provoke inactivity and inertia.

Closed problem framing

Writing a closed framing of a problem can be more challenging, particularly in the early stages of a change process. This may be explained in two ways. First, the very act of writing something down can itself be challenging. Richard Rumelt argues that the bullet point format afforded by modern word-processing and presentation software has produced a tendency to compartmentalize and decompose issues. His view is that asking a group to set aside bullet points and write coherently produces a step change. 'Having to link your thoughts, giving reasons and qualifications makes you a more careful thinker' (Rumelt, 2007: 62). It can be difficult to overcome the writer's block that comes with having to start this process. In contexts in which organizational change is involved this is further complicated, because there are usually colleagues involved, creating the potential for confrontation and embarrassment.

The second challenge of writing a closed problem statement is that, in many ways, it requires you to have done some prior work. In order to know that the magnitude of the cost reduction required is 35 per cent and that the timescale is two years, those within the vacuum manufacturer had probably done some work on the problem beforehand. Our experience of working with change teams in a number of organizational settings is that closed problem statements are almost like self-fulfilling prophecies in which the eventual solution is embedded in the problem statement. We have developed a particular exercise to produce closed problem framings.

First, we suggest that these statements need to be reasonably succinct. Our suggestion is that they should run to no more than fifty words. Although this is not cast in stone, we find it a useful upper target. Second, work conducted with large numbers of change teams leads us to suggest that problem statements feature certain common themes. These include a view of some *objective or goal* that is amenable to calibration and measurement, an indication of the *process* by which the change is to be delivered, the *resources* that are likely to be involved and the *time frame* within which the change must be delivered.

W – the objective or goal of the change process.
X – the process by which change will be delivered.
Y – the resources or skill set involved.
Z – the time frame for the change to be completed.

The change challenge facing this organization is to achieve **W** by doing **X** with **Y** in time frame **Z**.

Figure 3.2 Closed problem framing using WXYZ

These four key components can be set out in the form WXYZ, as shown in Figure 3.2.

Applying the WXYZ structure to the closed problem statement from the vacuum cleaner firm, we can see that some components are missing. The objective is set (W = a 35 per cent reduction in costs) and a time frame has been specified (Z = within two years), but there is no mention of the process or the skill set required. In this particular example, the process actually involves relocating production facilities to a low-cost economy in eastern Europe (i.e. X = relocation). As the relocation process got under way, it also became clear that the firm's ability to train new staff on the assembly lines was critical. The firm used quality circles and a number of other practices to ensure the efficient operation of its manufacturing activities. Training new staff quickly and efficiently allowed the firm to transfer production to a new site with minimal disruption (i.e. Y = training and human resources (HR)).

Since problem definition is an iterative process, it is easy to see how the pieces of a problem statement might fall into place over time. Such iteration is precisely what the enquiry–action framework is intended to facilitate. The realization that a significant cost reduction is needed might flow first from a financial analysis of the firm and its competitors. Next, the realization might come that a reduction of this size is possible only if labour costs are addressed. The potential difficulties of losing tacit knowledge from a skilled and experienced workforce may flow from here, leading to the conclusion that training skills are central. Finally the two-year time horizon may arise in the light of negotiations with key stakeholders, such as corporate headquarters, the banks and the unions, and the availability of facilities in the new location.

As a result, it is not always possible to tie down all four components at the outset. Indeed, our experience is that the iterative process described in Figure 3.1 means that those leading change gradually refine the problem statement as new evidence, data and experience become available. Paradoxically, the problem statement is both the first and the last thing that the change agent needs to write. The first iteration of the problem statement plays an important part in getting the process started, whilst the final version plays an important part in allowing those involved to agree that the change is coming to a close.

EXERCISE

Examine the three change challenges set out below. Each is set out using an open framing. For each challenge, make notes on the following questions.

Q1   Is this framing appropriate?

Q2   Apply the WXYZ format:

   (a) map which components are present/missing in each statement;

   (b) translate the statement to the WXYZ format by filling in any missing components.

CASE 1

Admiral Insurance was launched in 1993 by a group of five people who had previous experience in the insurance industry and saw an opportunity to secure a profitable niche (see Extended Case 5 for further details). Whilst most competitors focused on those who would traditionally be seen as safe drivers, Admiral aggressively pursued people paying high premiums such as younger drivers, those with high-performance cars and those living in cities, or some combination of all three. The business was formed by a group of MBA-qualified managers who wanted to create a unique culture in which hard work, fun and high performance lived side by side. Following early success, the business began to grow rapidly, eventually becoming a multi-site business and one of the largest private sector employers in Wales.

Problem framed as:
the change challenge facing Admiral is retaining its culture whilst growing rapidly.

CASE 2

Babcock Infrastructure Services is one the market leaders in providing facilities management to a range of clients. The mainstay of the business consists of several long-term contracts (ranging from five to over thirty years) to support the UK defence sector, including military bases. Two issues troubled the management team. First, defence budgets were under pressure and were unlikely to increase in real terms. Second, the defence market was fixed in size, since there were a finite number of army, navy or air force locations and Babcock already had high market share through what were called regional prime contracts. However, growth opportunities did exist beyond the defence sector, and the firm hoped to secure further contracts by using its existing skills and staff to target other markets, such as schools, hospitals, universities, prisons, etc.

Problem framed as:
the change challenge facing Babcock Infrastructure is to diversify.

CASE 3
National Health Service (NHS) Greater Glasgow and Clyde
Four separate organizations provided healthcare in west and central Scotland. A new initiative came from the Scottish government, which meant that these four organizations were to merge, producing a single organization employing over 45,000 staff and providing services to over 1 million citizens. The change challenge facing the organization is to consolidate three sites into a single location. Each constituent organization had its own management teams, meaning, for example, that the new organization would have four medical directors but only one role to fill. The same was true in finance, personnel, estates, logistics, planning, etc.

Problem framed as:
the change challenge facing NHS Greater Glasgow and Clyde is to integrate four organizations without interrupting service provision or increasing costs.

You may also wish to try framing the change challenge facing one or more of the organizations in the extended cases at the rear of the book.

WHO TO READ

Two scholars offer thoughtful and helpful voices in relation to this chapter. First, Ian Mitroff has written extensively on issues of problem formulation, and his 2009 book *Dirty Rotten Strategies* (with Abraham Silvers) offers a reasonable overview of his work. The second scholar to read is Richard Rumelt. A strategy scholar, in his later career Rumelt has drawn attention to the role of writing clearly in producing coherent analysis and action. The article from *McKinsey Quarterly* listed below is a good starting point for a much wider body of work that Rumelt has produced.

USEFUL WEBSITES

If you would like to follow up the vignettes introduced in this chapter, the following sites would be useful starting points.

- www.admiral.com has an 'about us' section that provides an overview of the company and insights into the changes that it has undergone.
- www.dyson.co.uk; the 'inside Dyson' section explains the 'Dyson story' and how the company developed and changed over time.
- www.babcock.co.uk's 'about us' section explains the business strategy and lays out the strategic objectives, which you might like to compare to your answers to Case 2 above.
- www.nhsggc.org.uk – in the 'information and publications' section more information can be found about the NHS in Glasgow and Clyde. In particular, the annual reviews and reports available on the site give an insight into their change priorities and explains some of the objectives they have been pursuing.

REFERENCES

Burnes, B. (2009) *Managing Change*, 5th edn. Harlow: Pearson.

Dutton, J. E. (1993) Interpretations on automatic: a different view of strategic issue diagnosis. *Journal of Management Studies*, 30(3): 339–57.

Kahneman, D., and Tversky, A. (1979) Prospect theory: an analysis of

decision under risk. *Econometrica*,
47(2): 263–91.

Lyles, M. A., and Mitroff, I. I. (1980)
Organizational problem formulation:
an empirical study. *Administrative
Science Quarterly*, 25(1): 102–19.

March, J. G. (1994) *A Primer on Decision
Making: How Decisions Happen.*
New York: Free Press.

Marshak, R. (2009) *Organizational Change:
Views from the Edge.* Bethel, ME:
Lewin Center.

Martin, W. (1986) *Recent Theories of Narrative.*
Ithaca, NY: Cornell University Press.

Mitroff, I. I., and Featheringham, T. R. (1974)
On systemic problem solving and the error
of the third kind. *Behavioral Science*,
19(6): 383–93.

Mitroff, I. I., and Silvers, A (2009) *Dirty
Rotten Strategies: How We Trick
Ourselves and Others into Solving the*
Wrong Problems Precisely. Stanford
University Press.

Rittel, H., and Webber, M. (1973) Dilemmas
in a general theory of planning. *Policy
Sciences*, 4(2): 155–69.

Rumelt, R. (2007) Strategy's strategist: an
interview with Richard Rumelt. *McKinsey
Quarterly*, November.

Schön, D. A. (1983) *The Reflective Practitioner:
How Professionals Think in Action.* New
York: Basic Books.

Shotter, J. (1983) Duality of structure and
intentionality in an ecological psychology.
Journal for the Theory of Social Behaviour,
13(1): 19–43.

Starbuck, W. H. (2006) *The Production of
Knowledge: The Challenge of Social
Science Research.* New York: Oxford
University Press.

Weick, K. E. (1995) *Sensemaking in
Organizations.* Thousand Oaks, CA: Sage.

4 Engagement and vitality

This aims of this chapter are to:

- explain the relationship between individual vitality and organizational engagement;
- explore the ways in which our experience change in organizations can shape our sense of engagement; and
- investigate the concept of health as an organizational process.

When we walk into an organization for the first time we quickly pick up something of the ambience and atmosphere of that organization. Much like viewing a home or interviewing a candidate for a job, we form first impressions quickly. In some cases it may be the creative sparks of an energetic and innovative workplace that we discern. In others it may the dour and somewhat lifeless sense that the organization is failing in some way. Since organizations are populated by people, it is natural to question the relationships between individual and collective moods. Does, for example, working in a great organization make you happy, or can a bad workplace lower your mood? Robert Quinn feels that there is a need for a 'new and larger concept called organizational vitality' (1978: 395). For Quinn, this concept would incorporate elements such as motivational climate, and other aspects that we might relate to organizational culture (see Chapter 6). In our own research we continue to be struck by the markedly differing accounts of organizational life that we have heard over many years of interviewing members of a variety of public, private and third sector organizations. Indeed, it has been argued that health is inherently an organizational and relational phenomenon (MacIntosh, MacLean and

Burns, 2007). In the early part of the last century Alfred North Whitehead observed that 'prolonged routine work dulls the imagination' (1929: 144) and that 'it is a libel upon human nature to conceive that zest for life is the product of pedestrian purposes directed toward the narrow routine of material comforts' (140). Vitality might therefore have its roots in the nature of our organizational experience, since health and disease have both been conceptualized as organizational phenomena (MacLean and MacIntosh, 1998).

Since Quinn's work, there has been relatively little research in organization and management studies that has sought to understand the idea of vitality, and empirically based studies of organizational vitality are few and far between. This might not be surprising, as vitality itself is an ambiguous concept, used in a variety of ways. We explore some of the work that relates to vitality and engagement before introducing a simple vitality diagnostic that we have developed for use in change processes.

Lynda Gratton's study of organizational 'hot spots' (2007) sought to explain why some organizations have a sense of internal energy and others do not. She looked at a sample of seventeen firms and at fifty-seven separate groups or organizational units within those firms. Inside the same organization she found some groups, units, departments or teams in which vitality was high and others in which this was not the case. Her observations led her to conclude that hot spots were created by three things. First, they occurred where there was a collaborative culture that permitted or incentivized cooperation (culture is dealt with here in Chapter 6). Second, those working in the hot spots were likely to be engaged in conversations that spanned traditional boundaries in the organization. This meant that those in the hot spots continued to be exposed to new thinking, new problems and opportunities and new people to talk to. Interestingly, Gratton suggests that 60 per cent of what we say in conversations with those whom we already know is repetitious. She argues that this explains the importance of breaking into new conversations (dialogue is dealt with here in Chapter 13). Finally, Gratton's hot spots seemed to cohere around what she calls 'an igniting purpose'. Whether this is Bill Gates claiming that there would be a computer in every home (long before this seemed at all likely) or Southwest Airlines' vision of providing the convenience and speed of air travel for about the cost of a car journey, clarity of purpose seemed important in galvanizing vitality (clarity was dealt with in the previous chapter).

Jane Dutton (2003) argues that the energy and vitality of individuals and organizations alike depend on the quality of the connections between people in the organization. In her view, high-quality connections can enhance the vitality of the individuals concerned and the wider organization within which they operate. Likewise, corrosive or toxic interactions can reduce vitality. The nature of the conversations taking place in an organization can be subjected to analysis and change (as we show in Chapter 13). Within the enquiry–action framework, then, the second way of diagnosing the change challenge facing an organization is to consider the levels of vitality and engagement that those working in the organization display. In today's competitive environment, success or failure is increasingly dependent on the creative capacities of individuals working within the organization. Since creativity and innovation are inherently voluntary activities, we would argue that people need to want to be there. Interestingly, this is a key aspiration for both Oticon and Admiral (Extended Cases 4 and 5, respectively). We describe this as the level of engagement between the organization and its members.

Advertising agencies, software firms and research and development (R&D) settings are just some examples in which creativity might be seen as essential, yet in other work situations, in which safety, repeatability and control are key, creativity might seem less relevant. That said, even in highly routinized work it is helpful to achieve some level of engagement. At work some people are perceived as disengaged, or perhaps even disruptive. However, outside work these same individuals are engaged in a variety of creative and productive activities, often on a voluntary basis. One senior manager in a large manufacturing firm commented: 'It is as if they leave not just their brain at the reception desk but their soul too.' Our argument is that a lack of engagement is not simply a neutral result but, rather, that any form of disengagement has corrosive consequences.

This is a real challenge, since our organizational interactions often take place within a context of countermanding tensions with frequent pulls in opposing directions. Although a free exchange of ideas might sound ideal, the political realities of many situations mean that there are times when colleagues and friends cannot be completely open (Krantz, 2006). For instance, in seeking to gain political backing for a creative venture, it may be necessary for team members to be able to 'absorb the tensions' of the need for openness to uncertain futures and the need to create or portray sufficient confidence in an outcome to warrant the time, budget and resources being spent on the creative effort. Therefore, in this view, creative vitality occurs through interaction and dialogue, and, although this partially entails a mutually positive micro-environment, it also entails the ability to absorb and manage tensions and cope with a range of individual and organizational demands. As changeful situations in organizational life often entail paradoxes, such tensions are commonplace (Beech et al., 2004).

Our research has convinced us that vitality is an emergent phenomenon, much like strategy or culture. As such, vitality can be influenced, particularly by change. However, vitality is not just about creativity and change. Most organizations need repetition in order to be efficient, and they need control in order to achieve targets. This becomes problematic only when control and repetition come to dominate.

Low vitality

Ed works as a senior manager in a large public sector organization. A peak period of work occurs once per year. This happens each year, and, in order to meet the deadlines, the staff are encouraged to work overtime. In turn, this means that the building needs to be open on a Saturday, and this incurs a fee of £150 for paying security costs. However, the security firm's fee was held in the budget centre that related to overtime, and payment to an external security firm was permitted to come only from a different type of account called an estates budget. Internal financial rules mean that the minimum amount transferrable from one budget category to another is £1,000. Despite having requested and secured money to cover both the staff costs for overtime and the costs of paying security to open the building outside normal working hours, there was a problem. In order to pay £150 for a security guard you would, in effect, have to pay £1,000 from one budget to another in an irreversible transaction. In Ed's words:

I've been through this kind of rigmarole before. It's completely absurd in the context of trying to deliver the business results that we have to deliver. This is what it is like, and its one of a long litany of these kinds of examples trying to get small things done. They don't want you to pay £150; they would far rather that you had to pay more for something. [...] The attitude starts to become one which is unhelpful.

Ed recounts this example in the context of a discussion about the low levels of engagement and vitality in his workplace. The frustration at having to work around the internal rules is exacerbated by the fact that Ed is trying to help the organization hit key performance targets.

High vitality

Joe is an entrepreneur in the food sector. He holds a position as chair of an industry body that represents a particular type of food production. In this role, he has attended many meetings with government officials. Following a change of government in Scotland, Joe attended a meeting with the new minister and his team. As he says:

I've been going to these meetings for years. Up until this one it had always been the same old thing – you know, familiar faces, the usual suspects and one or two government ministers with responsibility for our sector. We'd all sit there. The great and the good would be on the stage. The chair would conduct things; questions – polite questions – would come from the floor. Everything that might be misconstrued as a criticism of government would be met with an explanation as to why things were the way they were. The closest we got to change was undertakings to 'look into things'. It was always like that: going through the motions, everyone there because they felt they had to be there – but expecting nothing more than a good informal chat over the dinner that followed. But last time it was different. Obviously, given the political changes [a change in government], it was two new ministers – but we were all expecting the same thing. First thing we noticed was there was no stage, no top table. When the ministers were asked questions, they answered them directly. They expressed opinions and asked others there directly what they thought of this or that, what could be done about this situation or that, what was needed, who was going to do what by when. It really felt like they meant action. It was infectious; you could feel the energy levels rise in the room. People started moving around – gesturing to one another. Some ties loosened – some came off! We were getting excited, hopeful that we might be on the edge of a breakthrough – and all because the conversation was open and we all felt that everyone in the room actually cared enough to do something new, take some risks – get moving. It was magic!

In contrast to the story told by Ed, Joe is energized by the interaction with others in the meeting he attends. The sense of optimism is in stark contrast to the perceived futility of the rules and regulations in Ed's situation. Ed seems locked into a pattern of interaction that prevents obvious solutions being produced. Roles and systems that had been devised to make processes more efficient seem now to have the reverse effect. Conversely, Joe's interaction at the consultation meeting features tangible excitement, as government ministers are able to step outside their traditional identity roles and move into a different form of dialogue. In our research on vitality, aspects of identity dynamics appear to play an important part in framing the attribution of agency to self and others (typically, with vitality being experienced when agency is located in or close to the person telling the story).

Vitality diagnostic

As a means of instigating a dialogue about vitality and engagement, we use the prompt questions below as a diagnostic.

Q1 What we do

(i) Give examples of the sort of action/performance that you have seen in the past that you would like to see more of in the future.

(ii) Give examples of the sort of action/performance that you have seen in the past that you would like to see less of in the future.

(iii) Which of the types of action/performance in questions (i) and (ii) are more typical of your normal working day?

Q2 How we fit together

(i) Do people know what is happening in the organization (and does it make sense)?

(ii) Do you feel connected to the people you work with?

(iii) Do you feel connected to your manager?

Q3 How we are developing

(i) Do people know where the organization is going, and do they buy in to that direction?

(ii) Are you supported in your own development?

(iii) How many of your colleagues are 'stuck' in their current roles?

(iv) Are achievements rewarded?

(v) Does the organization celebrate successes?

Q4 How we make decisions

(i) Where are the main decisions made in the organization?

(ii) Do people throughout the organization have an input into decisions?

(iii) Do people feel that they make decisions and choose actions in their own jobs?

Q5 How we innovate

(i) Is the organization good at innovating and changing (e.g. developing new services or improving procedures)?

(ii) Do people feel that they have the freedom to make innovations in their own jobs?

(iii) Do people have an input into innovations and developments in the business more generally (e.g. suggestion schemes)?

Q6 How we communicate

(i) Do people receive good information from the organization (e.g. what is happening, future direction, current issues)?

(ii) Can people make suggestions/raise issues with their managers?

(iii) Do people make suggestions/raise issues with their managers?

(iv) How open are conversations with your manager?

(v) How open are conversations with people who report to you?

EXERCISE

Use the six questions in the vitality diagnostic to explore the ways in which Admiral Insurance (Extended Case 5) maintains the creative drive and energy that the senior management team see as central to its success.

WHO TO READ

Aaron Antonovsky (1987a, 1987b) is a sociologist who has studied the relationship between stress, health and well-being. His 'sense of coherence' framework seeks to explain why some individuals cope much better with stressful environments than others.

USEFUL WEBSITES

- www.lyndagratton.com; this site offers a brief overview of the hot spots study.
- www.bestcompanies.co.uk; Best Companies is the organization behind the *Sunday Times* list of the 'Best places to work' awards. The site gives details of the methodology used to generate the rankings.

REFERENCES

Antonovsky, A. (1987a) *Unraveling the Mystery of Health: How People Manage Stress and Stay Well.* San Francisco: Jossey-Bass.

Antonovsky, A. (1987b) Health promoting factors at work: the sense of coherence, in Kalimo, R., Eltatawi, M., and Cooper, C. (eds.)

Psychosocial Factors at Work and Their Effects on Health: 153–67. Geneva: World Health Organization.

Beech, N., Burns, H., de Caestecker, L., MacIntosh, R., and MacLean, D. (2004) Paradox as invitation to act in problematic change situations. *Human Relations*, 57(10): 1313–32.

Dutton, J. E. (2003) *Energize Your Workplace: How to Create and Sustain High-Quality Connections at Work.* San Francisco: Jossey-Bass.

Gratton, L. (2007) *Hot Spots: Why Some Companies Buzz with Energy and Innovation, and Others Don't.* Harlow: Pearson.

Krantz, J. (2006) Leadership, betrayal and adaptation. *Human Relations*, 59(2): 221–40.

MacIntosh, R., MacLean, D., and Burns, H. (2007) Health in organization: toward a process-based view. *Journal of Management Studies*, 44(2): 206–21.

MacLean, D., and MacIntosh, R. (1998) Health and disease in organisations. *Journal of Alternative and Complementary Medicine*, 4(2): 185–8.

Quinn, R. E. (1978) Toward a theory of changing: a means–ends model of the organizational improvement process. *Human Relations*, 31(5): 395–416.

Whitehead, A. N. (1929) Universities and their function, reproduced in (1962) *The Aims of Education and Other Essays.* London: Ernest Benn.

5 Stakeholder positioning and dynamics

The aims of this chapter are to:

- introduce the concepts of stakeholders and influence;
- explore an approach to mapping stakeholders;
- identify the potential dynamics of stakeholders; and
- consider the implications for strategic and tactical action.

As a change idea or programme is introduced people will naturally align themselves with various positions with regard to the change. For some the change may represent a step in the right direction, and so be something to be supported. For others it could constitute a threat, for example by rendering their current competencies redundant, and so they may oppose the change. In many change situations there are a great variety of possible positions, and the complexity is increased as stakeholders change their positions over time. Therefore, when leading change it is helpful to understand the positions that stakeholders may adopt and what the consequences of this can be for change outcomes. In this chapter we explore a technique for mapping stakeholders' positions, recognizing the influence that they might exert and the dynamics that emerge as people act and react to each other.

We illustrate some of these points by drawing upon a case from the French film industry, and we conclude that, whilst 'managing' stakeholders may not be possible, the techniques discussed can provide a route to engaging with stakeholders.

Stakeholder positioning

Two of the fundamental questions of change management are 'What space do we have to act in?' and 'How can we increase that space?' (Freeman, 1984). The space for acting is defined by the relative position of the individual or group seeking to make change happen and others around them who could be relatively supportive or obstructive towards the change intention. Stakeholder mapping has often been used to work out how to develop organizations in the midst of a network of others who may want to see different outcomes (Schneider, 2002). Stakeholder analysis can be used for a variety of purposes during a change project (Peltokorpi *et al.*, 2007). These include assessing expected benefits (Strong, Ringer and Taylor, 2001), understanding implementation challenges, analysing the capability of an organization to change and gaining insight into stakeholders' influence over implementation. The technique we discuss is often used both for large-scale strategy formulation (Eden and Ackermann, 1998; Bryson, 2004; Ackermann and Eden, 2011) and for immediate action. In the first case, it is often conducted by a strategic team and takes place over a prolonged period of time, normally being revisited on a regular basis to update movements. In the latter case, it can be used by individuals or groups as they prepare for a particular interaction and can be kept simple enough to be borne in mind as the interaction is proceeding.

The first step is to define the change that is to be analysed, as stakeholders will align differently depending on the issue at hand (Savage *et al.*, 1991). This topic was discussed in Chapter 3, where we explored the balance between clarity and ambiguity in defining change objectives. However, at this stage in the management of change the implications of the change objectives need to be spelled out in terms of the likely/possible responses of others. 'Role thinking' (Huxham and Vangen, 2004) or putting oneself 'into the shoes of the other' can be very revealing when carried out seriously. It is not uncommon for this process to lead to a significant modification of either the objectives or the timescale/ resources that are envisaged as being necessary for the change.

Having defined the change issue or problem that is being considered, the first step of mapping is to produce a list of stakeholders (Bryson, 2004). This is normally achieved through dialogue within an internal team (van der Heijden, 2005). The stakeholders can be defined as relatively broad groups, such as 'competitors', or they can be smaller collectives, such as a specific competitor, or a particular individual, such as the chief executive officer (CEO) of a supplier. The rule of thumb is that the stakeholders should be defined in the smallest aggregate required to understand who could act in relation to the change issue being addressed. Thus, it might be appropriate to consider suppliers as one stakeholder group if they are all likely to react in a similar manner, but to consider a number of separate suppliers if some might react strongly to a change in the focal organization whilst others may have little interest. It is also worth considering whether or not the stakeholders you group together would regard themselves as a group (Rowley and Moldoveanu, 2003). There is a difference between suppliers happening to respond in a similar way and deliberately reacting as a collective. If they are acting as a collective you may need to identify those playing a leadership role and note them separately when producing a stakeholder map.

Once the stakeholders have been identified, the next task is to map where they sit with regard to your organization. This is done by considering their position on two axes (Eden and Ackermann, 1998; Ackermann, Eden and Brown, 2005). The first axis is the degree of interest the stakeholder is judged to have in the change issue. At a simple level, interest can be positive or negative towards the change. The range stretches from stakeholders who are directly affected by the change to those who have only a passing interest, or for whom the change is a relatively unimportant part of their context (Finlay-Robinson, 2009). In some cases there is a 'vicarious interest', in which case the stakeholder is concerned with the interest of an ally or person connected to him or her. For example, first-tier suppliers may not have very much direct interest in the choice of a second-tier supplier by the customer, but they might have a preference for one that they have a relationship with, and hence they have an interest in who is appointed by the customer. In a looser form, a trade union might be concerned with the impact of a change on non-members if it could simulate them to join the union. Interest therefore comes in a variety of forms: positive, negative, direct, passing and vicarious.

The second axis relates to the level of influence that the stakeholder could have over the progress of the change. Some stakeholders might have a great deal of influence and be able either to accelerate or to prevent the change, whilst others might have little power to alter the way that things will develop. Influence takes several forms. Some stakeholders will have the ability to have a direct influence on decisions and how the change proceeds. Direct influence can be based on position (for example, chairing a committee or being a CEO), the ability to allocate or withhold resources (controlling the purse strings, as Huxham and Vangen, 2004, put it), or the ability to issue instructions that others will follow. Indirect influence occurs when stakeholders are not in a position to make the decision themselves, but are able to delineate or give direction to the shape of the decision. This can occur, for instance, through the use of expertise when a stakeholder's knowledge is acknowledged and used by the decision makers. Such knowledge can be technical, business-related or derived from analysis or data that others do not have. Hence, one way of gaining influence in a group is to find information or analysis that they do not have and bring it into the decision-making 'arena' (Hardy and Clegg, 1999). These forms of influence are observable and occur during the decision-making phases of change management.

However, influence is also exercised around the decision-making arena, in order to produce a covert or indirect impact on how the change proceeds. This is when influence can be more subtle and difficult for the change managers to counter, and so it is often the case that successful change management entails considerable use of influencing skills and relationship building outside meetings and beyond the formal process. Some people regard such activities as unacceptably Machiavellian whilst others see them as a necessary component of change management. Certainly, it is worth keeping in mind one's ethical stance on openness of communication, involvement and the justification that ends can provide for the means employed (or not, depending on your stance). Influence outside the decision-making arena can be built upon relationships and trust. For example, when there is information overload, decision makers may have trusted colleagues whose opinion they will seek as a short cut to understanding the issue at hand. Therefore, knowing who these trusted colleagues are and what information or evidence they value, or supplying them with perspectives that they do not currently have, can be ways of indirectly influencing the decision makers. For example, it might be that the decision makers are remote from the customers and make judgements based on sales figures and complaint levels, but that a stakeholder with interest but little direct influence could supply examples of customer suggestions that are known on the shopfloor to the analysts/decision makers. Although they are not able to change the agenda directly, by supplying information on a topic that is of interest but that potentially leads to a different way of thinking, the stakeholder is able to exert indirect influence. Thus, influence can be direct, within the decision-making arena, or indirect and subtle or covert. It is often the case that when stakeholders lack direct and overt influence they will seek other forms of influence. Hence, the change manager needs to be aware of how such a line of influence can develop and flow.

When these two axes are taken together, it is possible to map some stakeholders as having strong potential influence and high interest (see Figure 5.1). These stakeholders (the 'players': Ackermann, Eden and Brown, 2005) are likely to notice changes that you introduce and to be active in taking steps of their own in reaction. Other stakeholders (the 'observers') might have a keen interest

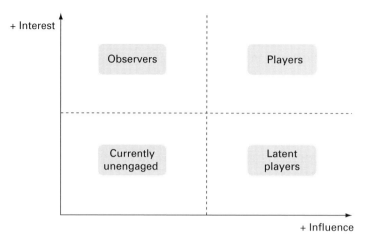

Figure 5.1 Basic stakeholder map

in the way the change progresses, but have relatively little influence over the speed and direction of change. The observers will pay attention to the change process and may be active in communicating their views to other groups. However, they command a different type of attention from the players, as they are likely to wield indirect influence outside the decision-making arena. In the diagonally opposite quadrant are stakeholders who have power to influence the speed and direction of change but have relatively little interest in the issue (the 'latent players'). For those managing the change, the issue with the latent players is the extent to which they become interested in the change topic. The latent players can be lobbied by the observers or can become interested because of changes in their own context. Hence, they can migrate into being engaged players. Therefore, they often command particular attention from the organization. The last quadrant is low on both influence and interest (the 'currently unengaged'). These are not people with no interest whatsoever, but their primary focus is on other topics. Stakeholders in this group can be significant either when players seek to engage them, or when they become part of the tactics of another stakeholder group.

Putting the mapping technique into action

As stakeholders are identified, they are recorded on the first 'rough take' of the map. In the process of discussion it is normal to identify more stakeholders, so the list expands. It is important to be aware of the subtleties of how the stakeholders define themselves and their values and aims (Hillman and Keim, 2001), as these will influence their reactions and behaviour. In addition, stakeholder identities are often dynamic (Ybema *et al.*, 2009). As a change progresses, alliances can form (**aggregations**) and differences or disputes can lead to separations (**disaggregations**). Equally, the analysis can lead to aggregation or disaggregation, as, for example, the distinctions between suppliers become less important for the change (and hence they are aggregated in the analysis) or a particular leader amongst suppliers is identified as an 'opinion leader' (in which case he or she is disaggregated and given his or her own position on the map). The stakeholders are positioned on the map according to their relative interest and influence, and this gives an initial picture of the socio-political environment of the change. However, as Neville and Menguc (2006) point out, the stakeholders rarely keep a single position. In reality they interact and move in terms of both interest and influence, and tracing such movement over time is a source of particular value in stakeholder mapping. These dynamics are recorded by drawing arrows of movement on the map.

Aggregations are coalitions of stakeholders with shared interest.

Disaggregation is a process whereby groups separate because of differences in interest.

The dynamics are recorded in two ways. **Descriptive dynamics** show how stakeholders actually move. **Prescriptive dynamics** are actions to be taken in order to influence a change in position. For example, one may want to move a powerful player out of the players' box by reducing his or her interest in the change issue so that the field is more open for your action. Conversely, one may want to move a latent player up into the players' box where he or she can offer active support for the change. Such moves might be achieved by seeking to divert attention to other issues of importance or by lobbying. These prescriptive dynamics are recorded by numbering the relevant arrows and having a separate list of associated actions.

Descriptive dynamics provide a record of how stakeholders actually move.

Prescriptive dynamics are actions that one takes in order to influence how others move.

As the change progresses, the initial map becomes covered in descriptive and prescriptive arrows, and so new maps are constructed showing both the descriptive state of affairs and the aspired-to outcome. The closeness of the fit between aspiration and description provides a way of assessing how the change activities are progressing and where the next phase of effort needs to be expended.

In the next section we illustrate the process by discussing a case from the creative industries. This case is based in France and relates to the film industry. It follows the stakeholder engagement process adopted by a group of senior managers as they faced a significant change. The company asked to be anonymized, and so we have given it the pseudonym 'Film de France'. The diagrams are ones that the company produced, which we have then simplified for presentation here, and the analysis of the case comes from our experience of working with the managers as they went through this process.

Mini-Case 5.1: Film de France

Film de France is a company that provides marketing and strategy consulting services to companies in the cinema/movie sector. It has a specialism in the use of IT, and many of its clients are high-tech companies that operate in the production and distribution chains. Film de France's mission is to help companies achieve growth through the use of technology and it has a history of supporting the development of small companies from local operation to national and international levels. The production of films typically involves a range of companies supplying specialist services, and the distribution of the final product entails complex logistical, technical and contractual management. As well as supplying some technical services, Film de France occupies the key broker role in several networks. It operates in the export market of French films to international customers and the import and distribution of overseas films into the French market. It works in a successful and growing industry, with one-third of the French population going to the cinema at least once a month, and in 2010 a new French film was released every day on movie screens around the world; some forty French films are aired each day on televisions worldwide.

Film de France was established by a charismatic entrepreneur, and he is currently still the chief executive and a major shareholder. However, as he nears retirement, the debate over his succession has been intensifying within the company. Decision making is seen as autocratic and the style of working is very traditional. This was successful in the past, and senior managers estimate that at least 40 per cent of their clients are with Film de France because of direct personal relationships with the CEO. However, the senior managers feel that the company is in need of modernization but the CEO is reluctant to plan seriously for retirement. The senior managers are aware that it will be a difficult process, for personal and business reasons alike, and they have met without the CEO to consider how to bring about change. Figure 5.2 shows a simplified form of their initial analysis of stakeholders.

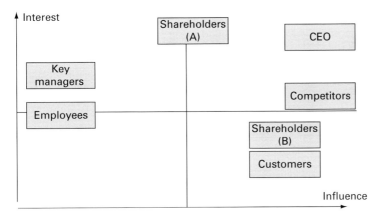

Figure 5.2 Initial analysis

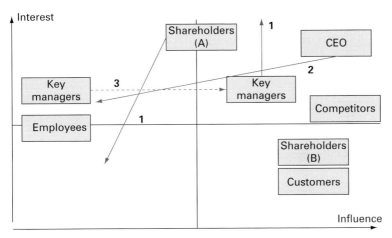

Figure 5.3 Actions by senior managers to encourage stakeholder movement

The chief executive is placed highest in both influence and interest, and the managers and employees have almost no influence attributed to them. One group of shareholders (A) is thought to be highly interested in the change of leadership, but moderate in their degree of influence. A second group (B) is thought to have significant influence (partly because of the number of shares they hold) should they choose to use it, but as the chief executive has particularly close relationships with these shareholders (some of whom are family members) their interest in acting is seen as fairly moderate. Competitors are seen as very influential and fairly interested, because the sector has been subject to a series of mergers and acquisitions and a change of leadership could herald a change in ownership structure.

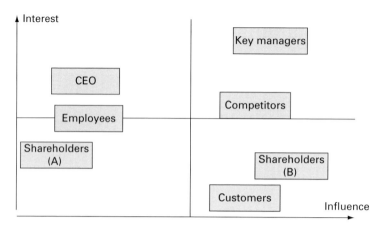

Figure 5.4 Target stakeholder map for succession

Having drawn up the initial map, the next stage is for the managers to consider dynamics and decide what actions to take in order to change the shape of the map. In undertaking this exercise, they recognize that they have already moved in terms of interest (see arrow 3 in Figure 5.3) but that key targets are to reduce the interest and influence of shareholders A, as they could block change in order to increase their own influence (arrow 1 in Figure 5.3). The managers plan to reduce the influence of shareholders A by highlighting the results they achieve, by persuading the chief executive that giving them some voice in decisions would not lead to poor decision making and by convincing him that he needs them to have greater interactions as primary contacts with certain clients. They also need to shift the CEO's interest and influence in maintaining his current position as autocratic leader. They aim to do this by persuading him that he needs to enable a smooth handover in two years' time by starting early and mentoring the senior managers so that he can be confident in them. Hence, his interest will increasingly be in mentoring rather than leading (arrow 2 in Figure 5.3). The senior managers have key allies in some shareholding family members, who want the CEO to retire but are somewhat sceptical about how genuine his intentions are. Hence, some of the shareholder B group could help with persuading the CEO into the new way of understanding his role.

Figure 5.4 depicts the desired 'end state' stakeholder map, in which the senior managers would be able to strongly influence succession planning. Their intention is to establish greater relationships with clients, to generate evidence of their ability to perform and hence to be able to persuade the chief executive and shareholders that they are competent to lead the company into its next phase of development.

Twelve months on from their initial analysis, the senior managers have had some success. The chief executive has stated openly that he intends to retire and has started to introduce senior managers to key clients as the *leaders* of projects. He still finds it difficult not to be present at key meetings with these clients, but does seem to be accepting that there will come a time when he will no longer be there to oversee his staff. Informal contacts with some of the shareholders have revealed that they are aware that the CEO will need to be replaced and are keen that this should be achieved in a way that preserves the business. The employees did not feature strongly in the analysis of the senior managers, and this is also something that has changed in practice. The managers have conducted an internal communication exercise, which identifies a degree of concern amongst the staff about the succession and the future of the company. The plan is to take a more engaged approach to strategic renewal and seek to give the employees more voice. This is clearly in contravention of the autocratic and hierarchical culture that has existed until now. Another dynamic that the senior managers did not expect but that can be observed is the increasing tension and competition between them as the possibilities of a change come closer to reality. There is a certain amount of personal positioning, and an outside analysis would disaggregate the senior manager group as individuals start to make contact with key shareholders and clients in order to bolster their own position.

This illustration is a simplified version of what has been happening in Film de France, but it highlights certain aspects of stakeholder mapping. It shows that identifying the stakeholders can have an immediate impact on how the change issue is understood and defined. Over time there is a dynamism to the stakeholders, as they form alliances (such as the one between some of the stakeholder B group and the senior managers) or disaggregate (for example, as the senior managers start to do as the change proceeds). It also illustrates the different forms of influence and indirect power through which one stakeholder group can mobilize the power of another group by shifting its level of interest and focus. Although stakeholder mapping is both descriptive and prescriptive, one of its values is in recognizing the differences between aspired-to states and those that pertain. Hence, it can be helpful in planning action and reviewing the impact of the action. In this case the change is strategic and personal. In other cases stakeholder mapping can be a crucial phase of programmed change. When conducted in a group it can be used as a way of engaging employees and enabling them to see other perspectives on their organization (see Chapter 4).

EXERCISE

Read Extended Case 7: Nokia.

(1) Construct a stakeholder map from the point of view of Nokia before the collaboration with Microsoft was established.

(2) Construct a stakeholder map from the point of view of Microsoft before the collaboration with Nokia was established.

(3) From a stakeholder/influence perspective, what advantages do Nokia and Microsoft gain by collaborating?

(4) Would Microsoft gain a useful advantage by taking Nokia over? What reaction might they expect from stakeholders to such a move?

WHO TO READ

John Bryson (1995, 2004) has provided a series of practical and theory-informed insights into stakeholder analysis and mapping. He discusses associated actions such as problem formulation and solution search and explores collaboration and coalition building in some depth.

USEFUL WEBSITES

There are many forms of stakeholder mapping, and the following websites are helpful in providing some alternatives.

- www.csrvadergio.net focuses specifically on corporate social responsibility (CSR) and the engagement of stakeholders in pursuance of ethical aims. The site uses a similar grid to the one discussed above but suggests generic action for stakeholders in the four quadrants. Those in the high-interest, high-influence sector should be partnered with, those in the high-influence, low-interest sector should be involved, those in the high-interest, low-influence sector should be consulted and those in the low-interest, low-influence sector should be informed (see Figure 5.5).

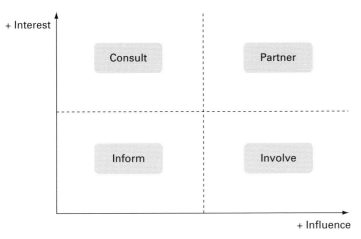

Figure 5.5 CSR stakeholder mapping

- www.stakeholdermap.com links stakeholder mapping to mind mapping and provides helpful examples.
- www.changingminds.org focuses on power and resistance and may be particularly appropriate when a degree of conflict is involved in the change. The site features a scale of stakeholders: active opponents, passive opponents, fence-sitters, passive supporters, active supporters. Each is then rated in relative power – high, medium, low – and hence actions can be prioritized and decided.

REFERENCES

Ackermann, F., and Eden, C. (2011) Strategic management of shareholders: theory and practice. *Long Range Planning*, 44(3): 179–96.

Ackermann, F., Eden, C., and Brown, I. (2005) *The Practice of Making Strategy: A Step-by-Step Guide*. London: Sage.

Bryson, J. M. (1995) *Strategic Planning for Public and Non-Profit Organizations*. San Francisco: Jossey-Bass.

Bryson, J. M. (2004) What to do when stakeholders matter. *Public Management Review*, 6(1): 21–53.

Eden, C., and Ackermann, F. (1998) *Making Strategy: The Journey of Strategic Management*. London: Sage.

Finlay-Robinson, D. (2009) What's in it for me? The fundamental importance of stakeholder evaluation. *Journal of Management Development*, 28(4): 380–8.

Freeman, R. E. (1984) *Strategic Management: A Stakeholder Approach*. Boston: Pitman.

Hardy, C., and Clegg, S. R. (1999) Some dare call it power, in Clegg, S. R., and Hardy, C. (eds.) *Studying Organizations: Theory and Method*: 368–87. London: Sage.

Hillman, A. J., and Keim, G. D. (2001) Stakeholder value, stakeholder management and social issues: what's the bottom line? *Strategic Management Journal*, 22(2): 125–39.

Huxham, C., and Vangen, S. (2004) Doing things collaboratively: realizing the advantage or succumbing to inertia. *Organizational Dynamics* 33(2): 190–201.

Neville, B. A., and Menguc, B. (2006) Stakeholder multiplicity: toward an understanding of the interactions between stakeholders. *Journal of Business Ethics*, 66(4): 377–91.

Peltokorpi, A., Alho, A., Kujala, J., Aitamurto, J., and Parvinen, P. (2007) Stakeholder approach for evaluating organizational change projects. *International Journal of Health Care Quality Assurance*, 21(5): 418–34.

Rowley, T. J., and Moldoveanu, M. (2003) When will stakeholder groups act? An interest- and identity-based model of stakeholder mobilization. *Academy of Management Review*, 28(2): 204–19.

Savage, G., Nix, T., Whitehead, C., and Blair, J. (1991) Strategies for assessing and managing stakeholders. *Academy of Management Executive*, 5(1): 61–75.

Schneider, M. (2002) A stakeholder model of organizational leadership. *Organization Science*, 31(2): 209–20.

Strong, K. C., Ringer, R. C., and Taylor, S. A. (2001) The rules of stakeholder satisfaction. *Journal of Business Ethics*, 32(3): 219–30.

Van der Heijden, K. (2005) *Scenarios: The Art of Strategic Conversation.* Chichester: John Wiley.

Ybema, S., Keenoy, T., Oswick, C., Beverungen, A., Ellis, N., and Sabelis, I. (2009) Articulating identities. *Human Relations*, 63(3): 299–322.

6 Culture, habits and unlearning

The aims of this chapter are to:

- introduce the concept of integrated, differentiated and fragmented cultures;
- explore an approach to analysing culture using Gerry Johnson's 'cultural web' as a diagnostic tool;
- consider the implications of culture for how change might be planned, enacted and reacted to;
- identify the distinction between single- and double-loop learning and consider which might be appropriate in different circumstances;
- introduce the concept of defensive routines and highlight the ways in which they can inhibit change; and
- make readers aware of the dangers of oversimplifying the concept of culture as it applies to organizations.

Organizations are social settings in which individuals and teams interact in the conduct of business. As they do so they construct meanings associated with their activities and the objects that they use. For example, a senior manager with a large office might symbolize his or her status rather than simply providing a venue for meetings. The meanings associated with such a symbol can vary. For example, some might regard a large office as something to aspire to and a mark of achievement, whilst others might see it as symbolizing the separation of senior managers from the rest of the workforce (as discussed in the ITS Canada case, Extended Case 2). The ascription of such meanings is variable and is beyond the control of management, yet it will have an impact on how people behave. For this reason, organizations are often ascribed cultural characteristics as a helpful means of describing what the organization is like. Some organizations are described as entrepreneurial, others as bureaucratic; some may be aggressive, others collaborative; some may be characterized as innovative whilst others are seen as traditional. Of course, a singular description is unlikely to capture every aspect of the organization, or to be universally true. Perhaps the most commonly cited definition of organizational culture is 'how things are done around here' (Drennan, 1992: 3), which resonates with many people's experience and nicely captures a view of what is communicated to those inside and beyond the organization. If nothing else, such descriptions help us make sense of the organization, particularly as a newcomer. New members of an organization must establish what is acceptable in their new surroundings. As an example: it's your first day in a new job and you're invited to a team meeting. Should you question decisions that are being made? In some settings this would be seen as a way of demonstrating your commitment, intelligence and engagement. However, the same behaviour in another setting might be read as inappropriate, disrespectful and even career-limiting. In fact, there are probably nuances at play that will take some time to spot. It may be acceptable to question decisions with some colleagues but not with others. There may be odd hierarchical reversals whereby questioning more senior managers is good for your career but questioning your direct line manager is distinctly bad.

Over time, we become socialized into our organizational settings such that we no longer need to think about the nuances of acceptable behaviour. It is for this reason that Edward Hall argues that 'culture hides much more than it reveals, and strangely enough what it hides, it hides most effectively from its own participants' (1976: 53). A major danger for those inside the organization is becoming so steeped in the culture that even subjective judgements of whether things are normal, acceptable, helpful or limiting are difficult. Organizational culture gradually recedes from the view of those most familiar with it, yet culture can drive decision making, change and strategy in significant ways. For this reason, organizations are often considered as 'solutions looking for issues to which they might be the answer' (Cohen, March and Olsen, 1972: 2). Of course, from this standpoint, the most comfortable and reassuring thing to do is to repeat tried, tested and familiar processes. From the perspective of those charged with managing change, the question that must be answered is: does the organization's current culture enable or inhibit the change that we are planning?

First, we should make clear that we are assuming that culture is not beyond influence, and for this reason we include culture as the fourth area of diagnostic work in the enquiry–action framework. However, neither would we see culture as being controllable by managerial effort. Most scholars agree that culture evolves slowly, often in response to unplanned events. For this reason, Edgar Schein is critical of the idea that culture can be changed from the top down (1984), whilst Emmanual Ogbonna and Lloyd Harris (2002) suggest that culture scholars can be divided into three groups: optimists, pessimists and realists. In their terms, realists hold the view that culture as a whole cannot be changed but that certain elements can be adapted or edited (e.g. artefacts or norms). Working on change from a cultural perspective requires us to have some means of articulating or describing the culture and considering whether it needs to change. There are a number of competing frameworks and typologies that claim to help capture and characterize organizational culture. Here we draw on two such frameworks.

Joanne Martin (1992) suggests that organizational culture can be conceptualized in one of three ways: integrated, differentiated or fragmented. An **integrated culture** implies consistency across different levels within the organization and across different functional or structural groupings. For instance, in an integrated culture junior staff in the sales department would espouse similar values, norms and behaviours to senior staff in the finance department. This consistency may well be reinforced by formal statements of mission, values, reward systems, etc. Hence, in integrated cultures the meanings associated with actions or objects will be generally agreed by organization members, and shared values will be deeply held. For example, in an entrepreneurial company it might be possible to find many people who are dedicated to innovation and share a view of what good-quality innovation would look like. Integrated cultures can be effective at achieving certain types of change. What is termed 'evolutionary change' in Van de Ven and Poole's (2005) model (introduced in Chapter 1) is likely to be acceptable to organization members, because this is seen as a development of existing norms, values and ways of doing things. Similarly, in Marshak's (2009) model, the metaphors of 'fix and maintain' and 'build and develop' are most likely to be acceptable. Because meanings are shared in an integrated culture, it is possible to arrive quickly at a shared understanding of the change objectives, often in a 'closed' framing (see Chapter 3), and for people to agree what should be done. The danger for integrated cultures is that they can be resistant to more radical forms of change that would involve challenging some of the accepted ways of doing things, or that require people to 'think outside the box'. Hence, innovation can become somewhat linear and radical change can be delayed until a crisis looms, at which point change can be characterized by conflict (or a 'dialectical process', in Van de Ven and Poole's terms).

A **differentiated culture** is composed of nested subcultures that coexist and may, over time, co-create each other. Interventions to change aspects of the organization may be read differently within each of the subcultures. In an airline, for example, pilots, cabin crew, maintenance staff and sales teams would probably have different cultures. An attempt to change promotion procedures might be read as encouraging by one group whilst being seen as threatening by one or more of the other groups. Although differentiation implies difference between groups, consensus and cohesion within groups is to be expected, creating both 'in' and 'out' groups that drive the dynamics of inter-group interaction. Research in the health service suggests that interactions between managers and clinicians are influenced by these 'in'/'out' group issues to the extent that clinicians who take on managerial roles are left in a hybrid position, which marginalizes them from other managers and their fellow clinicians alike (see Llewelyn, 2001). One consequence of a differentiated culture is that disagreements would be commonplace and tolerated in ways that might be unacceptable in an integrated culture.

Finally, a **fragmented culture** would see ambiguity and disagreement as the defining feature of an organization in which individuals and groups share little in the way of common ground. Any attempt to establish consistency or consensus would be seen as misguided or oversimplified, partly because the individual members of the organization are simultaneously members of other organizational settings in their social and domestic lives. One example might be a global organization such as the British Broadcasting Corporation (BBC). The BBC has journalists working in many countries and covering many specialist topics, from economics to sport and politics. Some staff are full-time employees, others will be part-time and many will not spend time at BBC offices or headquarter on a regular basis. The likelihood of a news correspondent in a remote war zone having much in common with someone covering financial affairs in New York is low. The loose coupling gives great strength to the organization, making it capable of adapting to multiple environments, but it also means that centrally planned change is extremely difficult. Some organizations have fostered a fragmented culture in which organizational members share more values with long-term clients that they do with each other. This can have the result that good client relations are maintained, but with the potential cost of a high degree of diversity within the organization. In fragmented cultures there is a high degree of dynamism, such that 'in' groups and 'out' groups become changeful themselves. In a differentiated culture one would expect the subculture groups to be reasonably consistent over time. However, in

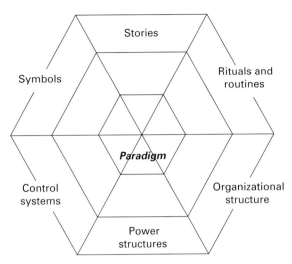

Figure 6.1 The cultural web

a fragmented culture the make-up of subgroups can change quickly and alter in relation to different issues that are current for the organization. For example, when considering the reward system there might be three main groups, but when considering the strategic direction of the company there might be five or six different groups. Hence, communication of change and reaching agreement on objectives is much more difficult in a fragmented culture. Leading change is therefore a considerable challenge in such settings and an understanding of internal politics is vital, as was discussed in Chapter 5.

Regardless of which type of culture an organization has (integrated, differentiated or fragmented), it may be helpful to describe aspects of that culture in more detail. For this purpose, we use Johnson's cultural web (Johnson, 1988); see Figure 6.1.

The cultural web attempts to summarize organizational culture by capturing observations about the physical, symbolic and social/organizational aspects of a specific setting. The model uses six overlapping but separate dimensions as a means of establishing a sense of the **organizational paradigm**.[1] The other six aspects of the model represent a set of interlocking activities, beliefs and structures that form a cultural web. This means that changes to the overall

---

[1] For Johnson, the paradigm is a set of assumptions that might be regarded as being held in common within the organization. To that extent, the paradigm might be taken for granted within the organization. In some cases this is relatively obvious; a newspaper, for example, might see itself as centrally concerned with news in terms of journalistic research, reporting and presenting. However, in other cases it may be less obvious to those outside the firm. For example, a firm selling financial services could be seen as a bank but might operate with a self-conception of the organization as about direct sales.

paradigm may be problematic, since changing one or more of the other aspects may not be enough to break the web of interconnections currently in place.

For Johnson, culture tends to persist and can be thought of in terms of six related but distinct categories. First, organizations develop ways of doing business that quickly become embedded as **routines**. How firms recruit staff, develop products, manage suppliers, etc. might be conceptualized as routines, and these routines characterize and form part of the organization's culture, as the routine is repeated again and again over time. Some routines represent commonplace and everyday activity whilst others carry more significance. Johnson's early training as an anthropologist sensitized him to the importance of **rituals**, which he would describe as special events that highlight or reaffirm aspects of the organization's culture. In his most recent work he has examined the rituals associated with strategy awaydays (Johnson *et al.*, 2010). Rituals of this type are also repeated, perhaps less frequently than routines, and may be associated with rites of passage, celebration or reprimand. Other examples of organizational rituals might include the wrap party that follows the completion of a movie, graduation ceremonies that mark the achievement of a new status, celebrations for retirement or long service, the way that failure or rule breaking is dealt with, etc.

These routines and rituals often form important aspects of the **stories** that circulate within the organization. Storytelling in organizations is an established area of research, and scholars argue that stories need to be succinct enough to be retold, have some memorable point or moral and be engaging or entertaining. Larger complex narratives are summarized down into snippets[2] to facilitate storytelling (Sims, Huxham and Beech, 2009), and the most powerful stories are viral. You do not need to have been there to interpret the story of a young entrepreneur striking a deal with a global firm and redrawing the map of an entire industry. Only a handful of individuals were actually involved in the interactions between a young Bill Gates and IBM, but many of us have subsequently heard snippets of the story in which he persuaded IBM to allow Microsoft to provide the operating system for personal computers. The story is short and has heroes and villains, who may be interchangeable depending upon the point of view from which the story is told, and the story itself tells you something about the ambition, vision and entrepreneurial drive that many see as characterizing Microsoft.

---

[2] A snippet is a short extract or fragment from a longer narrative. A snippet from Tolkien's epic trilogy *The Lord of the Rings* might be as follows: there's this ring that can make you invisible, but overuse is unhealthy for you.

Next, Johnson's model draws our attention to the symbolic aspects of the organization. These **symbols** are likely to be artefacts or events that hold meaning beyond their functional purpose. A named parking space is intended to ensure that you can always get parked outside the office, but it also symbolizes importance and status. Company credit cards, frequent flyer lounges, numbers of direct reports, the use of first names or nicknames and jargon all operate at a symbolic level. Hence, many other aspects of the cultural web, such as organizational structure, also operate symbolically to reinforce the culture and paradigm of the organization.

These first three parts of the cultural web (rituals and routines, stories and symbols) are common to all members of the organization. In many ways, these three aspects of organizational culture pervade organizational life. However, the next three (power structures, organizational structures and control systems) tend to be more prominent in the minds of those in managerial positions. **Power structures** say something about the extent to which individuals, teams or groups can exert influence on others within the organization. This influence can be formal and directive (e.g. I am giving you an order) or informal and coercive (e.g. I am persuading you that this is the right thing to do). Power structures are therefore related to but distinct from organizational structures. Someone further up the organizational hierarchy may have formal power over a more junior group of staff while, in reality, being unable to use that power. **Organizational structure**, then, relates to the formal organization charts that set out which groups and individuals report to each other as a means of capturing roles, responsibilities and authority. Organizational structure also says something about the number and frequency of meetings, who attends those meetings, etc. Again, it may be that, in formal terms, key decisions are taken at monthly management meetings but, informally, everyone acknowledges that these formal proceedings simply rubber-stamp outcomes agreed in some other forum. Hence, the sixth and final category in the cultural web is that of **control systems**. These are the mechanisms that formally and informally monitor behaviours and outcomes throughout the organization. Examples might include performance indicators, bonus systems and promotion procedures. For example, the way that people are rewarded encourages certain types of behaviour and also expressed the values of the organization. In the financial services example above, the reward system is highly individualized, and increased rewards are accrued by individuals who are able to act in an entrepreneurial way to attract new clients and earn commission. This reveals the underlying assumption that people are motivated by money and work best when focused on their own performance. In other settings, in which teamwork is important, such as bringing different skills together to achieve a creative product that could not have been produced by any of the individuals working on their own, team-based bonuses or rewards that accrue to the whole team on the basis of outcomes achieved encourage a different kind of behaviour and reveal different assumptions about how people are motivated – in this case by the ability to make a contribution to an outcome that is valued and to be a professional who is highly regarded by his or her peers. Such arrangements exist, for example, in parts of the creative industries, such as some music productions in which groups agree to share rewards on the basis of the joint effort going into the product.

Using the cultural web, it is possible to make some aspects of organizational culture explicit. This is not to say that the model offers a complete, or necessarily an accurate, representation of culture. For example, different subgroups within an organization might produce completely different cultural webs if a differentiated or fragmented culture is in place. For instance, Beech, Coupland and MacPhail (2009) describes just such a setting, in which different groups within the same organization experience very different norms, routines and expectations. Many scholars are critical of overt attempts to manage culture on the basis of oversimplified models. Mats Alvesson (2002) suggests a number of ways in which culture is oversimplified, including a tendency to reify culture as something that exists and is amenable to intervention, because our mode of explaining it is superficial. Taking such reservations on board, the cultural web can form a useful basis for further discussion if it is simply taken as one account, at a point in time, of how culture is read by those involved in the analysis. It can often be helpful to construct several cultural webs of the same situation as it is understood from the different subcultural perspectives. This can lead to a further phase of analysis, in which the similarities and dissimilarities of understanding can be explored. Our suggested approach to diagnosis with respect to culture is described in Figure 6.2.

A related body of work considers learning processes in an organizational context. One of the most influential scholars in this field is Chris Argyris (see, for example, Argyris, 1990). As a species, a large part of our success in evolutionary terms is because of our capacity to learn. From early childhood we learn new tasks, internalize them and recall the stored solutions on future occasions. Argyris defines learning as a circumstance in which 'the use of the programme necessary to perform the requisite action is so much under control that the control over the performance does not have to be conscious or explicit' (1977: 114). That is to say, we have truly learned something when we can execute tasks without

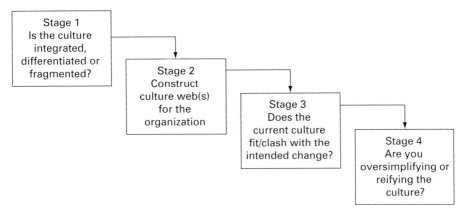

Figure 6.2 Diagnosing cultural aspects of change

giving them too much thought. A simple example, such as learning to walk, ride a bicycle or drive a car, reinforces this sense that the activity sinks below our conscious awareness. We may drive a car, changing gears, lanes or speed, without 'thinking' about it. We may even be able to hold a conversation, think about our destination or admire the scenery whilst driving. However, to achieve mastery of the task such that it can be recalled in this way involves the ruthless generalization and storage of routines (Sussman, 1973). The storage of routines is therefore hugely beneficial, but it introduces new problems.

In Chapter 12 we revisit the concept of learning by introducing the model of learning developed by David Kolb. However, here we concentrate on Argyris and Schön's (1978) explanation of what happens as we learn something for the first time. The experience often involves failure, errors and disappointment. That is the essence of what is called learning by 'trial and error'. Argyris and Schön recognize two different modes or models of learning, which they label 'double-loop' and 'single-loop' routines. Double-loop learning is learning from first principles. As described in Figure 6.3, the learner considers what Argyris and Schön call the governing values of the problem. Imagine trying to strike a golf ball for the first time. One must conceptualize how to hold the golf club, how far away from the ball to stand, how fast to move, etc. These various 'governing values' form part of our initial attempt to strike the ball. As we execute the task for the first time we may well make a mistake in one or more aspect of the problem. Perhaps we stood too close to the ball and missed altogether. Perhaps we were also trying to hit the ball too quickly and lost balance. The disappointment of missing the target would, in the terms of Argyris and Schön's model, be seen as a mismatch or error in relation to expectations.

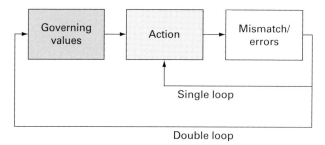

Figure 6.3 Single- and double-loop learning

Our learning process would take us back to reconsider the governing values of the problem, conceive a new plan for action, try this out and judge whether the results are acceptable. As we proceed, we hope to reduce the mismatch or error that we experience to a point at which results meet our expectations even though the outcome may not be perfect. For example, we may eventually develop a method of striking the ball that means that it travels fairly straight but perhaps not as far as we had hoped. Once the mismatch or error reduces to a level that we can tolerate, Argyris and Schön suggest that we switch to a fundamentally different mode of learning. Single-loop learning may continue to involve modest adjustments to the actions taken but no longer revisits the governing values of the problem. For example, our stance when striking the ball begins to become fixed and is no longer subject to revision. This is the ruthless generalization and storage process that Gerald Sussman refers to, since we need standardization in order to memorize and categorize with any efficiency. A useful diagnostic test is to consider how much spare mental capacity you have when executing a particular task. If the task demands all your attention, it is likely that you are engaged in double-loop learning. If the task can be executed whilst you think of other things, engage in conversation or other activities, it is likely that you have transitioned from double- to single-loop learning.

Argyris and Schön apply the same distinction between single- and double-loop learning when they consider organizations. When an organization begins to grow and eventually undertakes its first acquisition, it is likely that double-loop learning will occur as the organization discovers how best to integrate the two organizations (see Extended Case 6: Power Provision). If the organization continues to undertake a series of acquisitions over time, a single-loop routine will develop such that the task is not learned from first principles every time. The routines from a cultural web would simply be single-loop learning activities that the organization has at its disposal. These routines would represent 'how things are done around here' but, as the environment in which the routines are used changes, some routines become obsolete. This is problematic, since, by definition, we are not consciously thinking about the single-loop routines that we use, and when they become inappropriate we struggle to notice. Accordingly, a third category of learning is introduced to signify those subconscious routines that are actually unhelpful or inappropriate. Argyris suggests that we invoke 'defensive' routines when the social consequences of double- or single-loop learning are unpalatable. Here we simply suggest that defensive routines are those single-loop routines that have become unhelpful in the way that many subconscious habits can. As such, defensive routines offer a good explanation of the difficulties many organizations experience when trying to change organizational culture. Historical, embedded and habitualized patterns reassert themselves despite overt attempts to move beyond them.

The proposition we are making here is that organizational life tends to involve a life cycle. First there is double-loop learning, when new circumstances or problems are encountered. Next we engage in single-loop learning, as we master these new problems and develop reliable, repeatable, routinized solutions. Finally, we invoke defensive routines, when we are unaware that our single-loop routines are no longer appropriate. Each stage in the cycle is driven by a strong evolutionary tendency to codify, 'to ruthlessly generalise and store'. All defensive routines were, at some prior stage, highly functional single-loop routines and were therefore probably associated with past success, or, at least, with the lack of failure. To get some sense of the level of comfort and reassurance that a routine can provoke, try this simple exercise. Sit with your arms in front of you, then cross your arms. After a few moments, place them in front of you again, then cross them the other way around. The second time around there is usually some hesitation and sense of awkwardness about the simple process of folding your arms. Argyris's argument is that, for more complex organizational tasks, a similar phenomenon occurs, and we struggle to move beyond established patterns or habits. Working with change from a learning perspective requires that we answer the following question: will the change that we are planning require us to displace or overcome any defensive routines? If the answer is 'Yes', then a key challenge will be to create circumstances in which unlearning past routines can go hand in hand with attempts to learn new solutions. The diagnosis of the type of learning that is required relates to actions concerning how we do things (the subject of Chapter 10) and in more radical forms changing who we are – for example, changing attitudes (covered in Chapter 8).

EXERCISE

Read Extended Case 2, ITS Canada. The case concerns an effort to change culture in a breakaway organization that features some aspects of a start-up yet some cultural inheritance from the large international bank from which it was spun off. The aspirations of the senior management are quite clear in seeking a more flexible, fast-moving and team-based culture. Consider the first eighteen months covered in the case and answer the following questions.

(1) Construct a cultural web for ITS Canada.

(2) Do you see the culture as integrated, differentiated or fragmented?

(3) Do you think the effort to change culture has been a success eighteen months into the process?

(4) What factors have influenced the outcomes to this point?

(5) What style of learning (single- or double-loop) do you regard as necessary for the next stage of development in this case?

WHO TO READ

This chapter covers two related bodies of work. In the learning literature, the work of Argyris is highly influential. His first publication in the *Harvard Business Review* appeared in 1958 (titled 'The organization: what makes it healthy?'), and since then he has produced a stream of highly cited books and papers. Similarly Geert Hofstede's work on culture, and in particular his research on national traits and cultural differences, is frequently cited by those working on the cultural aspects of organizations.

USEFUL WEBSITES

- www.strategyexplorers.com includes a number of 'white papers', and Johnson provides one in which he discussed the concept and application of the cultural web. This paper gives a particularly helpful introduction to using the web in practical settings, such as management workshops.

- www.infed.org/thinkers provides an accessible introduction to the work of Argyris and organizational learning. This covers single- and double-loop learning and a range of other concepts from Argyris's work.
- www.geert-hofstede.com offers a good resource for those wanting to understand the way in which Hofstede claims to map and understand national differences on issues such as power distance, uncertainty avoidance and individualism.

REFERENCES

Alvesson, M. (2002) *Understanding Organizational Culture*. London: Sage.

Argyris, C. (1977) Organizational learning and management information systems. *Accounting, Organizations and Society*, 2(2): 113–23.

Argyris, C (1990) *Overcoming Organizational Defences: Facilitating Organizational Learning*. Englewood Cliffs, NJ: Prentice Hall.

Argyris, C., and Schön, D. A. (1978) *Organizational Learning: A Theory of Action Perspective*. Reading, MA: Addison Wesley.

Beech, N., Coupland, C., and MacPhail, S. (2009) Anti-dialogic positioning in change stories: bank robbers, saviours and peons. *Organization*, 16(3): 335–52.

Cohen, M. D., March, J. G., and Olsen, J. P. (1972) A garbage can model of organizational choice. *Administrative Science Quarterly*, 17(1): 1–25.

Drennan, D. (1992) *Transforming Company Culture: Getting Your Company from Where You Are Now to Where You Want to Be*. London: McGraw-Hill.

Hall, E. T. (1976). *Beyond Culture*. Garden City, NY: Anchor Press.

Johnson, G. T. (1988) Rethinking incrementalism. *Strategic Management Journal*, 9(1): 75–91.

Johnson, G. T., Prashantham, S., Floyd, S., and Bourque, N. (2010) The ritualization of strategy workshops. *Organization Studies*, 31(12): 1589–618.

Llewellyn, S. (2001) 'Two-way windows': clinicians and medical managers. *Organization Studies*, 22(4): 593–623.

Marshak, R. (2009) *Organizational Change: Views from the Edge*. Bethel, ME: Lewin Center.

Martin, J. (1992). *Cultures in Organizations: Three Perspectives*. New York: Oxford University Press.

Ogbonna, E., and Harris, L. C. (2002) Managing organizational culture: insights from the hospitality industry. *Human Resource Management Journal*, 12(1): 22–53.

Schein, E. H. (1984) Coming to a new awareness of organizational culture. *Sloan Management Review*, 25(2): 3–16.

Sims, D., Huxham, C., and Beech, N. (2009) On telling stories but hearing snippets: sense-taking from presentations of practice. *Organization*, 16(3): 371–88.

Sussman, G. (1973) A computational model of skill acquisition, Technical Report AI TR-297. Massachusetts Institute of Technology, Cambridge.

Van de Ven, A. H., and Poole, M. S. (1995) Explaining development and change in organizations. *Academy of Management Review*, 20(1): 510–40.

PART C
Enacting Change

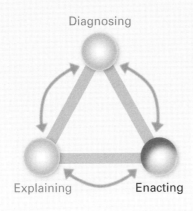

Diagnosing

Explaining   Enacting

Taking action is clearly central to managing change, and this is the focus in Part C. Some actions are clear and overt, as when, for example, the organizational structure is altered. In this case, the change is observable and it is possible for everyone to know what has happened. Other actions are less obvious. For instance, changing through gradual development or changing the way that ideas are framed can be subtle processes that are not recognized by everyone. Change managers need to balance the overt and the subtle, as both are needed. Even when a structural change is observed by everyone it can take a longer process of subtle attitudinal change before people genuinely believe in the change. Equally, subtle changes over time need to be symbolized and made explicit in order for them to be strongly embedded. Successful change managers tend to be good at judging how quickly to push things and knowing when to allow time for debate and disagreement. Change actions are, therefore, almost never 'one-offs'. Rather, there is an ongoing process in which different ways of enacting the change are marshalled over time in order to speed up or allow time to reflect, make overt changes or allow subtle (sometimes psychological) shifts. In this section we explore seven forms of change action. Having read the section you should be in a position to reflect on the appropriate blend of actions for different change management tasks as you encounter them.

7 Changing structure

The aims of this chapter are to:

- discuss the relationship between the business environment and the structure of organizations;
- explore the alternative structures that companies can adopt and consider their relative strengths and weaknesses;
- suggest a framework for redesigning structure; and
- enable a critical discussion of a mini-case and of the Oticon case study.

Introduction

LucasArts is the company, headed by George Lucas, that is behind the special effects used in the *Star Wars* movies, amongst other digital technology products. In the last decade competition in the special effects industry has increased dramatically, but so have the opportunities in line with the increasing quantities and qualities of digital games, some of which use techniques that only companies at the top end of the market, such as LucasArts, can achieve (Jones, 2009). However, LucasArts had a problem. They employed a large number of creative digital artists, who would be well placed to take advantage of new market opportunities, but the digital artists worked independently within departments that focused on specialist activities, often communicating only between departments that were geographically remote from each other via video conferencing systems. Lucas decided that it was necessary to restructure in order to change the process and output of the company. He relocated the digital artists into a single site that was designed to encourage interaction. It included open areas, lounges and high-quality communal facilities. He asked them to develop a common digital platform so that people currently working in different departments could potentially collaborate. The operational leaders introduced temporary project teams and challenged the workers to develop new products for both the film and games industries. The result has been an increase in the sharing of skills between individuals and departments. LucasArts has subsequently been even more innovative, and, in addition to producing the film special effects for which it was famous, it has developed notable successes in the games industry, including products such as 'Star Wars: The Force Unleashed'.

In this short example we can see certain elements of structural change. **Organizational structure** is, in part, a response to the business environment, and, in this case, changes in the environment presented both threats from new competition and opportunities in new markets. However, the old way of structuring the organization, which had worked very well for the previous product line, was less suited to the more flexible demands of the new environment. Therefore, a new strategy was devised – to innovate, develop new products and enter new markets. However, this required a new way of working together, and hence a first step in the strategic change was to alter the way that work was coordinated, from specialists working in functional departments to collaborative teams focused on bringing different skills to bear on the development of a new product. These are the central questions of structure.

The organizational structure is the arrangement of people in reporting/authority relationship lines.

First there is the question of separation: how far are tasks split between highly specialized units and carried out by specialized practitioners, or are tasks and people more generic? Second: how are activities coordinated? Should there be a clear set of rules that everyone follows? Should everyone report directly to his or her manager and have a distinct role, or should workers report to different people depending on the task they are doing at any particular time, and should they vary what they do depending on what the current goals are? Third: where should decisions be made? Should decisions be centralized and carefully controlled, or should there be greater autonomy for workers and the ability to make decisions in a decentralized way? Different ways of structuring the organization provide alternative answers to these questions. We do not suggest that one set of answers is correct, but as a manager of change there is a need to understand the questions and the advantages and disadvantages of the various possible answers. The business environment[1] has a significant impact, and we now discuss its relationship to organizational structure.

Structure and the environment

The business environment of an organization can have a significant impact on the way it is structured. The environment includes levels of stability, complexity, diversity and hostility (Mintzberg, 1993). These can be defined as follows.

- The level of stability relates to how much is known about the environment and how much it is changing. A stable environment would be gradually changing in a fairly predictable way, and companies would have a reasonable degree of certainty about the speed and direction of change. Conversely, a variable environment would be typified by erratic change that is difficult to predict in speed or direction.
- The level of complexity relates to the number of environmental factors that impact upon an organization and the way in which the factors are interconnected. Some environments can be dominated by a small number of factors that operate in clear ways. For example, a particular form of technology might dictate an industry standard of cost efficiency, and hence it is adopted by all or most firms, and this can impact on the way the organization is structured. For instance, work can be structured around the technology of a production line that requires operators to work in a particular way. This can also require supplies, logistics and quality assurance to function in a specific place and temporal order. That is, there is a clear and understood arrangement of the elements in the process. The elements may be complicated, but their interconnectedness is not completely unpredictable and uncertain. At the other end of the scale, some environments have many factors that interact with each other in uncertain and complex ways. For example, a company that operates around the world might have to respond to changing political circumstances, which relate in turn to religion, local alliances and hostilities, the struggle for ascendancy of alternative ideologies, and so on. As political shifts occur, there can be significant impacts on security, legislative structures, exchange rates, credit ratings, etc.

---

[1] The business environment includes the socio-political context of the organization, along with economic actors such as competitors and customers.

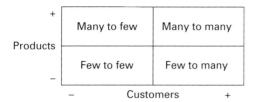

Figure 7.1 Level of diversity

- The level of diversity relates to the range of activities the company undertakes. There can be a relationship between the number and the standardization of products and the number and the nature of customers. Companies may have a small number of products, often that are relatively standardized, or they may have many products, which might be a broad range of standard products, or they may have an approach based on the customization of products or services. Equally, the company may have a small number of key clients (which may act as intermediaries en route to end customers), or sales may be made to a large number of individual customers. Various combinations are possible: few products/few customers, few products/many customers, many products/few customers or many products/many customers (see Figure 7.1).
- The level of hostility relates to the degree of competition and other environmental factors that could be a threat to the company. When there is a high degree of hostility, cost control, protection against takeover and a sufficiently diverse portfolio to be able to withstand downturns in one area of business may be priorities. When there is low hostility, the industry may be typified by more networking and collaborative agreements.

When deciding how to respond to the environment, options include imitating the dominant forms and working in line with the perceived environmental forces, seeking to 'buck the trend' and be different from the norm or adopting a hybrid position in which innovation is blended with a degree of mimicry. This approach to change can be related to Van de Ven and Poole's (1995) framework, which was covered in Chapter 2. Here change originates outside the organization and can be 'prescribed' or evolutionary. Different types of environment can highlight particular questions, and these are illustrated in Figure 7.2.

In a relatively stable environment the obvious question for change managers is 'How can we increase efficiency?'. The answer to this has often been found in standardization and the installation of routines – the idea being to work out the best practice possible and duplicate this throughout the organization. Thus, change may focus on incremental improvements in the speed of operation, the

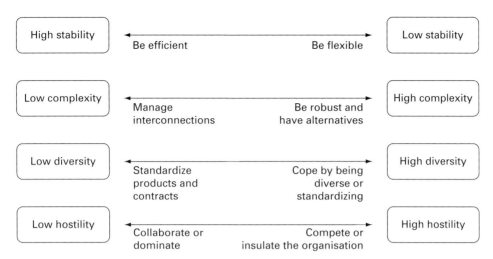

Figure 7.2 Questions of how to structure prompted by different environments

reduction of waste or cutting costs. At the other end of this scale, faced with unpredictability, the question may be 'How can we increase the flexibility of the organization?', such that it can adapt to changes in a timely manner. At this end of the scale, the management of change might focus on equipping people to problem-solve and innovate so that they are not entirely reliant on established routines.

When there is low complexity in the environment the question can be 'How do we effectively manage the interconnections of the elements in the system?'. The answer may be, for example, to structure carefully and, when possible, control the elements in the supply chain so that the flow is smooth and predictable. Conversely, in high-complexity environments, it is difficult to predict what effects activity in one part of the system might have in other places in the system. Therefore, the question might be 'How can we increase the robustness of our activities and have alternatives?', such that, when the unexpected happens, all is not lost, because either the system can cope or the organization can switch to other activities. Therefore, change management activities at one end of the scale may be about increasing coordination and control. At the other end of the scale the focus may be on enhancing capacity and the ability to recognize and react to occurrences in the system that were unexpected or that are the unintended consequences of actions the organization has taken.

Considering the range of activities leads to the question 'How should processes be structured: around production or around customers?' (see Chapter 10 for a discussion of changing process). Structuring around customers can be particularly advantageous when there are relatively few key customers. At the extreme, this can entail company employees working in an embedded way inside the customer company. An alternative is that project teams are organized around delivery to a particular customer. If the company organizes itself around products, this typically means that specialist activities are carried out in production and the product is then added to the range available to customers, and the focus of training and operational tasks is the product. The organization is more likely to be arranged around production when there are many customers.

A hostile environment is one in which competition is exacting and there are other potential threats, such as a political environment in which tax might be increased or favour might be given to competitors. However, a benevolent environment is one with less competition and favourable conditions, such as tax breaks for investment. A question that arises is the extent to which the company should compete and seek to dominate or, instead, collaborate. It is not immediately obvious which approach should be taken at each end of the spectrum. In a benevolent environment there can be advantages to collaborating with others and building strong and open relationships with customers and suppliers. This can reduce the competitive costs of doing business. Alternatively, as the company has advantages in a benevolent environment, it could seek to maximize these and further reduce the power and position of competitors. At the other end of the scale, an obvious option is to compete or try to gain a position that competitors cannot easily match. However, sometimes there is an alternative: building partnerships, either with competitors or along the supply chain. Either way, there are impacts for managing change through the structure. In particular, there is the question of whether or not to form partnerships or collaborations with others. Alternatively, when the competitive option is chosen, there will be structural impacts to pursuing low-cost or high-quality routes.

Types of organizational structure

Organizations can adopt different types of structure, either in response to particular environmental conditions or as an internally driven strategy. In many cases, the structure of the company changes as it grows and develops. Organizational change is often aimed at redressing imbalances that are perceived to have occurred or at bringing the company back into line with the business environment. Four significant ways of structuring are as follows.

Entrepreneurial and simple structures

Entrepreneurial structures typically centre on one core individual or a small group of people who jointly direct the company. The structure can be envisaged as a web of relations around the central person or group. When entrepreneurs start companies they typically cover most if not all of the tasks. They design and deliver services or products, they develop strategy and marketing and they build relationships with suppliers and customers. If they grow they may take on people to duplicate some of their functions, such as delivery or marketing, or to free them from back-office activities. However, this does not normally result in strong functional separation. Because of the small numbers, people can help each other and develop an understanding of the whole operation of the company. This can lead to considerable flexibility and an 'all hands to the pump' attitude when there is a need for a specific task to be completed. The advantages also include the ability to communicate directly and a minimal need for formality. As people are in direct touch with each other, decision making can be speedy and motivation can be enhanced through having a variety of tasks with clear purpose. When it works, this can result in a positive psychological contract (a concept that is discussed in Chapter 11). Disadvantages include the possibility of the company becoming power-centric. If all decisions have to go through one person or a small group, it is easy for their views to prevail such that defensive routines can emerge and there can be a lack of critical questioning (see Chapter 6 for a discussion of these issues). Nevertheless, on balance, many people regard the simple structure with its informality and flexibility as a good structure within which to manage change. However, this is difficult to maintain as the organization grows.

Entrepreneurial structures have simple lines of reporting arranged around a central person or group.

Functional and divisionalized structures

As companies grow, they often introduce more formality and standardization. This typically means that a hierarchy is established. The organizing principle that drives this type of structure is that work is best done in specialized units, which can increase the efficiency and effectiveness of the company's operation. The role of management therefore has two main aspects. First, it is to develop the specialized groups, ensuring that change is focused on their being up to date and sharing cutting-edge learning about their specialization. Second, it is to manage the process of interaction between the specialized functions. Within functions, the way that things are done can be standardized as a way of ensuring the quality and predictability of outcomes. Often standardized operating procedures are captured in statements of 'best practice' or manuals that enable workers to maximize the use of their skills. Back-office functions are dealt with by separate departments, and the ideal is that those in the functional departments are supported by others so that they can spend most of their productive time on core activities. For organizations in which uniformity and control of process and outcome are important, the **functional structure** can work very well. However, the disadvantage is that it can lead to a lack of creativity and innovation and the predominance of rule following as the normal mode whilst at work. When the process works well, the outputs of one function feed in as the inputs for another function in a seamless fashion. However, the potential disadvantage is that functions can become very focused on their own objectives and what is important to them, and can lose sight of the need to cooperate with others and for shared goals. This style of organization is sometimes regarded as being difficult to change and as having the potential to operate with what is known as a 'silo mentality' – that is, a concern only for one's own area, to the potential detriment of the organization as a whole.

Functional or divisionalized structures are arranged around people who perform a specific function working in the same department together. This increases specialization but also increases the need for integration between the different functions.

Matrix and project-based structures

In a **matrix structure**, employees report in two directions. The normal arrangement is that people are responsible to a functional manager for the technical aspects of the work and to a project or product manager for the way their day-to-day work is coordinated with other people and for tasks relating to the same product/project. The advantage of this arrangement is that each employee has a specialist manager who looks after the different aspects of his or her work and development. The functional manager can oversee training, and because the employee is part of the functional group he or she can keep up to date with new practices and learn with others about the techniques that are being applied in different parts of the organization. The project/product manager, on the other hand, can guide and coordinate the way the employee performs so that he or she is an effective part of the team and can make an effective contribution. The obvious disadvantage is trying to 'serve two masters'. It is fully possible for the employee to be pulled in two directions at once or to have contrary requests on their time. This can be solved by either the functional or the project manager retaining primary authority. If the functional manager retains authority, the arrangement is referred to as a 'coordination' matrix, and the functional manager liaises with the project manager to agree a certain amount of time that will be spent on tasks. The alternative is the 'secondment' matrix (Thornhill *et al.*, 2000), in which the project manager has primary authority during the time the employee is working on the project.

A matrix structure is one in which people report in two directions – to a project leader and to a functional head.

Project-based structures can be formalized as matrices, or, alternatively, the organization can be arranged in a functional form, with people chosen in an ad hoc way to work on projects for a fixed amount of time. It is not uncommon for knowledge-centric companies to work in this way. For example, consulting companies and pharmaceutical companies may operate by developing a series of projects, such as conducting an enquiry and making recommendations for a client or developing the marketing strategy for a new product. In such instances, a range of skills and experience are needed. This might draw people from different departments and also with different skills or experience of working in a sector or marketing to a particular segment. The advantage of this style of organizing is that it can be an effective way of getting a range of knowledge deployed on a single project, which thus becomes the coordinating mechanism. The disadvantage is that, if people are constantly moving to new project teams (forming the team, starting to work together, completing the project and then moving on), a lot of time and effort can be lost in group/team processes. However, in organizations that are effective at project working, people can become highly efficient in moving into a new team and reaching the required level of performance within a couple of hours (Beech et al, 2002). This can be achieved by routinizing the process of team formation, such as by including it in training or having manuals and advice available, or in some cases the culture can foster a team orientation such that people are naturally oriented towards collective work (Ekvall, 1997).

Network structures

Networks can be either internal or external. Internal network structures exist when companies establish separate profit (or cost) centres that interact with each other on the basis of an internal market. The idea behind this arrangement is that costs can be driven down and savings made when one unit supplies services or components to another, which thereby acts as its customer. This approach is taken in large companies, and it can have the advantage of helping people focus locally on what they are producing and becoming more aware of how their products fit into the overall flow of value through the company. The disadvantage is that this approach can introduce an instrumental and separatist attitude. As different units are measured separately, they are incentivized in terms of their individual performance, and hence cooperative action can become limited and there may be an unwillingness to share costs between units.

Network structures normally incorporate several organizations that cooperate or that are coordinated, for example by an agreement about their relative positions in a supply chain and how they will interact.

External network structures are links between separate companies. 'Vertical' networks are typically centred on a core organization. The network operates to supply a good or service in a cooperative supply chain. This arrangement can be seen in car manufacture and distribution (Thornhill *et al.*, 2000). The core organization may be the manufacturer. It has structured agreements with first-tier suppliers, which provide specialist components that are assembled by the manufacturer. (The first-tier suppliers normally have second-tier suppliers that work with them.) The arrangement is more than a traditional supply and purchase arrangement, and the manufacturer will have an input into the quality, processes and arrangements of the supplier. In some circumstances the supplier operates within the physical facilities of the manufacturer on the basis of long-term agreements. In such cases, although the companies remain separate, they are closely interconnected and to an extent are mutually reliant. After manufacture, other parts of the network distribute and retail the cars. Although the companies may be formally separate, marketing, pricing, employee training and other practices are agreed at the centre and put into operation throughout the network. The advantage of such network arrangements is that there can be long-term control over quality, pricing and process such that specialist expertise is coordinated between companies that would otherwise be going through regular tendering and competitive processes (Hibbert and Huxham, 2010). The disadvantages are that the network as a whole can be susceptible to problems experienced by one part of the network, and that short-term savings achieved by driving down prices within the supply chain may not be as available to the core organization as they would otherwise be.

An alternative is termed the 'loosely coupled' network. These networks tend to be shorter-lived and may arise in response to an opportunity. For example, construction companies that normally compete with each other can form a partnership in order to win a contract for a job that is bigger or more complicated than they would be able to tackle alone. This is different from a vertical network, in which each partner plays a particular role in the supply chain. In a loosely coupled network the companies may well duplicate each others' capacities, but do so in a deliberate way to enable them to achieve an agreed goal. Such arrangements have the advantages of being flexible and targeted at specific purposes. In some industries they are normal, and hence companies become skilled at acting in this way, even when they might be simultaneously competing for other smaller jobs elsewhere. The disadvantage is that collaborative networks can take considerable political effort to form and maintain, and it is not uncommon for them to end up in a degree of 'collaborative inertia' (Huxham and Vangen, 2005) unless effective leadership operates.

Organic and mechanistic structures

Some classic research on the relationship between environment and organizational structure by Tom Burns and George Macpherson Stalker (1966) and Paul Lawrence and Jay Lorsch (1967) has identified two broad approaches: mechanistic and organic. This model is still useful in enabling change managers to consider what the nature of their structure is, and how well it is suited to the strategy and environment. Some structures tend more towards change and flexibility whilst others are more adept at taking advantage of a relatively stable setting.

Lawrence and Lorsch studied the internal structures, rules and procedures in the production, R&D and sales departments of companies operating in three industries: plastics; food processing and container manufacturing. Environmental uncertainty was highest in the plastics industry, with a rapid pace of technological and product change, and lowest in the container industry, which produced standardized products that changed little over time. Lawrence and Lorsch were interested in how coordination happened within and between the departments they studied. They found that, when all departments perceived the environment to be complex and unstable, each developed a different set of attitudes and way of doing things that suited the part of the environment that it was dealing with, and hence there was a high degree of differentiation between departments. Conversely, when the environment was perceived to be relatively stable and certain, successful organizations tended to have more centralized and formalized structures.

Burns and Stalker also found that organizations sought to operate differently in different environments. In changeable environments they found that the successful companies had organic structures that were complex and entailed decentralized decision making and a fairly continuous process of mutual readjustment, as individuals and departments had to adapt what they did to meet the demands of the environment. Communications could flow in many different directions and each person could have several different tasks, which would become prioritized and deprioritized depending on, for example, the needs of production and the demand of customers. In stable environments, companies favoured centralized decision making and simple lines of coordination that were principally vertical. Rather than having information flowing in many directions, people focused on one task and became highly skilled in its execution. They reported to one manager, who assigned priorities and ensured standardization in terms of products or services. Organic structures tend to be less hierarchical, with decisions being made either by people with relevant expertise or by the person closest to the customer. This has the advantage of being able to change quickly. However, the disadvantage is that the company could be producing contradictions and losing control of quality or cost because of the individual decisions that people take in ignorance of what others are doing. There is also the potential to spend a lot of time and effort on communication. The reverse is typical in mechanistic companies. Here there is little debate and discussion, but decisions are made by the person in authority rather than by the person who knows the most about an issue. Standardization means that the same thing can be done efficiently, but it can also mean that change is more difficult because people are trained in only one way of doing things, and the organization can be less effective at recognizing and responding to ideas from customers, competitors and employees.

McDonald's provides an example of a company that has moved from a mechanistic structure towards more organic principles. McDonald's initial commercial success was based on a highly mechanized approach in which entirely standardized products were sold in the same way, using the same marketing and operations through its network of carefully controlled franchises. The principle was that the same burger would be available on the same conditions of sale in any outlet, so that customers would know exactly what they were getting. However, in the early 2000s the environment became more complicated. Competition increased both at the upper end of McDonald's market and at the budget end. In addition, the variety of fast food available increased considerably. At the same time, McDonald's was criticized severely for its approach to the natural environment. The response was to allow franchises more freedom to innovate. The company increased the range of products, and local restaurants served products from barbecues and guacamole to pizza and lobster. McDonald's also adapted the look of its restaurants, including, for example, having a grand piano in the Wall Street branch. However, there was a problem, because, although there was greater freedom and innovation at the restaurant level, the central production operations were still mechanistic, and the changes that they were working on were aimed at increasing efficiency in the way that one would in a standardized environment. Customer behaviour was continuing to change, with a greater emphasis, for example, on healthy eating. As a result, McDonald's continued to lose market share and its stock price fell.

At this stage the change became more extensive. There was a change of leadership, and a new top management team that was more oriented towards an organic way of working was appointed. Teams of food specialists were decentralized and allowed to test out new products with customers and a greater emphasis was placed on the natural environment, the image of the company and the variety of products. However, in other areas, such as restaurant cleanliness and quality, there were problems, and in these areas decision making was recentralized. Hence, McDonald's moved from the extreme of a mechanistic structure towards a more organic approach, but, as is the case with many companies, it now occupies a hybrid position.

Enacting structural change

Structural change can be conducted incrementally, but is more often a radical shift in which the alteration needs to have a high profile and be clearly communicated and determinate (Burnes, 2009). However, it can be conducted in more top-down or bottom-up ways. As we have seen above, the decision to change is normally a combination of reacting to changes in the business environment and an internal strategy that entails doing things radically differently. Change can be conducted incrementally, for example by introducing project teams in a piloting study in a mechanistic organization. This might be done when the change managers believe either that the introduction of radical change will be strongly resisted or that people will not have the skills and abilities to work in a new way. It has the advantage of not forcing everyone to change at once, and the more willing volunteers can be chosen for the pilot. In addition, if the pilot works it can produce concrete evidence of the change in terms that are meaningful to the organizational population. The disadvantage is that such an approach can be partial, and there can be a fall-back into the old way of doing things if the pilot is unsuccessful or the change leadership is inadequate.

A radical form of change is more typical when it comes to organizational structure, because it often requires everyone to change in tandem so that tasks and processes fit together in a supportive way. This would constitute a rapid speed of change on a broad scope, according to Burnes's (2009) model (see Chapter 2). For example, changing to a more organic structure entails people having more autonomy in their roles and encompassing more than one specialized task. If some people are doing this but others are still working in a very mechanistic way, it is likely to be difficult to integrate the two. When making radical change it is important for all involved to know very clearly what they are going to do, why and how. This can be related to Andrew Pettigrew's model (1985), which focuses on establishing the reasons for change, the 'content' that will be changed and the process by which it will be changed. This can be achieved in a top-down strategy by the central managers deciding on a new direction and negotiating it and then directing the change, as was the case in the LucasArts and McDonald's changes considered above.

An alternative is to adopt a bottom-up approach, in which employees are involved in deciding on the nature and outcome of the change (Beech and MacIntosh, 2008; MacIntosh, Beech and Martin, 2012). This can be carried out through role analysis technique (RAT). This entails people in a focal role working in a group (a) to list and prioritize what they think they should be doing in their job and (b) to list what others who interact with them should be doing so that the process will work best. At the same time, the others who interact with them are in a separate room defining what they should be doing and what they expect of those in the focal role. Once both groups have completed their lists the whole group gets together to compare notes. It is not unusual to find substantial differences between the expectations of the two groups, and in addition there may be crucial activities missing from all the lists. The significant process is the facilitated discussion, in which the different groups work out what their impact is on others and redefine their activities in order to take account of shared goals. In effect, this is a form of facilitated dialogue, in which the self can change because of taking in serious feedback from others through whom the consequences of actions are better understood. In traditional forms this technique was used to fix the details of roles, as would be the case in a mechanistic structure, but it works equally well with organic structures, in which the roles still need to be defined but typically are broader and entail more innovation. In such circumstances, the dialogue aims to increase awareness of the implications of one group innovating for the operation of other groups.

EXERCISE

Consider the role of identity in the Oticon case.

(1) How would you describe the environment of Oticon?

(2) Using the mechanistic-organic model, analyse the structural changes that Oticon went through.

(3) What would you see as the principal advantages and disadvantages of (a) mechanistic and (b) organic structures?

(4) What are the pros and cons of a hybrid approach that seeks to have either:

    (i) some parts of the organization structured in an organic way and other parts in a mechanistic way; or

    (ii) people working sometimes in a mechanistic way and sometimes in an organic way at different times or whilst engaged in different tasks?

WHO TO READ

Henry Mintzberg's (1993) book *Structure in Fives* is a classic text on organizational structure. He explores the forces that impact on organizations and the alternative ways that organizational attempts to coordinate activities are realized in their structures. More recent research has linked structure, new forms of organization and politics (Morris, Hassard and McCann, 2006; Hassard, McCann and Morris, 2010). Collaboration and networks are of increasing interest, and Chris Huxham, Siv Vangen and Paul Hibbert have carried out longitudinal and insightful research on these issues (Huxham and Vangen, 2005; Hibbert and Huxham, 2010).

USEFUL WEBSITES

- www.hrmguide.net. This website covers types of organizational structure and draws upon Alan Price's (2007) book, which takes an HR management perspective.

- www.pathfind.org/...organizationalstructure. This website include a 'how to' guide that offers a broad template that could be adapted for different circumstances. It is perhaps most applicable to mechanistic structures, but it will serve to provide some useful questions for those working in organic settings.

REFERENCES

Beech, N., MacIntosh, R., MacLean, D., Shepherd, J., and Stokes, J. (2002) Exploring constraints on developing knowledge: on the need for conflict. *Management Learning*, 33(4): 459–75.

Beech, N., and MacIntosh, R. (2008) 'Managing complex change: challenges in the National Health Service – Greater Glasgow and Clyde', in Klewes, J., and Langen, R. (eds.) *Change 2.0: Beyond Organizational Transformation*: 137–58. New York: Springer.

Burns, T., and Stalker, G. M. (1966) *The Management of Innovation*. London: Tavistock.

Burnes, B. (2009) *Managing Change*, 5th edn. Harlow: Pearson.

Ekvall, G. (1997) Organizational conditions and levels of creativity. *Creativity and Innovation Management*, 6(4): 195–205.

Hassard, J., McCann, L., and Morris, J. (2010) Management restructuring in Britain: the case of UK auto. *Transforming Management*, 1st quarter.

Hibbert, P. C., and Huxham, C. (2010) The past in play: tradition in the structure of collaborations. *Organization Studies*, 31(5): 525–54.

Huxham, C., and Vangen, S. (2005) *Managing to Collaborate: The Theory and Practice of Collaborative Advantage*. London: Routledge.

Jones, G. R. (2009) *Organizational Theory, Design and Change*, 6th edn. New York: Pearson.

Lawrence, P. R., and Lorsch, J. W. (1967) *Organization and Environment: Managing Differentiation and Integration*. Boston: Harvard University Press.

MacIntosh, R., Beech, N., and Martin, G. (2012) Dialogues and dialectics: limits to clinician-manager interaction in healthcare organizations. *Social Science and Medicine*, 74(3): 332–9.

Mintzberg, H. (1993) *Structure in Fives: Designing Effective Organizations*. Hemel Hempstead: Prentice Hall.

Morris, J., Hassard, J., and McCann, L. (2006) New organizational forms, human resource management and structural convergence? A study of Japanese organizations. *Organization Studies*, 27(10): 1485–511.

Pettigrew, A. (1985) *The Awakening Giant: Continuity and Change in Imperial Chemical Industries*. Oxford: Blackwell.

Price, A. (2007) *Human Resource Management in a Business Context*. London: Thompson.

Thornhill, A., Lewis, P., Millmore, M., and Saunders, M. (2000) *Managing Change: A Human Resource Strategy Approach*. Harlow: Prentice Hall.

Van de Ven, A. H., and Poole, M. S. (1995) Explaining development and change in organizations. *Academy of Management Review*, 20(1): 510–40.

8 Identity and change

The aims of this chapter are to:

- discuss the connections between change and personal identity;
- develop a model of identity work;
- encourage the critical evaluation of a mini-case of a construction company; and
- suggest guiding questions and considerations for working with issues of identity work when managing change.

Introduction

The question of identity – 'Who am I?' – is a deceptively simple question. The answers are manifold and complex. Identity has traditionally been thought of as that which is essential and unchanging – that which pervades over time and in different circumstances. For example, a person who is essentially extrovert may be outgoing both at work and with friends, and may have this identifiable characteristic throughout life. Other aspects of who they are might be more transient; for example, the same person, whilst remaining extrovert, may not think about politics in the same way or associate him- or herself with the same occupational groups throughout life, because he or she is focused on, and influenced by, external sources of ideas and information.

Although there may be aspects of the self that are relatively unchanging, in the context of organizations and work much research has focused on aspects of identity that have degrees of fluidity that are affected by change and that themselves stimulate change. At a simple level, as people move through different roles (e.g. team leader, manager, director) they often take on differences in persona. With experience they look at the world in a slightly different way, and they have a different repertoire of skills to draw upon. Equally, as they have experiences, both positive and negative, they can come to think of themselves in new ways and can recognize themselves as members or outsiders of identifiable social groups.

Who people think they are has a significant impact on what they do and how they relate to others. For example, Dan Karreman and Mats Alvesson (2001) tell the story of senior newspapermen, who have a regular meeting to review the front pages and sales figures of the previous month's papers. Although they know at an intellectual level that sales relate to whether there has been a holiday or not, notable events in sport (on the back page) or key political events, such issues are absent from their analysis. As 'newspapermen' they are interested in 'the headlines that sell papers', because they associate with journalists and do not see themselves as ordinary businessmen. For change management, the interesting questions are how people give themselves identities, how they attribute identities to others and what the consequences of these identity beliefs are for what they do. Consequently, there can be significant implications for change. When change is seen as fitting with a positive self-identity, the process may flow more smoothly. Conversely, when a change is perceived as presenting a challenge to a self-identity, a struggle can emerge in which the person resists change because of its negative impact on him or her (Thomas and Davies, 2005). Either way, identity change can be highly emotive (Coupland *et al.*, 2008), and so it should not be trivialized. Neither should change managers expect to be able to deal with such matters only through explanation and persuasion, as there is a strong experiential and reflexive element to such change. One way of understanding identity change and its relationship with broader organizational change is via the theory of identity work, and we now discuss this approach.

Identity work

Identity work has been defined as involving 'mutually constitutive processes whereby people strive to shape a relatively coherent and distinctive notion of personal self-identity and struggle to come to terms with and, within limits, to influence the various social-identities which pertain to them' (Watson, 2008:

129). This way of thinking emphasizes process. Rather than each of us being a fixed and unchanging entity, the identity we see ourselves as having is changeable, both through our own effort and the social constraints of our environment. The social constraints and possibilities come from what Tony Watson (2008) identifies as 'discourses' – that is, patterns of language/thought/action/symbols that have social currency and effect. For example, it could be said that there is a *discourse of management*, which incorporates, for instance, the concern to run companies effectively, language about markets, products, accounts and behaviours, symbols including dress codes, and assumptions about how to run meetings or minimize bureaucracy. Within something as broad as management, a variety of sub-discourses are likely to emerge, and so, for example, variants include macho-management, entrepreneurial management and humanistic management. These discourses interact with social identities, in this case various notions of what it is to be 'a manager'.

Identity work is a set of processes undertaken to create and maintain a sense of self.

One understanding of 'doing identity' is that it is about claiming membership of **identity categories** (Parker, 2007), and by claiming a category the person thereby differentiates him- or herself from others. For example, in claiming the 'humanistic manager' category, one rejects the self-identity of a 'macho-manager'. However, as Martin Parker points out, there is segmentalism, or multiple identification with diverse categories. Accordingly, the humanistic manager may also claim identities as, for example, a professional accountant, an executive of the company, a person who is 'in the know' about the industry, and so on. The discourses and categories also spread more broadly, in that there are aspects of identity and how identity is performed in the workplace that relate to the social context in general. Such factors can include gender, family, age, ethnicity and religious – or other – beliefs.

Identity categories are labels associated with people or groups, such as 'managers', that imply membership of the category. Categories have distinct boundaries that denote some people as included and others as excluded.

In the theory of identity work, these categories are not seen as 'complete and finished' and subsequently imposed on the individual. Like people's identities, they are also in a process of construction and change, and they are influenced by the self-identities of the people who populate them. For example, the identity category 'father' is rendered meaningful by one's experiences of being fathered, media images and writing about fathers, discussions and shared experiences, and the influences on these experiences of other categories such as 'mother'.

People are not seen as being passively subject to the imposition of social categories. For Stefan Sveningsson and Alvesson (2003), identity work is a fundamentally active process in which people seek to create and maintain a sense of self, acknowledging that this can entail work, and even struggle, as they are immersed in a social environment. They can choose to make certain identity claims central to themselves and other identity claims peripheral. They may seek to add nuance and interpretation to the categories, for example being a humanistic manager with added business acumen. Thus, as people enter a role in the workplace or go through a change programme, there are some aspects of identity that 'await' them. These include language, expected behaviours and roles and embedded ways of seeing the activity, as well as broader discourses such as fashions in management (in order to be seen as a competent manager, one should be conversant in whatever the current trendy notions are in the industry – ideas and practices as diverse as lean methods and corporate social responsibility). The person does not have free choice, as to claim an identity that goes too strongly against the grain will lead to social sanctions in many organizations. These range from gentle suggestions by friends to more overt condemnation of types of behaviour and attitude by seniors. However, normally people have some choice and are able to reinterpret roles and ways of being. Hence, hybrid categories emerge, and people become recognized for 'their take' on a role.

When identity work is 'going against the grain', people can meet resistance to their identity claims as others seek both to deny a claim or to project a different identity onto the person. Hence, Robyn Thomas and Annette Davies (2005) note that identity work can be a political process in which there is an effort to exert power, and this can meet with resistance. In some settings, when the organizational context is strongly dominant, identity work can be a way for people to seek to resist or avoid the consequences of hegemonic power in which they are required to have a certain identity or *be* in a certain way (Brown and Humphreys, 2006). In extreme forms, this can be highly invasive for people; for example, Creed, DeJordy and Lok (2010) explore how gay, lesbian, bisexual and transgender ministers in the Protestant Church engage in identity work so as to cope with the perceived contradictions between their institutional role and their personal identity. In this case, they move from being marginalized individuals to being agents of institutional change. In this way, as Mark Learmonth and Michael Humphreys (2011) point out, identity changes might be regarded as 'positive' or 'negative' depending on the perspective taken. However, when considering change, we should not neglect the 'struggle' part of Sveningsson and Alvesson's (2003) definition. We should also be aware that, when instituting change, it is possible for change managers to be acting as part of a hegemony or to be making unreasonable demands for personal change, and the ethics and efficacy of such demands are worthy of reflexive questioning. In general, change that relates to identity is likely to entail difference, and for the change manager the question is often how differences between people can be accommodated without resulting in conflict and opposition. This may be preferable to seeking to impose uniformity. One way of addressing this issue is through dialogue.

We can think of these identity-forming interactions as a process of dialogue (Beech, 2008). Some input to the identity work dialogue starts from the self. These inputs are seen as being the result of internalized interactions that can come from childhood, notable experiences and resonant encounters (Beech, MacIntosh and MacLean, 2010), in which utterances, images, snippets of stories and the feelings associated with events become absorbed and taken as being part of the self. For example, early and repeated experiences of rejection could lead to a fear of exclusion and a self-identity as an 'outsider'. Equally, repeated experiences of success and reward could lead to a 'natural' view of the 'self-as-winner'. These self-identities enter a process of dialogue – that is, interaction in which the self can be open to change. Change can result from input and resources from the social context, such as roles, discourses and the utterances and behaviours of others. These social processes can be confirmatory or can lead to the self-identity modifying or changing more significantly (Pullen, Beech and Sims, 2007). For example, the 'self-as-winner' can be depleted by negative criticism and repeated failure. This can lead to modification ('I don't seem to be able to win in this particular environment') or significant change ('I used to be a winner, but not any more').

As a person's work life is often important in terms of the position and meaning it gives to him or her, the identity work that goes on at work is non-trivial and often bound up with emotion (Coupland et al., 2008). For example, Thornborrow and Brown (2009) give the example of a paratrooper who goes through induction and training, is deployed and completes several missions and eventually, whilst sitting on a battlefield concludes, finally, that he is 'a Para'. Coupland (2001) provides another example, in which management trainees begin a graduate trainee programme as one group, adopting the category 'management'. Partway through the training the 'cool' group, who are seen as the high-flyers, refine their identity, dropping the management label and reconstituting themselves as 'strategists'. The 'out-group' are unaware of this and unintentionally confirm their un-cool status by continuing to use the 'management' label. These examples draw on resources in the current working lives of the people. However, at a personal level they may draw upon more longitudinally embedded aspects of the self, such as a fear of being left out or branded un-cool, or, conversely, a deep belief in the 'self-as-winner'.

The dialogue is not a one-way process. The identity claims and actions that people make impact on the social context. So, for example, Coupland's in-group not only claim an identity for themselves but also produce an out-group identity for the others, and then act as if this were true. They bring about an 'us and them' situation and start to produce and reproduce hierarchical divisions. These play a role in knowledge flows (who you tell and who you don't), and ultimately in who gets the better assignments, the better experience and, hence, the better jobs. This produces a next generation of managers (or strategists) who have relatively positive experiences of this type of segmented approach and so in future they may have a predisposition to preserve it. As a result, the individual and the system can be seen as mutually constructing each other. This dynamic is emphasized by Mary Jo Hatch and Majken Schultz (2002, 2004), who explore the relationship between context and organizational identity. They identify some processes as **expressing**, in which identities are projected outwards, and others as **impressing**, when identity projections from the outside are internalized. They recognize that an excess of either dynamic can be problematic. If expressing dominates, the people or organization can exhibit narcissistic tendencies in which they assume that others see them as they see themselves, and this can lead to too much self-importance. Conversely, if impressing dominates, 'hyper-adaptation' can occur, in which a sense of self is sublimated to the projections of others and consequently there is too little self-worth. What is required, according to Hatch and Schultz, is a balance, and when managing change it is worth considering the state of this balance, and hence deciding whether to encourage more impressing (for example, through benchmarking or using external role models) or more expressing (for example, through mentoring to help people appreciate their own position and develop skills in explaining it and maintaining the position in the face of pressure to change).

Expressing is the process whereby identity claims are projected from the self outwards into the social context.

Impressing is the process by which identity projections from the social context are internalized by a person who alters his or her self-conception as a result.

Figure 8.1 provides a diagram of identity work processes. In the diagram, various aspects are represented as distinct, and, analytically, it can be useful to

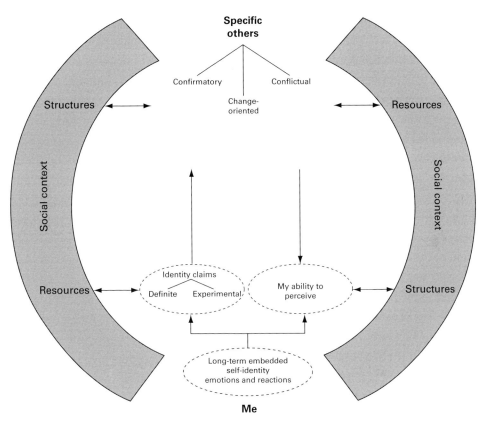

Figure 8.1 A model of identity work

treat them as separate in order to focus on how they interact. However, the assumption of this approach is that, in reality, there is continuous internal and external dialogue. The interaction occurs within the social context, which provides resources and imposes social structures. Resources are used when people make identity claims, and they include, for example, **professional identities**, which enable people to make claims that are broadly understood and accepted. Social structures permit and encourage some identity claims and discourage others. For example, there are macro social structures around gender, and in the early part of the twentieth century there was an association between maleness and leadership. (This is not a point about the physical aspect of being male, but the social aspect, in which certain characteristics are believed to be masculine and are then extrapolated into fields of practice such as business.) At that time, it would be easier for a man to make identity claims of being a rightful leader than it would be for a woman (and this problem may still be prevalent in some cultures and organizations).

Professional identities are identity categories that people have at work, and they are generally associated with particular occupations in which having the occupation, or being a professional, is an observable identity – such as, for example, being a police officer (Thomas and Davies, 2005) or an accountant (Coupland, 2001).

Within the social context, the self develops certain long-term, embedded beliefs about self-identity. These can originate, though not exclusively so, in childhood experiences, and may relate to interactions with others who were very significant for us. There is an interplay between the long-term embedded self-identity and the person's emotions and reactions. The composite that is 'me' makes identity claims. Some are definitive, for example when defending the long-term embedded self-identity or when making a strongly held aspirational claim – who I see myself becoming. Other claims may be more experimental, tentative or even playful, such as trying out taking a role in a new group that one does not normally have, such as the joker or the leader. If it works, the person may extend the experiment; but nothing is lost if it fails.

There is a two-way interaction with others in the context. Others may be judged to be insignificant and ignored, but those who are significant can have a major impact. This may be proactive, in which case the others are projecting an identity onto the self or seeking to persuade the person that he or she is or should be a particular way. For example, a senior manager may seek to influence how a newly promoted protégé embodies the role of manager. Alternatively, others can interact reactively. They can respond to an identity claim by the self in a confirmatory, change-oriented or conflictual way.

The impact of the others, whether proactive or reactive, is filtered through the self's ability to perceive, recognize and react. Sometimes this is a straightforward process, but, because identity is involved, people can filter reactions so strongly (either positively or negatively) that the person is reacting as much to their preconceived expectation as the message transmitted by the other; in the extreme, the other can be a fantasy that is generated from the self (MacIntosh and Beech, 2011) and that is used to confirm the self-identity.

We now explore a mini-case in which identity work and organizational change are both present.

Mini-Case 8.1: Green Circle Construction

Green Circle Construction (GCC) was a medium-sized company that had recently expanded by taking over a smaller organization that was based in a geographical area about fifty miles away. GCC's main activity was road and footpath construction. The takeover expanded the number of key customers but also created some duplication, and so there was a restructuring and the creation of a new management team with a new CEO. The new approach was to focus on 'action not words' and to increase quality and decrease bureaucracy through an 'openness principle'. Rather than working in hierarchical and formally remote ways, the idea was that people could just speak to each other to get the job done. This change was implemented by the new CEO with no compromise:

The way we operate has got to improve. We'll start off by telling the truth. We're not trained to trust each other, but straight away we'll behave this way. We'll shove all the old baggage out of the door. We'll come in fresh and we'll operate in this new style.

There appeared to be much need for this approach. These are the comments of some of the workers:

We don't see the management much. I've never seen them out. They don't come and say 'Oh, that's a good job'. If you do a bad job they'll come and say 'That's a bad job'.
    Management's remote to us. We're just a wee pleb somewhere.
    They're just folks making decisions that's never actually been out there working. They're making decisions that's actually ridiculous.
    They've got no bloody clue how it works. There is two ways of doing things: their way and the wrong way.

The CEO was away on holiday, and the senior managers held a meeting, at which there was a lot of criticism of the CEO for failing to make the change a reality. The senior managers decided to confront the CEO, in line with the openness principle. The commercial director said:

I got the unpleasant job of telling him [the CEO] at the next meeting. I sat there, and if one of the directors was going to give a different story to what they told me I was going to crucify them. But everyone told the CEO the same thing. You could actually see his head going down... I said: '[Name], don't take that in a negative way. Take it positively, because I would never have been able to say that in [name of previous company]...' And he came back, and he changed the whole thing around and made it so positive. It was amazing.

In a separate conversation, the CEO reflected on the same event:

I had a painful corporate team meeting two weeks ago, when they were slagging me off for 'It's not good enough'... I mean, the openness is actually not nice. It's actually quite hurtful at times, but, you know, you've got to bounce ahead as a result.

The response was to be more radical in the changes. The restructuring was taken beyond senior and middle management to changing team formation and simplifying reporting relationships. Some redundancies were made, and there was a belief that they had the right people in 'leadership roles throughout the organization'. A senior manager said: 'I would say we are the "can do" people.' The CEO tried to become more visible: 'I'm a very active person going out and about; visited 150 facilities and depots in the last year.'

There was some evidence of this having an impact. These are the comments of two middle managers:

I can see the change right from the top. [Name of CEO] is trying for a more human relations, open sort of culture, and involving everyone from the bottom up.

"I think these work groups are quite a good thing. I was able to put my side across to these people [workers] who had never had that opportunity. Because you're a manager, they wouldn't speak to you in [the old company], but we sat there and had an informative meeting in both ways.

The maintenance workers also thought that the job got done, and that problems were solved by working as a team. However, their definition of who was in the team varied somewhat from the managers' espousal:

Everyone pulls together, everyone knows each other.

'[Name], I could do with a hand in here.' 'No problem.' We are all working boys together, we'll help out our working mates. I mean, you'll do it for nothing, just for giving a pal a handout.

If we can get a wagon out on the road for the next morning we will work till we do it. I had two men and myself one night – four o'clock in the morning – to get the wagon out. And we were grafting. The management had said it was ready, but it wasn't ready. They knew it wasn't ready. [. . .] It would have been done no matter what; we would have worked till it was finished.

In GCC the intention was to change how they did things by being different. They recognized a problem with the old identity categories of 'us' and 'them'. In the words of a senior manager, 'They don't trust us, which was our fault at the end of the day, but we are trying to get them to build up a relationship.' The post-merger organization needed to integrate across old boundaries of competition and to win contracts by having good relationships with key customers and delivering a high-quality product. It was not that the previous company had been unsuccessful, but its success had been achieved in spite of relatively poor communication and a lack of genuine teamwork. In the new setting the CEO wanted the company to be open and action-oriented. A crucial moment was when he was faced with the criticism that his own actions were out of line with his rhetoric. This was painful for the CEO and felt dangerous to the senior managers. However, the response was to try to bring behaviour into line with the espoused way of being. In effect, this was an effort to occupy a different identity from the old management. Whilst this does not lead to an overnight change, it encouraged others to move as well in terms of their relationships, attitudes and behaviours. Sometimes the style of language used can sound evangelistic or manipulative, but there seemed to be a high degree of authenticity, and this came across to others in the company.

Analysing Green Circle Construction using the identity work model

We can use the model of identity work presented in Figure 8.1 to analyse the Green Circle Construction mini-case. The CEO can be seen to have made definite identity claims to be a new sort of manager: open, trustworthy and action-oriented. In making these claims, he had the advantage of drawing upon resources in the management discourse that would espouse the direction he is adopting, and because the company had just changed through a takeover the social structures were also relatively supportive of a new way of doing things. Others reacted – some positively, some negatively – but largely in private. This is why the early signals the CEO picked up were that things were going well and that he and the organization were in the process of becoming new identities. However, the challenge from the senior managers after his holiday constituted an interaction with a significant other. It seems that he had failed to live his espoused identity, and so initially it appeared to be a conflictual interaction and the CEO felt defeated. However, the commercial director helped the CEO reinterpret the interaction as being confirmatory/change-oriented. He explained that the interaction could not even have happened in the previous regime, and that the answer was to push ahead with greater vigour. This turned out to be a resonant encounter, and the CEO was changed by it. He felt that he had received reinforcement from a significant other.

Because we had privileged access to the 'backstage' talk of some of the workers we can see that the CEO's identity claims were not fully accepted by all. This relates to some of the workers' long-term embedded assumptions about 'us' and 'them'. This will be difficult to change, not least because before some workers can accept the new identity of the CEO they will have to change certain aspects of their own identity. That is, they will have to give up some of the oppositional construction of self that positions them as the problem solvers and the doers who compensate for the remote 'folks making decisions' with 'no... clue how it works'. If the managers stopped being the negatives that had to be compensated for by the workers' positive, there was an inadvertent attack on the workers' raison d'être. Therefore, it is important to think through the dialogical implications when seeking to understand and enact identity-related aspects of change.

Enacting change and engaging with identity work

The question of identity – 'Who am I? – can be prompted during organizational change. People can recognize aspirational versions of themselves that they could become. Alternatively, there can be significant threats to their identities, as, for example, 'competent professional', 'member of the in-crowd' or even 'anti-management'. Therefore, when introducing change that could impact on people's identities, it is worth asking:

(1) Will the change introduce, or be perceived to introduce, identity claims on the part of management? If so, are these the claims that we want to make and can they be substantiated?
(2) Will the changes be a form of interaction with the self-identities of others? If so, will they be perceived to be confirmatory, change-oriented or con-flictual? Are they likely to be perceived as a different message by different people?
(3) What resources from the social context can be drawn upon to aid the change?
(4) What social structures are likely to have an impact, and will they be positive or negative for the change?

Not all changes are a matter of identity. It is fully possible to make changes to tasks and procedures without impacting on people's self-identities. However, there are changes that need people to *be* different. There are forms of change leadership that require the leader to be authentically different and 'live' the change. There are also changes that may not have been intended to have such a deep impact, but for some organizational members they do. In such circumstances it is worth considering the application of the identity work model and the ethics and efficacy of engaging in change that has identity impacts.

EXERCISES

(1) Consider the role of identity in the ABB case. To what extent do you see identity work occurring on the part of successive CEOs? To what extent do the changes appear to be linked to their identity projects? Does it matter?

(2) Read the Island Opera case. Explain the activities that Bella undertakes in order to make identity claims on what could be seen as her aspirational identity. What resources does she draw upon to strengthen her claim? How do others' reactions reinforce or work against her claims? Discuss the identity work that Jeremy undertakes. What factors impact negatively on his efforts at identity work?

WHO TO READ

Identity work as a concept and way of understanding change at work has developed into an interesting dialogue in the literature. Rather than focusing on one author, it is worth being aware of the community that is engaging in the dialogue. Sveningsson and Alvesson (2003) and Watson (2009) offer helpful definitions of the core concept. Sierk Ybema (2004, 2010) elaborates this and draws particular attention to temporal scales looking both forwards and backwards. Identity as a site of struggle and resistance has been explored by Andrew Brown and Michael Humphreys (2006) and Thomas and Davies (2005), Christine Coupland *et al.* (2008) have emphasized emotion and its connection to identity, and Nick Ellis and Ybema (2010) have discussed the dynamics of identity formation in modern organization forms.

USEFUL WEBSITE

- www.plato.stanford.edu; this website discusses personal identity from philosophical and psychological perspectives. It is part of the Stanford Encyclopedia of Philosophy and offers a good-quality discussion.

REFERENCES

Beech, N. (2008) On the nature of dialogical identity work. *Organization*, 15(1): 51–74.

Beech, N., MacIntosh, R., and MacLean, D. (2010) Dialogues between academics and practitioners: the role of generative dialogic encounters. *Organization Studies*, 31(9): 1341–67.

Brown, A. D., and Humphreys, M. (2006) Organizational identity and place: a discursive exploration of hegemony and resistance. *Journal of Management Studies*, 43(2): 231–57.

Coupland, C. (2001) Accounting for change: a discourse analysis of graduate trainees' talk of adjustment. *Journal of Management Studies*, 38(8): 1103–19.

Coupland, C., Brown, A. D., Daniels, K., and Humphreys, M. (2008) Saying it with feeling: analyzing speakable emotions. *Human Relations*, 61(3): 327–54.

Creed, W. E. D., DeJordy, R., and Lok, J. (2010) Being the change: resolving institutional contradiction through identity work. *Academy of Management Journal*, 53(6): 1336–64.

Ellis, N., and Ybema, S. (2010) Marketing identities: shifting circles of identification in inter-organizational relationships. *Organization Studies*, 31(3): 279–305.

Hatch, M. J., and Schultz, M. (2002) The dynamics of organizational identity. *Human Relations*, 55(8): 989–1017.

Hatch, M. J., and Schultz, M. (2004) *Organizational Identity: A Reader*. Oxford University Press.

Karreman, D., and Alvesson, M. (2001) Making newsmakers: conversational identities at work. *Organization Studies*, 22(1): 59–89.

Learmonth, M., and Humphreys, M. (2011) Blind spots in Dutton, Roberts and Bednar's 'Pathways for positive identity construction at work': 'you've got to accentuate the positive, eliminate the negative'. *Academy of Management Review*, 36(2): 424–7.

MacIntosh, R., and Beech, N. (2011) Strategy, strategists and fantasy: a dialogic constructionist perspective. *Accounting, Auditing and Accountability Journal*, 24(1): 15–37.

Parker, M. (2007) Identification: organizations and structuralisms, in Pullen, A., Beech, N., and Sims, D. (eds.) *Exploring Identity: Concepts and Methods*: 61–82. Basingstoke: Palgrave Macmillan.

Pullen, A., Beech, N., and Sims, D. (eds.) (2007) *Exploring Identity: Concepts and Methods*. Basingstoke: Palgrave Macmillan.

Sveningsson, S., and Alvesson, M. (2003) Managing managerial identities: organizational fragmentation, discourse and identity struggle. *Human Relations*, 56(10): 1163–93.

Thornborrow, T., and Brown, A. D. (2009) Being regimented: aspiration, discipline and identity work in the British Parachute Regiment. *Organization Studies*, 30(4): 355–76.

Thomas, R., and Davies, A. (2005) Theorising the micro-politics of resistance: discourses of change and professional identities in the UK public services, *Organization Studies*, 26(5): 683–706.

Watson, T. J. (2008) Managing identity: identity work, personal predicaments and structural circumstances. *Organization*, 15(1): 121–43.

Watson, T. J. (2009) Narrative, life story and manager identity. *Human Relations*, 63(3): 425–52.

Ybema, S. (2004) Managerial postalgia: projecting a golden future. *Journal of Managerial Psychology*, 19(8): 825–41.

Ybema, S. (2010) Talk of change: temporal contrasts and collective identities. *Organization Studies*, 31(4): 481–503.

9 Choosing customers and competitors

The aims of this chapter are to:

- suggest ways in which customers can be segmented;
- describe the role of strategic groups in defining change challenges; and
- consider the choices that an organization faces when changing customers and competitors.

Using some of the diagnostic approaches from the enquiry–action framework (presented in Part B of this book) may lead you to conclude that the change required tends to be externally rather than internally focused. In other words, that the change needs to reposition the organization in terms of the types of customers that are being served and/or which competitors this involves. Such externally focused repositioning may well cause or be caused by changes in organizational structure, self-image or business process. The direction of causality is far less important than the observation that there are interconnections, and that iterations may be required to arrive at a set of changes that help match internal organizational arrangements with the external organizational environment. Although the language of customers and competitors sits most comfortably in the context of private sector organizations, it is both possible and helpful to conceptualize customers and competitors alike in the context of public, voluntary and charitable organizations. We return to this theme later in the chapter, but we begin by considering two related but distinct changes that an organization may engage with: changing customers and changing competitors.

Choosing customers

In many ways, customers (private sector), service users (public sector) or donors (third sector) help define an organization. They configure key relationships and mark out the scope of what the organization does and does not do (Ellis *et al.*, 2010). Hence, in thinking about change, a natural consideration would be to ask whether your organization is embedded in a network of relationships that are helping or hindering its progress. In a private sector setting, it may be that there are too few customers willing to use your products or services. Since customers provide revenue to sustain the organization it is important that there are sufficient numbers of the right kind of customer, and that those customers are at least satisfied with the experience of buying from you. In a public sector setting, the question may be about the boundaries of provision between your organization and others – for example, the relationship between healthcare provision and social care. In charitable organizations, such boundaries are also important. Consider two charities, both of which support people living in poverty. One might focus attention on support for young children, while another may focus attention on education and training to help support adults as they seek employment.

A first step might be to identify current and potential customers. An approach called segmentation is used, in both marketing and strategy, to group customers using one or more characteristics, such as location, sales volume, pricing, etc. A single segment is typically defined as containing customers or potential customers who share some common traits. For example, when eating out we face a plethora of choices relating to food types, speed of service, pricing, location and any number of other criteria. Any individual restaurant is unlikely to match the demands of multiple segments, and it is helpful first to select those segments that you plan to target, then find ways of delighting those customers in the full knowledge that this is likely to mean that your offering is unattractive to those in other segments. Relating this simple example to the enquiry–action framework, we argue that one of the ways in which change might be enacted is to consider whether your current mix of customers is appropriate and sustainable as the organization moves forward. In public, charitable and third sector organizations, similar considerations can be made, though restraints in the form of mandatory obligations to provide service to certain service users or a strong moral commitment to the cause of a particular group of beneficiaries are more likely to feature.

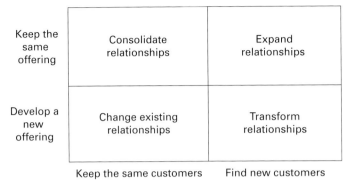

	Keep the same customers	Find new customers
Keep the same offering	Consolidate relationships	Expand relationships
Develop a new offering	Change existing relationships	Transform relationships

Figure 9.1 The adapted Ansoff matrix

A simple approach to structuring the decision about which types of customer relationships you need to foster is to use the Ansoff matrix. Igor Ansoff switched from a senior role at Lockheed, the US electronics and aviation firm, to an academic career and is regarded by many as the founding father of modern strategic management with his early texts on corporate and business strategy (1965, 1969). Many of the scholars who subsequently found themselves researching the development of strategy became sceptical about the role of planning and planners (see, for example, Mintzberg, 1991), but Ansoff's work remains influential. One of his key contributions is to pose two questions about the relationship between an organization and its customers. First, will the future centre on relationships with the same group of customers or some new group? Second, will the basis of these relationships be the current products and services or new products and services? Figure 9.1 is adapted from Ansoff's original two-by-two matrix.

The four categories in our adapted Ansoff matrix imply different change challenges. The decision to **consolidate** relationships implies limited or no change, since both dimensions of the model remain constant. In practice, changes in the environment are likely to mean that even this trajectory requires some incremental adjustment, to ensure that relationships with existing customers remain viable. Such incremental changes may require that you adjust operational processes (see Chapter 10) or maintain the vitality and enthusiasm of your staff (see Chapter 4). The Swiss watch manufacturer Rolex is one example of a firm that has consolidated its relationships within an existing segment. In 1910 a Rolex was the first wristwatch to receive the Swiss Certificate of Precision, in recognition of the accuracy of its timekeeping. The product has always been expensive, which means targeting a particular type of customer, and, over a century later, Rolex persists with offering the same basic product proposition to the same kinds of customer it has historically targeted. Of course, the products, processes, people and customers have each evolved over that period, but they remain similar enough to be placed in the 'consolidation' category.

In contrast, there are many examples of firms that bring new products or services to the attention of their existing customers. When buying your groceries, you may notice offers for a range of other services, including mobile telephony and financial services. These new offerings **change** the nature of your relationship with your existing customers. There may be little by way of overlap between selling one type of service and another, perhaps even to the extent that the customer is the only commonality. When UK supermarket giant Tesco was looking to continue growing, senior managers realized that they might have to look beyond their existing relationship with customers. One of a number of areas that was highlighted was financial services, and Tesco now offers banking services to customers who valued and trusted the Tesco brand; some 6 million Tesco customers also use Tesco banking facilities. One of the main challenges that this introduces is to reconceptualize the identity of the business (see Chapter 8), and there are significant decisions over whether to integrate the new activities into existing structures and lines of reporting or to separate these out (see Chapter 7).

Another strategy for growth is to retain the same basic product or service offering but to **expand** the network of customers that you interact with. NHS Greater Glasgow is a public sector provider of healthcare operating in Scotland. The National Health Service offers free healthcare and is funded by the government. During a round of reorganization in 2006, the Scottish government decided to reconfigure the geographic boundaries of the so called 'health boards' by dissolving one organization and splitting the territory between two other existing providers. This created a new organization, called NHS Greater Glasgow and Clyde, which expanded the network of service users that interacted with the organization. Whilst this public sector example does not fit with the desire to expand through acquisition and merger that may be seen in the private sector, many of the challenges remain the same. One obvious consequence was the need to reconfigure management roles to account for the duplication and overlaps that existed (see Chapter 11), as well as redoubling efforts to change the conversations within the organization about the relationship between the original organization and the much smaller organization with which it had merged (see Chapter 13). The resulting change processes that flowed from the merger had to overcome change fatigue, in that both of the organizations that were merged had been through several rounds of reorganization (MacIntosh *et al.*, 2007). In private sector settings, such expansion often involves exporting to new territories, which can introduce a range of cultural and legislative challenges.

The final approach suggested by the amended Ansoff matrix is to **transform** your relationships. This transformation implies changes in two dimensions simultaneously, in that relationships are now built with new customers on the basis of some new offering. Babcock International Group plc, with revenues in excess of £3 billion, can trace its roots back to the foundation in 1891 of Babcock & Wilcox. The firm's heritage in servicing and supporting military assets can be traced back as far as the First World War. Customers were often government defence departments, and the offering was relisted under 'support services' on the London stock exchange in 2000. A series of acquisitions have transformed at least some of the firm's relationships, whereby new activities are now delivered for new customers. One example would be the acquisition of a business that manufactures and installs baggage handling equipment for airports. The connection between this activity and maintaining a nuclear submarine is not easy to spot. The customers are different, the offering is different. In the words of one senior Babcock figure, 'The only thing they have in common is that they both involve doing complex things for complex customers.' The strategy literature suggests that such transformational change carries higher risk relative to the other categories in Figure 9.1, as it involves simultaneous change in both dimensions. To mitigate such risks, firms often combine this approach with consolidation, and the Babcock example is consistent with this observation in that the firm continued to invest in the original parts of the business.

Mike Saren (2006) points out that, when making choices about the strategic direction of change, understanding the behaviour of customers in terms of their own social constructions is vital. Their beliefs and actions may not always be the same. For example, when market researchers asked the public about their attendance at cultural events they found a tendency to considerably overstate the recency of attendance. It was not uncommon that people would think that they had been to a music event within the last six to eight months, when the data revealed that it had been nearly two years since they had purchased a ticket. One way of addressing this is to point out their error. However, an alternative that is increasingly used is to recognize that the person sees him- or herself as someone who attends music concerts at least twice a year, and this positive image can be used in selling more attendances. This constructionist approach also relates to the way that marketers come not only to understand their markets but to take a role in reconstructing them through their discursive activities, choices in image and representation of culture (Mason, Oshri and Leek, forthcoming).

Choosing competitors

One consequence of changing customers is that it may also introduce new competitors. Excepting the relatively rare circumstance when a completely new product category emerges, most customers that are new to one business are in existing relationships with other providers. Hence, growth for one firm often implies decline for another. This introduces obvious tensions and is true even in public, voluntary or third sector settings, as illustrated by policy debates about investing more money in social care and education in order to reduce the cost of healthcare.

We now introduce another technique from the strategic management literature to help structure the decision about which competitors to work with. Strategic group analysis was first introduced by Michael Hunt (1972), and it has gone on to become a widely recognized strategic analysis tool to help managers 'with the task of trying to position the firm in the strategic group which best fits the firm's strengths' (McGee, Thomas and Pruett, 1995: 258). Rather than think of every potential competitor, the logic here is that focus is important, and a strategic group of organizations is defined as that subset of firms in an industry with similar characteristics, following similar strategies and competing for the attention of similar customers. The implication is that firms compete far more intensely within their own strategic group than they do across different strategic groups (DeSarbo and Grewal, 2008). The strategic group analysis process draws on segmentation but focuses attention on competitors rather than customers. Characteristics that might be involved in mapping competitors could include geographical coverage, the distribution channels used, product range, scale, the ownership structure or pricing policy, to list just a few. Once conducted, strategic group analysis can provide subtle but significant insights (Flavian, Haverberg and Polo, 1999) that help frame important choices for an organization about who to compete with and the basis of that competition. Figure 9.2 sets out the steps involved in conducting strategic group analysis.

The newspaper industry provides a good example. There are dozens of newspapers on sale in the United Kingdom every day but they are not all in direct competition with each other. They vary in price, journalistic style and format. There are local, national and international titles to choose from, and one

(1)	List all potential providers of the product or service that you offer.
(2)	Identify criteria that differentiate between these competitors.
(3)	Check that you can source evidence/data in relation to these criteria.
(4)	Pick two criteria and use these as axes to map individual firms against.
(5)	Cluster the firms into strategic groups.
(6)	Consider the location of your firm in relation to the other strategic groups.

Figure 9.2 Steps in strategic group analysis

historic way of splitting the providers was to separate the broadsheets from the tabloids. In a mature market with sales in decline there is ever more fierce competition for customers. Worse, the internet and twenty-four-hour news channels are changing the ways in which consumers access news. The strategic group analysis shown in Figure 9.3 uses two dimensions to group newspaper titles into groups following similar strategies and competing on similar bases. First, the vertical axis considers the word count of the paper. This can be regarded as a proxy for journalistic quality, in that longer articles, more commentary, etc. might indicate greater emphasis on investigation and analysis. Second, the horizontal axis considers the breadth of topics covered, from thematic publications focused on sport or finance to titles that cover a range of news, politics, business and culture. In Figure 9.3, strategic group A contains a handful of titles with a specialist focus and high levels of content. One such example would be the *Financial Times*. Group B contains a larger number of traditional broadsheet outlets (many of which have since changed to tabloid paper sizes in a bid to win new customers). Examples in group B might include the *Times*, *Guardian* and *Independent* newspapers. Next, in group C, there are a range of titles that in the United Kingdom would be described as tabloid or 'red tops', such as the *Sun* and the *Daily Mirror*. These outlets still cover a range of topics, though perhaps slightly fewer than those in group B, and the titles in group C employ a different style of writing. This is only one mapping of the competitors in the newspaper industry, and other maps could be produced using circulation figures, the sales price or the percentage of revenue from

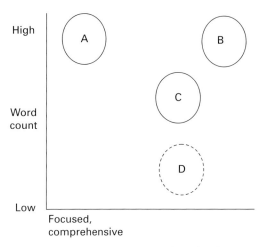

High

Word count

Low

Focused,
comprehensive

Figure 9.3 Strategic group analysis for the newspaper industry

advertising. It is also worth noting that some news organizations own multiple titles and/or operate in other news media such as radio and television. Nevertheless, the map in Figure 9.3 is helpful as an illustrative example.

When, in 1999, Associated Newspapers looked for opportunities to gain competitive advantage it was clear that something new was required. The *Metro* newspaper that Associated Newspapers introduced to the United Kingdom occupied a then unique position, shown as group D in Figure 9.3. The newspaper was initially distributed in London and now it is available in some fifty cities throughout the country. It has broad coverage of news, business, culture and sport but the word count is lower than that of its competitors, with short stories that are intended to summarize key points rather than offer in-depth analysis. However, the real innovation was that the *Metro* was distributed free to customers at rail stations, bus stations and other public transport venues. The target market was commuters, and the publication survived solely on advertising revenue. One senior executive from Associated Newspapers described the business model as follows: 'Basically, we rent out over a million pairs of eyeballs for somewhere between five and fifteen minutes every weekday. The reader gets free news on their journey and the advertisers get placement in and around short, punchy news stories.' Figure 9.3 shows how Associated Newspapers managed to identify and occupy an uncontested space in the strategic landscape, pursuing what some would call a blue ocean strategy (Kim and Mauborgne, 2005).

The decision to switch from one strategic group to another is not necessarily straightforward. Changing competitors may imply the need to change a variety of aspects of your organization. The basis of competition often varies from one strategic group to the next, and these differences form the basis of barriers to mobility between the groups. Switching from group C to group A in Figure 9.3 would require that an organization develop different skills, structures and relationships in order to succeed in its new strategic group. Further, just as you and your colleagues are planning to choose new competitors, other organizations may also be eyeing the same competitive space. In transitioning from one set of competitors to another, one of the main challenges may actually be to unlearn the habits and culture that relate to the strategic group that the firm is leaving (see Chapter 6).

Mini-Case 9.1: AVI Hi-Fi

Since the early part of the twentieth century it has been possible to record and reproduce music. From the introduction of the gramophone through to today's digital solutions there has always been a market for high-fidelity (or hi-fi) products that offer the highest levels of sound quality. Ashley James has worked in the hi-fi industry all his life, and he now runs a small hi-fi company based in England called AVI. For years the firm made specialist, and expensive, equipment that was sold through specialist retailers. Typically, when selling hi-fi equipment at prices in the range £500 to £1,000,000, retailers offer demonstration rooms in which customers can try out competing products before reaching a final decision. Faced with a significant investment decision, customers usually research their purchase thoroughly by studying reviews of the best amplifiers, speakers and sources at particular price points. The reviews help narrow the choice down to a few products, which are then auditioned at a specialist hi-fi retailer. As a result, hi-fi manufacturers need to manage relationships with both the hi-fi press and hi-fi retailers carefully.

AVI moved into digital music with the launch of their flagship CD player, which cost £999. Initially sales of CD players grew rapidly, but over time digital music began to escape the need for a physical format (i.e. the disc). When Apple launched the iPod and iTunes, digital music finally reached a mass audience. Why would customers need either the CD or a CD player when the music could be stored and copied using a personal computer, mobile phone or digital music device such as an iPod?

The hi-fi world was highly sceptical about the quality of sound that such systems could produce. James soon realized that technology was revolutionizing the industry he knew so well. 'By 2006 we'd noticed that people had stopped buying CD players, and we needed to think of a way to respond,' he says. This forced AVI to consider changing both customers and competitors. James and his fellow director Martin Grindrod experimented with an iPod using it as a source with AVI's own high-quality speakers. The initial experiment seemed to confirm the suspicion that compressing the digital recording to make it portable had also stripped out the richness and nuance required for high-quality sound reproduction. AVI persisted and switched to using iTunes as a source rather than an iPod. Using a Macintosh computer, James and Grindrod hooked the digital output from iTunes to AVI's own DAC (digital-to-analogue convertor), and the sound was much closer to the standard expected of premium-priced hi-fi. This led AVI to introduce a new product range and a whole new business model.

AVI developed a new range of active speakers that incorporated high-quality digital-to-analogue signal processors as part of an integrated and computer-based music system. Suddenly customers could benefit from all the convenience of computerized music, with libraries and playlists, whilst having the luxury of high-quality sound reproduction. The gap between this computer-centred music system and a traditional hi-fi source such as a CD player was small enough that AVI decided to change its product range markedly. Today AVI offers an integrated, digital music that is priced at the lower end of the specialist hi-fi market. The combination of relatively low pricing, greater flexibility and marginally reduced sound quality gave AVI the opportunity to serve a different group of customers.

However, there were still significant challenges, and AVI struggled to get traditional hi-fi retailers and distributors to stock their products. James notes: 'Hi-fi retailers regarded our new products as something that should be sold in PC World and certainly not in their outlet.' This signalled the need for a second change, whereby AVI would sell direct over the internet. This allowed the firm to reduce costs further, and it introduced AVI to a new group of competitors. Together, these changes resulted in a fivefold increase in sales volumes.

By changing customers and competitors, AVI is now better positioned to take advantage of the booming digital music environment. The changes made have involved technological moves in terms of new products and changing distribution models, partnerships and sources of competitiveness.

WHO TO READ

Ansoff is sometimes referred to as the father of strategic management. Born in Russia but raised in the United States, he was one of the first to write an account of the strategic planning process, and his early works still influence the field today.

USEFUL WEBSITES

Further details on the firms and examples used in this chapter can be found by visiting the websites of the individual firms. These are listed below for convenience:

- www.avihifi.com;
- www.babcock.co.uk;
- www.metro.co.uk;
- www.nhsggc.org.uk;
- www.rolex.com; and
- www.tescofinance.com.

REFERENCES

Ansoff, H. I. (1965) *Corporate Strategy: An Analytic Approach to Business Policy for Growth and Expansion.* New York: McGraw Hill.

Ansoff, H. I. (1969) *Business Strategy: Selected Readings.* London: Penguin Books.

DeSarbo, W. S., and Grewal, R. (2008) Hybrid strategic groups.

Strategic Management Journal,
29(3): 293–317.

Ellis, N., Fitchett, J., Higgins, M., Jack, G.,
Lim, M., Saren, M., and Tadajewski, M.
(2010) *Marketing: A Critical Textbook.*
London: Sage.

Flavian, C., Haberberg, A., and Polo, Y. (1999)
Subtle insights from strategic group
analysis. *Journal of Strategic Marketing,*
7(2): 89–106.

Hunt, M. (1972) Competition in the major home
appliance industry. Unpublished doctoral
dissertation, Harvard University,
Cambridge, MA.

Kim, W. C., and Mauborgne, R. (2005) *Blue Ocean
Strategy: How to Create Uncontested Market
Space and Make the Competition Irrelevant.*
Boston: Harvard Business School Press.

Mason, K., Oshri, I., and Leek, S. (forthcoming)
Shared learning in supply networks:
evidence from an emerging market
supply network. *European Journal
of Marketing.*

McGee, J., Thomas, H., and Pruett, M. (1995)
Strategic groups and the analysis of market
structure and industry dynamics. *British
Journal of Management,* 6(4): 257–70.

MacIntosh, R., Beech, N., McQueen, J., and
Reid, I. (2007) Overcoming change fatigue.
Journal of Business Strategy, 28(6): 18–24.

Mintzberg, H. (1991) Learning 1, planning 0:
reply to Igor Ansoff. *Strategic Management
Journal,* 12(6): 463–6.

Saren, M. (2006) *Marketing Graffiti: The View
from the Street.* London: Butterworth-
Heinemann.

10 Changing processes

This aims of this chapter are to:

- show how processes relate to other aspects of organizations, such as people and structures;
- locate process-oriented change research within the literature; and
- introduce basic techniques for process mapping and suggest ways in which process changes might draw on such modelling approaches.

As discussed in Chapter 7, it is apparent that as organizations grow they begin to formalize the way in which business is conducted, because all organizations reach a size at which an informal approach is no longer tenable. Everything from recruiting staff and choosing suppliers to designing products and managing quality can be described in terms of the sequence of activities involved. The larger, more established and more complex the organization is, the more formal the documentation of such activities can become, and many large organizations have lengthy documentation setting out the way in which tasks are accomplished. Whilst this is sometimes necessary for accreditation purposes, such as ISO 9001, such descriptions can be cumbersome. Partly because such documentation is long and detailed and has a number of interconnects with other aspects of organizational life, it can be very challenging to introduce change. Change to approved, accredited or simply familiar ways of doing things might need to involve multiple stakeholders (see Chapter 5) and can be time-consuming.

This chapter focuses on how to approach changing the sequence, location and timing of routine tasks. These bundles of tasks are often described as processes, or business processes. This view of processes as the operational mechanics of day-to-day business is an important aspect of managing change and draws on literatures that are rooted in computing science and operations management. This is a quite separate body of work from the process literature in strategic management, which more typically refers to longitudinal studies of strategy-making processes (see Pettigrew, 1992). The 1990s saw a trend whereby large numbers of organizations tried to maximize the efficiency of their business processes (see Hammer, 1990). This chapter reviews the origins of process mapping and introduces two mapping techniques that can be used to capture a description of a process.

To understand the genesis of process mapping, we have to return to the early development of the computing industry. With the benefit of hindsight, the first commercially available computers would now be regarded as rudimentary devices that had limited processor power and limited memory. The result was that they could execute only relatively simple instructions, and most computer programmes were designed and built by individuals. These simple instructions were written in a programming language, but they could also be described pictorially using a flow chart, such as the one shown in Figure 10.1, which sets out the simple steps in dealing with an order. This simple flow chart deals with

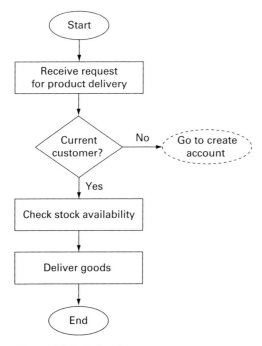

Figure 10.1 A simple process map

key steps in the process and can also reflect key decision points, such as the need to create a customer account when a new enquiry is received. Flow charts of this sort were invaluable in developing early computer programmes, since they could be translated into instructions of the style 'if'/'then'/'go to', which became code in computing languages such as BASIC. These forms have been adapted and used to study far more complex processes in organizational settings (see MacIntosh, 2003).

However, by the early 1970s computing hardware was developing rapidly, as predicted by Moore's law,[1] and more powerful machines were coming onto the market. This meant that more and more complex programmes could be written, and the software industry was born. A new challenge arose when programmes began to involve teams of programmers working together to build relatively complex code. Early pioneers, such as Douglas Ross (1977) and Ed Yourdon and Larry Constantine (1975), tackled this problem by introducing so-called **structured techniques**, which broke complex processes down into a series of simpler ones whilst ensuring that the pieces could be put back together again into an integrated whole. This meant that a team of programmers could divide work up amongst themselves safe in the knowledge that it would all fit together on completion of the work.

The term 'structured techniques' refers to a group of modelling techniques that are used to break complex systems or processes into a series of simpler ones. Although there are now more than 200 variants, most share three common themes. First, they adopt a formal approach to the development of process maps. Second, they focus on breaking processes down into simple steps. Third, they produce hierarchically ordered models.

As the name implies, structured techniques impose more structure than a simple process map. In most structured techniques two key innovations are introduced. First, as a complex process is broken down into sub-processes, it is vital to ensure that the inputs and outputs from the process remain consistent. Second, to manage the complexity, a hierarchy of processes is introduced. The task of checking stock availability in the process map shown in Figure 10.1 may in fact involve several sub-steps, such as assessing the importance of the

---

[1] In 1965 electronics engineer Gordon Moore (co-founder of Intel) predicted that the number of components that could be placed on an integrated circuit would double every year for the next ten years. In fact, this exponential growth in processing power is still happening; just compare your current computer, mobile phone or mp3 player with its predecessor to see Moore's law in effect. Indeed, it has been suggested that a smartphone of today would have been the most powerful computer in the world in the mid-1980s.

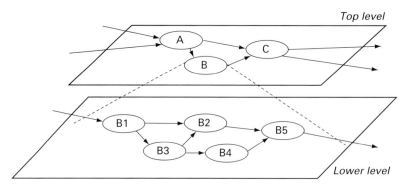

Figure 10.2 Process mapping using structured techniques

customer making the request and checking overall stock levels against other known and predicted demands. Whilst placing a new order is straightforward when there is sufficient capacity to meet demand, it may become a complex issue when some customers are going to have to be disappointed. When Intel announces a new processor or Apple launches the latest iPad or iPhone, demand may outstrip supply. Orders may not be met on a first-come, first-served basis, as strategic alliances, past relationships, profit margins, etc. may weigh heavily in the decisions about which orders to fulfil and which to refuse. Figure 10.2 illustrates the way in which a single process can be broken down into a series of sub-processes to produce a hierarchical model.

The process described in Figure 10.2 involves three steps, A, B and C. These three processes are described at the top level such that process B takes one of the outputs from process A and transforms it into an input for process C. Returning to the earlier example, process B may involve comparing the relative priority of one order over another, and this process is then broken down into a more detailed account of how this is achieved. This produces two levels in the process map (labelled 'Top level' and 'Lower level' in Figure 10.2). Process B is then described as consisting of five separate sub-processes, but note the consistency between levels in that the lower-level description of process B still takes only one input and produces only one output. This nesting of processes within processes is central to the use of structured techniques. In theory, subdividing processes in this way can go on and on. In practice, it is unusual to use more than three or four levels when dealing with organizational processes.

When Yourdon, Ross and others began to use structured techniques to map complex processes, collaboration was facilitated in the design of products and systems. Others soon realized that such approaches could also be used to analyse existing processes and to capture descriptions of how tasks were executed. This eventually led to the use of such techniques in change projects. In the summer of 1990 two papers were published that created widespread interest in the use of process mapping under the guise of business process re-engineering.

Michael Hammer (1990) and Thomas Davenport and James Short (1990) argue that information and communication technology (ICT) has the power to drive a second industrial revolution, in much the same way that automation and steam power drove the original revolution in the eighteenth and nineteenth centuries. Adam Smith (1776) drew attention to the processes involved in manufacturing pins to establish the notion that the division of labour into specialized tasks could dramatically improve productivity. This insight led eventually to the introduction of mass production, and a range of industrial engineering or scientific management techniques were developed by Fred Taylor (1911) and others to break operational processes down into steps so that maximum efficiency could be achieved. By focusing attention on business processes rather than manufacturing processes, the re-engineering movement was reconnecting with a much older heritage of developing and refining work (MacIntosh, 1997).

Hammer argued that computing technology had been used to automate outdated processes, inadvertently locking in inefficiencies. He cited the example of Ford, where 500 people were involved in the accounts payable process. When Ford took a stake in Mazda it became apparent that the Japanese firm used a completely different approach to the process, with only five people. Even accounting for the difference in scale between the two firms, Ford's accounts payable department was estimated at being twenty times larger. Rather than trying to improve the process, Hammer suggested starting with a clean sheet of paper and working out how best to achieve the same outcomes using new technology to enable new ways of working rather than simply automating the old way of working. His call was for a break from 'conventional wisdom and the constraints of organization boundaries' (Hammer, 1990: 108). Davenport and Short offered a similar message but with much greater emphasis on the need to understand the existing process. Their concern was that so-called 'clean sheet' approaches were often unrealistic, as so many legacy systems were in place. This implied that, before rupturing existing processes, it would be important to understand in detail how they operated.

Hammer and Champy and Davenport and Short had a huge impact on organizational life. By the mid-1990s up to 70 per cent of organizations either had or were planning to engage in significant process redesign (Grint and Willcocks, 1995). Consultancy businesses were keen to offer services that would support organizations through re-engineering or redesign projects, and a wealth of books, software and services were developed to support such efforts. However, the term 're-engineering' became stigmatized, for two main reasons. First, re-engineering projects were often used as a blunt device to reduce headcount. Whilst this produced financial gains, the human costs were unpalatable. Not only were large numbers of people made surplus to requirements but they often took valuable tacit knowledge with them. Second, re-engineering projects often struggled to deliver the ambitious targets set for them. Whilst Hammer and Champy could claim 'dramatic improvements in critical contemporary measures of performance such as cost, quality, service and speed' (1993: 32), many found more modest improvements that didn't match the hype. Failure rates for re-engineering projects were reportedly as high as 67 per cent (CSC Index, 1994) and interest in the approach had begun to wane by the late 1990s.

However, the importance of mapping business processes is a residual from this period. Our view is that understanding the mechanics of what happens and in what sequence is an important starting point but not one that should be separated completely from other factors, such as the people involved in executing the process, the supporting infrastructure involved and the performance criteria required of the process. A two-step approach helps ensure that nothing gets overlooked. Figure 10.3 sets out how to approach changing processes.

A major English university, ranked in the top 100 universities in the world, was concerned with the difficulties encountered when trying to keep track of student activities. With more than 30,000 students, this was a major problem. Everything from notification that a library book was overdue to exam results and health issues meant that the university needed to be able to manage contact with its students

Step 1 Mapping the existing process	Step 2 Fundamental questions
Using existing documentation and/or interviews and/or observations, map out the steps involved in the process under consideration.	Use the following questions to challenge the assumptions that underpin the existing process.
If the process is complex, consider using a structured technique to produce a hierarchical process map.	Q1 *What* are we trying to do? Q2 *Why* are we trying to do it? Q3 *Where* must it be done? Q4 *When* and *within what timescales* must it be done ? Q5 *How* will it be done – i.e. using which resources? Q6 *Who executes the process and does it need to be them?* Q7 *If you could start from scratch, how* would you set up a competitor?

Figure 10.3 Changing processes

quickly and effectively. The registry of the university kept a central student record, which was supposed to be the single repository for student information.

A process-mapping exercise was undertaken that drew in staff from every part of the university that had contact with students. This revealed that a number of separate record systems were being maintained within the university. In fact, the process-mapping exercise showed that if students wished to update something as simple as their address for correspondence they would have to request a change in seven separate record systems, including the academic department(s) in which they studied, the faculty office, the library and the accommodation office. On further investigation, each of these record systems was being maintained by different groups of staff within the university, who either felt that the outdated central record system did not meet their specific requirements or did not trust that the central record system was actually kept up to date. The net result was a plethora of independent record systems that often held conflicting information, since students wrongly assumed that if they told one part of the university the others would automatically be updated. Processes were mapped by those involved in keeping the record systems up to date.

In parallel with this process-mapping exercise, the management team at the university began asking the fundamental questions set out in Figure 10.3. The answers to Q1 and Q2 were reasonably obvious: the university was trying to manage student records in the most efficient and accurate way possible to avoid confusion and miscommunication. Q3 and Q6 threw up interesting answers, and the university realized that there was no longer a need for the process to be executed on university premises by university staff. Rather, a record system was constructed into which students input their own data directly, meaning that the process could be executed anywhere that students could access a secure internet connection. This reduced the resources required by the university (Q5) and meant that the process could be executed at any time (Q4), with any changes rolled over into a central record system within twenty-four hours. These changes made the process dramatically more efficient and reduced instances of formal letters being sent to old addresses, etc. Many of the changes that were made were instigated in response to Q7, which asks how you would set up a competitor business from scratch using the best available technology. Despite initial misgivings about data security and academic integrity, staff at the university began to realize that their students were used to dealing with online, instant access, joined-up systems in other aspects of their life (for their bank accounts and other services). Many aspects of the existing process for managing student records had developed as responses to prior mistakes in the organization. For example, the process for managing graduation records involved multiple checks and balances that had been introduced to eliminate embarrassing errors during graduation ceremonies. The tacit knowledge surrounding the process surfaced during the mapping of the process but the basis for a new solution was driven by asking the fundamental questions set out in Figure 10.3. The nature of tacit knowledge and the use of evidence are important issues when changing processes. As there may be cultural predispositions to what counts as evidence for change, there is a need for a rounded understanding of interpretations (Briner, Denyer and Rousseau, 2009), and the enquiry approach outlined above can assist with this.

EXERCISE

Mastering the art of process mapping takes a little practice. Consider two examples.

Example 1   Use a process map to describe a recipe from a cookbook.
Example 2   Use a process map to describe how a firm designs new products or services.

The two examples differ in a number of ways. In the first example, the recipe already exists and the mapping involves translating one explicit form of knowledge into another format. Whilst the process in the second example may well exist, it is likely that there will be differing accounts of what happens, the relative importance of key steps, the sequence, the time taken, etc. In that sense, the recipe may represent a more closed framing than the product/ service development process (see Chapter 3). In developing a process map for the second example you are likely to have to conduct a series of interviews to establish what is involved. It is also important to note that, in both examples, there may be one process for use under normal circumstances and another less formal process that is used when 'normal' circumstances do not allow – e.g. time pressures, a lack of funds, a lack of key resources, etc.

Figure 10.4 lists some useful interview questions. Use these questions to develop a process map of your own. You could choose a process from your own experience (e.g. booking tickets for the cinema) or from an organiza- tional setting (e.g. the process for forming a project team at Oticon; see Extended Case 4).

(Q1)   Starting at the beginning, what are the steps involved in the process?

(Q2)   Link these steps, what are the inputs and outputs at each stage?

(Q3)   Who does each step?

(Q4)   Who oversees the process and who has the power to intervene?

(Q5)   How long does each step take – typically and in an emergency?

(Q6)   Where are the decision points or branches in the process?

(Q7)   What major problems does the current process create?

(Q8)   Are there alternative processes used and in which circumstances – when no-one is looking, when time is short, when an important customer asks, etc.?

Figure 10.4 Interview questions

WHO TO READ

Hammer is credited by some as the person who drew attention back to the central importance of operations and logistics. The language he uses is often colourful and many of the claims he makes were subsequently contested by other academics, but it is easy to see why his work had such a significant following during the 1990s. From his first book (with James Champy: *Re-Engineering the Corporation*, 1993) to his last (with Lisa Hershman: *Faster, Cheaper, Better*, 2010), his focus was always on the ways in which processes could be improved in order to drive efficiency and competitiveness.

USEFUL WEBSITES

- www.hammerandco.com: the consulting organization that Hammer founded to commercialize the process re-engineering approaches discussed in this chapter.

REFERENCES

Briner, R., Denyer, D., and Rousseau, D. (2009) Evidence-based management: concept clean-up time? *Academy of Management Perspectives*, 23(4): 19–32.

CSC Index (1994) *State of Reengineering Report*. Cambridge, MA: CSC Index.

Davenport, T. H., and Short, J. E. (1990) The new industrial engineering: information technology and business process redesign. *Sloan Management Review*, 31(4): 11–27.

Grint, K., and Willcocks, L. (1995) BPR in theory and practice: business paradise regained? *New Technology, Work and Employment*, 10(2): 99–109.

Hammer, M. (1990) Re-engineering work: don't automate, obliterate. *Harvard Business Review*, 68(4): 104–12.

Hammer, M., and Champy, J. (1993) *Re-Engineering the Corporation: A Manifesto for Business Revolution*. London: Nicholas Brealey Publishing.

Hammer, M., and Hershman, L. W. (2010) *Faster, Cheaper, Better: The 9 Levers for Transforming how Work Gets Done*. New York: Crown Business.

MacIntosh, R. (1997) Business process re-engineering: new applications for the techniques of production engineering. *International Journal of Production Economics*, 50(1): 43–9.

MacIntosh, R. (2003) BPR: alive and well in the public sector. *International Journal of Operations and Production Management*, 23(3): 327–44.

Pettigrew, A. M. (1992) The character and significance of strategy process research. *Strategic Management Journal*, 3(1): 5–16.

Ross, D. T. (1977) Structured Analysis (SA): a language for communicating ideas. *IEEE Transactions on Software Engineering*, 3(1): 16–34.

Smith, A. (1776) *An Inquiry into the Nature and Causes of the Wealth of Nations*. London: W. Strahan & T. Cadell.

Taylor, F. W. (1911) *Principles of Scientific Management*. New York: Harper & Brothers.

Yourdon, E., and Constantine, L. (1975) *Structured Design: Fundamentals of a Discipline of Computer Program and Systems Design*. New York: Yourdon Press.

11 Aligning people and activities

The aims of this chapter are to:

- explore the nature and practices of selection decision making;
- introduce the psychological contract and discuss its importance for managing change;
- discuss approaches to selecting people to join change teams and organizations; and
- consider the application of practices contrasting environments.

Having the right people in the right place at the right time is important for the effective enactment of change. Whilst this might sound simple, in practice there are several potential pitfalls, and the process of effective selection decision making is a core skill of the change manager. For Kotter (1996), the ability to secure the right people for the coalition that will drive change is a foundational step in deciding the limits to the way the change will go. Marshak's (2009) metaphors of 'move and relocate' and 'liberate and recreate' (see Chapter 2) are pertinent here, as stopping doing things one way and moving to another can entail a change in the people; equally, the idea of liberation is that the people who are liberated will be able to move the company in a new and interesting direction. Accordingly, it is important for the people who are chosen to have both the right capabilities and the motivation for working towards the agreed goals. This can involve establishing a 'psychological contract' (Conway and Briner, 2005), or informal and unwritten agreement, over the direction of change and the willingness to exert effort towards the goals.

The processes of selection can be a one-way street, in which the manager decides about team or organization membership without consultation; or, in other circumstances, it can be a two-way process, in which the manager and the potential member are both involved in information exchange and decision making (McKenna and Beech, 2008). This depends to some extent on the nature of the role and the organizational circumstances. Open, two-way processes are more common when roles are flexible and can be developed in line with the attributes and aspirations of individuals (Taylor, 2010). On other occasions, particularly when there are very specific demands in a role or when the selection decision is about downsizing and possible redundancy, the process can be more managerially led. Either way, there is a need to make the best decisions possible, and in the second part of this chapter we explore some of the approaches to achieving this. Before that we discuss the nature and establishment of the psychological contract.

Establishing a psychological contract

The **psychological contract** is a tacit understanding between the employer and employee or between the manager and members of a project. It refers to what each party expects of the other and goes beyond the formal employment contract, which states the level of reward that will be received by the employee in return for fulfilling a specified job. The psychological contract relates to the relationship and degree of trust between manager and employee and is part of their mutual understanding. In short, it represents the extent to which there is mutual 'buy-in' between the organization and the individual.

The psychological contract is an unwritten agreement of what the employer and employee can expect of each other.

The psychological contract is fundamentally about perceptions, and so each side can have different understandings of what is reasonable (Rousseau, 1996), but when it is working well it is the source of mutual understanding about the purpose of the activities and the nature of the commitment flowing in each direction between the employee and manager. The state of the psychological contract is changeable and the degree of mutual trust and commitment can rise and fall depending on experience. When it is working well a virtuous cycle can operate, in which the employee's committed performance is recognized and rewarded, and this stimulates recognition on the part of the employee that he or she is valued. Conversely, if the employee feels undervalued, his or her motivation can drop, and this can lead to less positive feedback from the employer and the relationship suffers as a result. Employees' feelings and attitudes to work are influenced by how they perceive themselves to be treated. However, these feelings and attitudes are also related to how employees see themselves and the relationship (Conway and Briner, 2005). Hence, it is not a simple exchange process of employees' effort in return for reward from the employer. Rather, it is a complex and continuous managerial task to judge how far people are feeling connected to a change project and whether the level of goodwill is rising or falling.

Eugene McKenna and Nic Beech (2008) argue that one potentially useful way of thinking of the psychological contract is as a series of questions that employees could answer on the basis of their experience of the employment relationship. The questions are as follows.

(1) Where are we going (as an organization or on a particular change project)?
(2) Do I fit in?
(3) Can I contribute?
(4) How should I spend my time?
(5) Do I agree with (or am I committed to) what is expected?
(6) What can I do about it (to change or reinforce)?
(7) What will be the outcomes for people or objects that I care about (the quality of the product/service, clients, my colleagues and friends, the direction of the company, my current and future role in the company)?

At different stages of life and career, people might seek rather different answers to these questions, and the importance of different questions can rise and fall over time. Where the organization is going and how one fits in are significant questions in order to move beyond a merely instrumental attachment between the employee and the organization/project. People who feel that they are part of something worthwhile and that they are an integral part of the group may consequently feel committed to its aims. One way of enhancing this is to involve people in the setting of objectives, and in the context of change this distinguishes engaged approaches from top-down ones. The third question is the extent to which the person believes that he or she can contribute. In instrumental theories of motivation it is assumed that people are mainly concerned with what they can extract from the arrangement. Whilst people are concerned with what they get, and receiving a fair reward is an important part of a contract, people also want to feel that they are part of the group and that they can make a meaningful contribution. When people feel their skills have become obsolete they can become defensive or detached, and the intention of a positive psychological contract is the reverse of this: to ensure that people have goals that are meaningful to them and that they have the ability to make a genuine contribution to success. From the managerial perspective, this means that there is a need to 'negotiate' between the skills and knowledge of people, the tasks they are asked to do and the training they are given. Change projects sometimes entail people doing the same thing in a new context (for example, taking an existing service to a new market) but more often they entail people doing new things, which means developing their competences. This can threaten people's feeling that they are able to contribute effectively, and hence there is a need for managers to balance new requirements and training (this topic is covered in more depth in Chapter 12).

The question 'How should I spend my time?' is answerable in many ways. The expectation might be that work activities would be top of the list, but how work is done and what priorities are chosen can have an impact on performance, and, in addition, in times of change people can spend increased amounts of time on back-stage politics and defence mechanisms. If people feel threatened by the change they can spend their time trying to shore up the opposition to the change, which, in effect, can be a counter-change project in which coalitions are formed and there is an emotional investment in a vision of the future (typically, the same as the past). Even when people are positive about the change they might be idiosyncratic in what they prioritize, such as selecting the sections of the task that they like best or that they feel most competent in. Thus, this area is another management 'juggling act' in which careful attention needs to be paid not only to what people are doing, including the informal aspects of work, but also to why they are doing what they are doing.

The next two questions are about how far people are committed to the change objectives and what they can do to change or reinforce the objectives. If people feel that they cannot influence the objectives it may be more difficult for them to be committed to them, and hence they may seek to give the illusion of working hard rather than being genuinely engaged. However, there is a tension between allowing too much variation in expectations and too much top-down setting of expectations. The balance can be struck by having consistent top-level expectations but some local variation in how these objectives are met. The last question concerns outcomes. In change projects the outcomes can be very negative for people, including, for example, redundancy. Conversely, change can lead to promotion and more fulfilling roles. Similarly, others are likely to be affected by changes, and so people question what will happen to their friends, products or services that they may hold dear and have spent years working on. Hence, the manager needs to be aware of how outcomes are viewed and valued by people. When there are negative outcomes it is often best to be clear and deal with these first and with reasonable speed. Then it is possible to work on the good and the mixed outcomes. However, as Conway and Briner (2005) point out, it should be expected that people will differ as to what they value.

The psychological contract has sometimes been thought of as a calculative form of attachment between the individual and the organization, but in reality it entails emotion and multiple perceptions (McDonald and Makin, 2000). The aim of the change manager is to maximize the mutuality expressed in the psychological contract – that is, the connection and agreement between the individual and the project/organization. Once the person is in his or her post it is a tricky balancing act of perception, feedback and adjustment to influence the state of the contract for each individual. The point of selection into an organization or team is foundational for the psychological contract. When companies experience a high rate of staff turnover soon after recruitment (sometimes referred to as an **induction crisis**), this can indicate that expectations set at the point of selection have been at odds with the real experience of working for the company. Selection is the point at which it is easier to make the nature of the psychological contract explicit, and the forms of communication chosen can have a significant impact – for example, whether there is openness about the challenges and negatives as well as the positives and opportunities. Who does the communication is also important, and in some processes other team members are involved as well as managers. We explore selection processes that can contribute to the psychological contract in the next section.

An induction crisis is when a person leaves a job shortly after being recruited.

Selection decision-making processes

In broad terms, selection decision making is about answering three questions.

(1) Do the people have the **capability** to perform the role? (Can they do it?)
(2) Are they **motivated** to perform the role? (Will they do it?)
(3) Are they the best people available to do the role? (Should it be them?)

Capability includes the skills, knowledge and experience that a person brings to the job.

Motivation in this area relates to orientation towards the task – an attitude of willingness and a desire to perform in the job.

Assessing capability

The highest-quality answers to the first question tend to be based on the evidence of experience. Judgements about whether or not someone can perform in a role are most reliable when based on evidence of him or her having performed a similar role beforehand (Wood and Payne, 1998). However, in change programmes the aim is typically for people to do something different, and so there is a process of extrapolation from the past to the future, and the question may be one of seeking evidence of transferrable skills. In some cases there is a clear definition of what the role requires, but in others a degree of flexibility can be required, which means that the person and the role may have to coevolve. When this is the case, key attributes will include the ability to learn and adapt to new situations.

When the appointment is to a change project, there can be the possibility of making secondments or temporary transfers so that no permanent decision has to be made at the outset. The advantage of this is that it gives the managers the chance to see how performance develops and the employee the chance to see what the role is really like. On this basis, permanent moves can be agreed subsequently. If this 'testing out' approach is not possible an alternative is to use **work-based tests** to assess ability. These can be simulations of aspects of the role to be undertaken, such as working on an example of the sort of problem that is likely to be encountered in the role, to see what ideas and proposed actions the employee generates. Although such simulations provide less reliable information than observing someone doing the job, they do at least provide an insight into how the person thinks and acts.

Work-based tests are simulations of the activities performed in the role that are undertaken by candidates as part of the selection process.

When appointments are being made internally it is possible to use performance records and reviews to assess a person's ability. Such information can be very helpful but it should be remembered that performance is rarely an entirely individual matter. Achieving productivity, efficiency or a high-quality service normally involves several people playing integrating roles, and the intrinsic qualities of the product or service also make a difference. Hence, there is a danger of over-attribution of success to any one individual. When making internal appointments it is not uncommon to have several candidates all claiming to have played the central role in recent successes that are well known in the company. The selection process needs to 'get behind the headlines' and enquire as to the role they actually played and what others have contributed.

The traditional approach of interviewing candidates for a position is less good at accessing information on how people act. Interviews can be good at understanding people's thought processes, how they make sense of performance and what they have learned from experience. The crucial thing is for questioning to probe beyond the aspirational answer into the 'How?' and 'Why?' questions. For example, when asking about how people would lead a team it is appropriate to ask what changes they have previously led in a team, what they did, how it worked, why they did what they did, how others responded and what they did. By following such a trail of questions it is often possible to tell the difference in the quality of the experience that people have. Someone who gives the 'expected' answers, such as that everything worked out, may have less useful experience than those who can talk through the trials and tribulations of tasks and who can display that they have picked up problem-solving skills.

Assessing willingness

Interviews can be used as ways of assessing people's attitudes to a new role. The extent to which people have thought through what could be involved in the role, their ability to apply previous experience to new circumstances and their attitude towards flexibility can all be revealed at interview. It is useful to go beyond merely asking people if they are interested to ask how they feel the role would fit into their career aspirations and what it is about the content of the role that attracts them.

Given that people might pretend to be willing to do the job, one way of improving the decision making is to maximize the amount of information that the candidates have, as they are also in a process of selecting whether or not to take the role (if it is offered). This can be done by using the interview as an opportunity for two-way communication and to be open about the likely realities of the role (Newell, 2005). In some companies this is enhanced by the information being supplied before the interview by other employees. For example, candidates can spend time with people who currently perform the role, or who have performed it in the past, in order to get an insight into what it is like. In some cases employees can produce short case studies or video diaries to explain to others what their experience has been like. Although such information may be less than perfect, it can still be useful when others are trying to form an opinion of whether the role would be good for them or not.

Some organizations use **psychometric tests** to assess attitude and orientation towards the role. These can be helpful, particularly if it is administered professionally and followed up with proper feedback to the individual (Roberts, 2005). In this way they can be developmental for the candidates. However, there is a danger in assuming that even the best psychometric tests are measuring exactly what the organization needs to know. The more reliable tests have been used on a great number of subjects and hence their content tends to be fairly general, such as indicating levels of extroversion, agreeableness, conscientiousness, emotional stability, intellect and openness (McKenna, 2006). These might be useful indicators, but they should be used only as part of a managerial judgement that incorporates other information.

Psychometric tests are psychological assessments that give feedback on people's characteristics. This can be useful if the characteristics can clearly be linked to performance on the job.

Making a judgement: deciding on the best candidate

Selection decision making is generally uncertain. Even the best evidence of how someone has behaved previously is not a guarantee of what he or she will do in the future. Therefore, it is normally worth ensuring that there are several sources of information and that there is a genuine two-way process of information gathering and decision making. **Assessment centres** offer an appropriate process for two-way decision making. These are collections of activities, such as work-based tests, interviews and group activities, that can be used to build up a composite picture of the candidates.

Assessment centres are events that combine several selection techniques. They can take place over one day or more.

When selecting the people to join the team or organization it is important that the justice of the decision is transparent. This means enabling both the successful and the unsuccessful candidates to see the rationality of the decision and to know that they have had a fair chance. Therefore, it is important that all candidates go through the same process, and that they know who is making the decisions and on what basis.

One point of selection is to signal the nature of the change through the people who are appointed and those who are not. It is also an opportunity to establish the psychological contract. In essence, it is a form of dialogue via which both parties will make a decision, and it works best when each side is able to form an informed view of the other. Hence, it is important not to 'oversell' the role or the nature of the change but to try to establish realistic expectations.

We now look at two mini-cases. In the first, the Eden Project, an open and bottom-up approach is taken to selection decision making. There is minimal structure and a focus on experience. In the second, an NHS example, the situation is highly structured, with clear and extensive job descriptions and organizational structure. A different approach is adopted, using an assessment centre to enable extensive information gathering by candidates and the organization alike.

Mini-Case 11.1: the Eden Project

The Eden Project, based in the south-west of England, was started in 1999 by Tim Smit, who had previously worked in the music industry and horticulture. The project took over an old clay mine and derelict area and commenced with start-up funding from various agencies, including the European Union and the UK Regional Development Agency. It has transformed the area, constructing a venue that is an ecological leader and a commercial success. The Eden Project built a series of giant glasshouses that provide humid, tropical and temperate zones for the cultivation of rare and interesting plants: what they refer to as the 'global garden'. The Eden Project has become a major tourist attraction, and it also provides educational services for children; in addition, it has expanded to being a live music and performance venue, with a large outdoor stage, and it has run major festivals and the 'Eden Sessions', featuring headline artists. There is a strong environmental element to the project, and as well as the conservation of rare plants other schemes have included large-scale soil production. The Eden Project has been a considerable economic success. When it opened in 2001 the cost was put at £121 million for construction and operational set-up. By the end of 2010 (according to Southwestbusiness.co.uk, 10 March 2011) there had been 12.8 million visitors and the total economic contribution, including revenues accruing not just to the project but to local hotels and restaurants as well, stood at £1.1 billion.

This success relies on having staff who are committed and who have developed high-quality services and a series of innovations over the last ten years. The staff bring a range of disciplines to bear, including botany, archaeology, horticulture, engineering, arts and events management. The approach is to minimize bureaucracy, and job descriptions are kept to a minimum, with people being encouraged to take on leadership for ideas they develop and to challenge themselves to work in areas they are not yet experienced in. When making an acceptance speech for an award for quality in construction in 2006, Smit said (quoted by McKenna and Beech, 2008: 377):

I wish everybody could have the opportunity just once in their lives of working with a large team, all of whom enjoy each other's company and admire each other's talent, and from this they build something that surpasses even their own imaginings.

The aim is to foster a team-oriented approach to innovative projects that expand environmentalism, education and entertainment. Smit sees trust as the foundational organizing principle – 'to dare to treat people as you would yourself like to be treated' (quoted by Edwards, 2005: 31). His view is that what is needed is a shared attitude, not adherence to a set of regulations that would limit creativity.

Selection decision making in the Eden Project takes a radical but effective approach. The process has a minimum of paperwork, and potential employees are invited to join a team for between one and three days. The team gets to know the people and see how they work. Importantly, they also get to understand the people's attitudes and orientation to the values and ways of working at the Eden Project. The team then discusses the potential employees and makes a recommendation to management. In almost all cases the management then ratifies the decision. Because the potential employees have gained some working experience in the project they are also in a position to decide whether it is the right job and company for them or not. Hence, there is two-way selection decision making, based on experience, and there is a dynamic perspective. The view is that, if the candidates have the right attitude and appropriate foundational skills, they can be trained in the future capabilities that they need.

Mini-Case 11.2: reselecting the management population on NHS Greater Glasgow and Clyde

NHS Greater Glasgow and Clyde (NHSGGC) is responsible for the health provision for 1.2 million people and has a staff of over 44,000. Services provided include thirty-five hospitals, over 300 GP surgeries and more than fifty health centres and clinics. In addition, it has major operations in public health. The board was developed following a series of structural changes at the national level through which a number of smaller divisions that had previously been independent were merged. At the same time a new focus on partnership work-ing was emerging, both as the most promising form of practice in the field and as a requirement of policy and funding bodies. This meant working in a new way with local authorities, and charitable and voluntary agencies that provided services such as housing and welfare, which needed to integrate more effec-tively with healthcare. The aim was that service users, who typically drew upon a range of services, would have a less disjointed experience of care and support and that decisions made in one part of the system would work effectively with decisions made in another part.

These changes meant that there were considerable challenges for managers. They had to move into a new structure, there were dual expectations of efficiency gains and quality enhancement and there was a requirement to manage in a new way that entailed collaboration and facilitative leadership. This meant a significant change in management roles, with different skills and approaches being needed. In a commercial setting it would not be uncommon to deselect people who could not adapt to the new situation, and make redun-dancies when duplication was identified after the merger. However, in this setting there was a prior agreement that no involuntary redundancies would be made.

It was decided to run an assessment centre to allocate the top 400 managers to new roles in the merged organization. As these managers already worked for a constituent part of NHSGGC, information was available on their qualifications, the jobs they had done and performance information. However, this type of retrospective information did not fully capture the knowledge that was needed to make decisions about how they would perform in the new roles. The assess-ment centre sought to provide this information. It consisted of several activities. People filled in forms and expressed preferences for particular jobs in the new structure. Psychometric tests were used to assess the managers' fit with the new style of facilitative leadership that was expected. Having completed the test, each manager had a feedback session with consultants to discuss the results, and reports were submitted to the top management. Individual interviews were held and a group case study activity was conducted. The case study was written on the basis of observations of an area of activity that most resembled some of the challenges of the new way of working. People were asked to respond to the situation in the case study in small groups, and also to the actions they proposed, and their activities in the team were observed and fed back to them. As a result, there were multiple ways of accessing information about how the managers behaved and performed in the past and in situations designed to simulate the future. Interviews and psychometrics were used to gather information on their aspirations and their understanding of the new approach, and there were opportunities for feedback discussions, which influenced the reports submitted by the consultants.

Following the collation of this information from multiple sources, there was an exercise to fit people into the most appropriate roles. This meant a matching between individual aspirations and performance and the available jobs. Such a process is never likely to occur without some disappointment and disagreement. However, there were relatively few appeals, and the process could be seen as broadly transparent and thorough. In addition, those who had been through the process were quite clear on the new approach that was to be taken in the organization. Moreover, they received a considerable amount of feedback, which was subsequently fed into their management development activities, such as honing leadership and collaborative management skills.

Enacting change

These two mini-cases are set in quite different circumstances. The Eden Project is able to operate free of many rules and formal procedures. The project's managers are mainly concerned to recruit people with creative and environmentally oriented attitudes. Once people are in the role, both the person and the role are expected to develop and change, and so to be excessively formal or to assume a fixed job description at the outset would be counterproductive. The process is likely to be effective in establishing the psychological contract. A great deal of information about the Eden Project is available to candidates, and because they come and get direct experience they are able to assess how well they would fit in. The process is unusual, in the emphasis that is placed on bottom-up decision making, but this is an important symbol of the culture.

In the NHSGGC example, there is far more structure and a set of policy and legal constraints on how the organization can act. Therefore, the process needs to be more structured. However, the process still involved two-way information exchange, and the assessment centre sought to provide multiple sources of information for decision making. In addition, the process sought to exemplify the new forms of behaviour that would be expected. Thus, considerable effort was put into development (for example, using the psychometric tests as the basis for developmental feedback and subsequent training), and the case study deliberately modelled the sorts of situation that the managers could expect to find themselves in in the future. The process was also transparent, and there was an appeal process. The aim was to establish the right sort of psychological contracts and to make sure that people understood the nature of the changes.

Therefore, when making selection decisions to align people and activities, some action options to consider are:

- treat the selection process as a strategic decision for getting the right people in to build a coalition for change;
- see the process as a two-way dialogue that should lead to a positive psychological contract;
- when possible, build some work-based or experiential evidence into the process;
- use multiple sources of information;
- be aware of the message that is being sent out about the culture of the organization from the decisions that are made; and
- seek to maximize transparency and fairness.

EXERCISE

Read Case 6, Power Provision plc.

(1) How would you assess the state of the psychological contract as the case progresses?

(2) Do you think that the selection decisions to make redundancies were rational and fair? Could they be improved? If so, how?

(3) What do you think the processes adopted say about the culture at Power Provision plc?

WHO TO READ

The psychological contract is an important concept in management generally, and it can be applied to the management of change to understand motivation, engagement and the reaction of people to changes in the way that they work. Neil Conway and Rob Briner (2005) provide an insightful perspective on this.

USEFUL WEBSITES

- www.cipd.co.uk is the website of the Chartered Institute of Personnel and Development. It has many useful resources, and these include fact sheets and articles on selection decision making.
- www.peoplemanagement.co.uk: this is a journal dedicated to managing people. There are articles and interactive blogs and comment boards on this and related topics.
- www.businesslink.gov.uk is a governmental website that helps with legal issues when downsizing and making people redundant. It also provides helpful insights about avoiding redundancies, rights and obligations and how to plan effectively for redundancies, which are an important example of selection decision making.

REFERENCES

Conway, N., and Briner, R. B. (2005) *Understanding Psychological Contracts at Work: A Critical Evaluation of Theory and Research*. Oxford University Press.

Edwards, C. (2005) Paradise found. *People Management*, 11(19): 31–2.

Kotter, J. P. (1996) *Leading Change*. Boston: Harvard Business School Press.

Marshak, R. (2009) *Organizational Change: Views from the Edge*. Bethel, ME: Lewin Center.

McDonald, D. J., and Makin, P. J. (2000) The psychological contract, organizational commitment and job satisfaction in temporary staff. *Leadership and Development Journal*, 21(2): 84–91.

McKenna, E. (2006) *Business Psychology and Organisational Behaviour*. Hove: Psychology Press.

McKenna, E., and Beech, N. (2008) *Human Resource Management: A Concise Analysis*. Harlow: Pearson.

Newell, S. (2005) Recruitment and selection, in Bach, S. (ed.) *Managing Human Resources*, 4th edn.: 115–46. Oxford: Blackwell.

Roberts, G. (2005) *Recruitment and Selection*. London: Chartered Institute of Personnel and Development.

Rousseau, D. M. (1996) *Psychological Contracts in Organizations: Understanding Written and Unwritten Agreements*. Newbury Park, CA: Sage.

Taylor, S. (2010) *Resourcing and Talent Management*, 5th edn. London: Chartered Institute of Personnel and Development.

Wood, R., and Payne, T. (1998) *Competency-Based Recruitment and Selection*. London: Wiley.

12 Learning and developing

The aims of this chapter are to:

- show how the nature of learning includes different preferred styles;
- develop a model of learning for technique and insight;
- explain alternative methods of learning and development;
- illustrate the application of these methods in a mini-case study of the Boston Consulting Group; and
- establish the application of learning and development practices as part of change management.

Learning and development are central to change management. Most change projects entail people doing things differently, and major changes often mean that people need to understand the nature of the organization's processes, relationships with customers and clients and practices of delivery differently. Such changes mean that the change manager has to understand how people develop and what can be done to enable people to enact and understand the innovations that are aspired to (Antonacopoulou, 2006).

This chapter sits between the macro issues for learning that were raised in Chapter 6 and the more person-centred issues that are discussed in Chapter 14. In Chapter 6 the distinction was made between single-loop learning (incremental improvement) and double-loop learning (radical change). In Chapter 14 we explore the nature of reflection and reflexivity and the ways that learners can challenge themselves and come to a new understanding of who they are and what they do. In this chapter we focus on the distinction between technique learning – the focus on specific, defined skills outcomes – and insight learning – the focus on developing new ways of conceiving reformatory personal change. We discuss how the alternative methods of learning and development can be integrated and the change manager's role in selecting which methods to use to meet the demands of their situation (Easterby-Smith and Lyles, 2003).

The Chartered Institute of Personnel and Development conducts regular surveys of learning and development methods. The institute's 2010 survey found that there was an increasing integration of coaching, organizational development and performance management in which the aim was to increase innovation and effectiveness. Talent management was seen as a key driver of business, and 60 per cent of businesses in the survey were investing in talent management. This included in-house courses and coaching. In addition, mentoring schemes were on the increase, along with learning on the job. In this chapter we compare and contrast some of these approaches and offer advice on how they might be combined fruitfully. We start by discussing approaches to learning and explain the model of learning for technique and insight.

Approaches to learning

Audrey Collin (2007) builds on Don Binsted's (1980) earlier model of a **learning cycle**. For Binsted and Collin, there is not one cycle but a set of three interconnected cycles. One cycle is concerned with the reception of input. In this cycle the learner absorbs information, ideas and techniques from an external source. The source can be, for example, a demonstration of a new skill, reading a set of instructions or being told how to do something. Although the source of information is external there is an internalizing process, in which the learner fits the information or idea into his or her existing set of skills and schema of meaning. This internalization process can be one of extension, confirming and developing the way the learner currently understands a particular task, or can be a process of displacing and replacing the previous understanding. A second cycle is referred to as the 'discovery loop'. This is concerned with action and feedback. In this cycle the learner experiments with new ways of doing something, makes some self-discoveries about how well the new ways work and receives feedback from others about the success or otherwise of the new approach. This cycle also has an internalizing aspect similar to that of the reception of input cycle. A third cycle takes place purely internally. This is the reflection cycle. In this cycle the learner hypothesizes and conceptualizes his or her received input and experiences.

During this process the learner becomes more aware of the consequences of actions and approaches and considers how to approach the future.

Several theories are based on the idea of a learning cycle. These typically incorporate phases of action, feedback and reflection.

Collin's approach has some resonances with that of David Kolb, Irwin Rubin and James McIntyre (1984). For them, there are two main dimensions of learning: the degree of involvement–detachment and the degree of action–observation. In the cycle, it is envisaged that learning occurs as the learner becomes involved in concrete new experience (CE), then enters a phase of detachment through reflective observation (RO) in which he or she can reflect on his or her experience from different perspectives. This can lead to a further phase of detached activity in abstract conceptualization (AC), in which specific observations are linked to previous learning and formal or informal models of thought that could apply to the object of learning. Lastly, there is active experimentation (AE), in which the composite ideas that emerge from AC are applied to decision making and problem solving for future action. Subsequently, as the learner engages in new concrete experiences, that cycle can be repeated in such a way that the models and concepts he or she holds can be reinforced, refined or replaced.

Although this is envisaged as a cycle, Kolb, Rubin and McIntyre argue that many learners have a preferred phase and hence will learn better in particular ways, and this conceptualization was developed by Peter Honey and Alan Mumford (1992). 'Activists' are said to learn best when they are involved in concrete tasks. 'Reflectors' do not learn so well directly at that moment, but get much more from reviewing afterwards and understanding what has happened. 'Theorists' need to relate new ideas and practices to each other or to existing schema. Whereas activists learn the specific skill or aspect of knowledge, theorists need to understand the big picture in order to see how the specific new knowledge fits in. 'Pragmatists' learn best when what they are learning has relevance to them. They are less likely to be interested in the general 'big picture', or even one-off specific events. They are more interested in knowing how the learning they are doing will impact in the future; in other words, they are concerned with relevance.

These cyclical approaches to learning are useful in that they highlight the continuous, processual nature of learning. Sometimes one can experience learning as an immediate 'light going on' moment, but for much learning in organizations there is a set of activities that needs to happen. Some of the activities are social and others are more individual. Most entail thought and action, and often some degree of emotion, which can help or hinder the learning process. For example, the fear of looking stupid can lead to a defensive approach and difficulty in being open to new ideas. Conversely, excitement at encountering the new can be a good motivator for learning.

Given these complexities, the change manager needs to consider the nature of the learning that is required, how this might be enabled socially and individually and what methods of learning and development should be chosen. In Figure 12.1 we represent a processual approach that can be used by change managers when developing people. In the centre of the figure the oval represents the type of learning occurring. We draw a distinction between learning aimed at increasing the skill or knowledge in applying a **technique** and learning aimed at expanding **insight**. Learning a technique could be how to do a distinct physical or cognitive/ interactive task, such as producing a report from a database or carrying out a negotiation. These tasks have specific skills associated with them, and these skills can be learned through training. Learning/developing insight is more concerned with how techniques fit into the bigger picture, how current ways of under-standing what we do could be refined or reformed and the development of models that could result in double-loop learning (see Chapter 6). For example, developing as a leader entails technical learning such as techniques of communication, decision making and perceiving others, but beyond this it also requires a degree of self-understanding, recognizing how others see you and being able to juggle

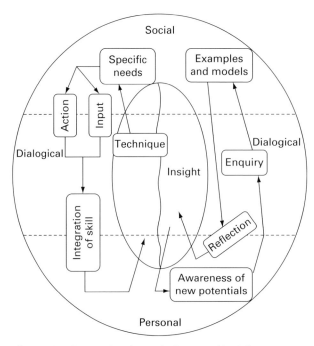

Figure 12.1 Learning for technique and insight

multiple social inputs at the same time as communicating to an audience composed of multiple sections. The latter requires insight into the self and the complexity of the social processes within which leadership takes place (Antonacopoulou *et al.*, 2006). The distinction between technical and insight learning is presented as a wavy line in the diagram as the boundary is blurred, with some new insights relating directly to techniques and some innovations in technique impacting directly on how the learner sees the world.

Learning a technique is concerned with discrete task learning.

Learning for insight is concerned with broadening ideas and enabling the learner to innovate.

The outer circle of the figure represents the context within which learning takes place. At the top of the circle is the social zone, where a learner can encounter examples, such as other leaders, models and theories of how a practice should be conducted, and can experiment with enacting a new skill or approach. The bottom of the circle is the personal zone, where there is inward reflection and analysis. Learning activities in this zone are about evaluating and internalizing learning. The middle section is the zone of dialogue, where the personal and the social, the inside and the outside, meet. In this zone, learning activities include questioning to understand how others conceive and practise the skill that is being learned. In addition, activities include enquiring and analysing, so as to develop a view of how a technique fits with others, or the nature of the meaning of an approach to a complex task such as leadership.

When a person is learning a technique, the need for the learning and specifying what needs to be learned is in the social zone, as the technique is already in existence and is defined. The initial learning can be through input or action/experimentation, both of which occur in the social zone and both of which cross into the dialogue zone as the learner questions and then starts to internalize the technique. Following this, there is a need to integrate the new technique with existing skills and parts of the task. Sometimes this is a straightforward integration but on other occasions it can demand some readjustment of other activities. For example, learning a new technique for closing down a negotiation is likely to have implications for how negotiations are initiated. The integration moves into the personal zone, as the learner absorbs the new technique into his or her style of performing the tasks – in this case, negotiating.

When a person is developing a new insight or way of seeing things, as well as social motivations (Antonacopoulou and Chiva, 2007), there is a need for the learner him- or herself to acknowledge that there could be value in exploring new potentials or challenging his or her current way of understanding. Having established a willingness to open up to new possibilities, the learner enters a dialogic phase of enquiring and questioning – exploring both his or her own way of understanding things and the potential of alternatives. The social zone can be drawn upon for examples of how others see the world and alternative models and theories that underpin the way that other people or organizations operate. For example, some forms of benchmarking, especially when they come from different markets, operate to shift people's thinking. It is unlikely that such comparators can be copied; rather, there is active learning to do to draw inspiration from the example provided by the other in developing one's own way of seeing. Hence, there is a process of reflection that includes dialogue with others and personal reflection, which then impact on insight.

This model comes with the 'health warning' that it is not intended to capture all types of learning and it is a considerable simplification of what can happen in reality. For instance, the spaces of learning can impact on both the content and the process of development (Macpherson *et al.*, 2003). However, its purpose is to help change managers to incorporate learning and development as part of the enactment of change. First, it is worth considering whether the learning is relatively closed and specific (technique) or more open-ended and potentially transformative (insight). Second, the question is about how the learning should be motivated or stimulated. For technical learning, establishing the need to learn is a social matter, for which examples of good practice or technical specifications can be used. For insight learning, there is a need to assist the learner to become aware personally that he or she might see things differently. There is a social role in both approaches, but the role is different. Technical learning tends to focus more on input and experimentation whereas insight learning tends to focus more on discovery and enquiry. Lastly, there is a need to move through dialogue into the personal zone for the learner to internalize the learning. This can entail feedback from the change manager and processes that allow for reflection. In the next section we discuss some of the methods that the change manager can use to stimulate these learning processes.

Methods of learning and development

There are many methods of learning and development available to the change manager and they have different strengths, weaknesses and applications. Therefore, the important thing is to be aware of the choices and when to deploy specific methods.

A popular method is **on-the-job learning**. This entails learning by doing, which fits with Kolb, Rubin and McIntyre's concrete experience and Honey and Mumford's activist style. People who benefit from this method are those who like to work a task out as they do it. They may have a low tolerance for learning the theory before entering the field of practice and have a preference for an experimental, trial-and-error approach. This method works well for technique learning, as it is normally focused on the skill needs of a particular task, and these can be defined and often codified. The advantage for the organization is that it is relatively low-cost, as it does not involve paying for courses or trainers, but there are potential disadvantages. As the approach entails trial and error it can be conducted only when the cost of error is tolerable for the organization. If the cost of something going wrong would be too great it is better for the learner to practise in the safe environment of the classroom or training course. On-the-job learning normally involves some instruction and demonstration by skilled practitioners. The skilled practitioner can also act as a coach for the learner. This can work well when skilled practitioners are also skilled in facilitating learning, but, when they are not, no matter how skilled they are themselves they may not be able to pass on the learning.

On-the-job learning is a practical approach in which people learn by doing.

A related method is job rotation or allocation to fixed-term projects. The purpose of this method is to expose learners to different task and skill arenas (Sims *et al.*, 2006), so that they can broaden their ability and understand how the different parts of the business fit together. In many companies, management trainees follow a plan of spending a certain amount of time in a series of departments so that they see and, hopefully, understand what is done in each area. The advantage is that this can provide the learner with a holistic understanding that is difficult to achieve when concentrating on one function. It is low-cost and can be an active style of concrete experience learning if the learner is doing some on-the-job learning in each placement. The potential disadvantage is that learning can be relatively superficial if the learner ends up just observing or undertaking menial tasks in the placements because of his or her lack of skill. When it works well this method can support insight learning, because the learner is being exposed to a variety of functions and is asked to reflect on how they integrate and how the system as a whole works. A practice that is increasingly common is the use of secondments. These may be part of companies' social responsibility programmes, and they entail an employee working for another organization, which might be a charity or voluntary sector organization, for a fixed period of time. Through doing this employees can broaden their horizons and learn from a quite different environment at the same time as contributing to their host organization. The learning intention of such secondments is to generate insight learning and challenge the taken-for-granted assumptions about how things should be done. In the mini-case below of Boston Consulting Group, learning of this style is facilitated by consultants moving through a series of projects. In some cases the learners develop an increasing depth of knowledge by focusing on a particular industry. In other cases learners develop cross-fertilizing insight by working across a range of business environments.

Many change programmes are associated with training courses. These can be either internally provided or external to the company. In many cases in-house courses are designed for technique learning. Particular skill gaps can be identified as part of a change process. For example, there might be a requirement for supervisors to become team leaders. This means that they will need to develop skills of leadership and two-way communication that may have been less prominent in a traditional supervisory role. Given this need for an identified population of learners, it is possible for the company to commission an in-house course that develops the skills required. The advantage of this method is that it can be highly tailored to the requirements of the job, so, although there is a cost implication, there is a direct relationship between the learning and the job. The difficulties include having a sufficient population with the same requirements to make the course provide value for money. When courses are designed effectively they will incorporate learning methods that work for all the styles: activist, reflector, theorist and pragmatist.

An alternative to in-house courses is to send employees on external-courses, which can be short (e.g. two-day) topic-specific courses or longer educational programmes. Short topic-specific courses are normally focused on technique learning. They have the advantage of the learner being off-site in a new environment where they can explore practices with specialist experts. In addition, they can be learning alongside people from other companies, and so there are other forms of dialogical learning available to the participants as they learn from each other's experiences. The potential disadvantages are that there is a cost associated with such courses and there may be limitations in transferring the learning back into the workplace. Sometimes the learners might have developed new skills, but when they go back into the same old system of their own organization it can be difficult to enact the new skills. For change managers, therefore, an important part of using this method is to be careful in planning the exit of learners from the workplace onto the course, and their return, so that they and those around them are able to benefit from the learning.

Educational external courses are longer courses aimed at achieving a qualification, either academic or professional. Such courses are normally used as part of individual development rather than short-term change programmes. They are used effectively as part of a strategy to develop organizational cultures (see Chapter 6) through a long-term investment in people. They can also be part of establishing and maintaining the psychological contract with employees, who feel that they have been invested in by being supported to go on a course (see Chapter 11). External educational courses are beneficial mainly for their facilitation of insight learning. They can expose participants to ideas of a challenging nature and can enable learners to reflect on their preconceptions and the established ways of doing things in their organization. Of particular value is meeting and studying with people from other companies over time and in connection with a series of topics. This enables some longitudinal learning about how things are done elsewhere. When it works well this goes beyond normal benchmarking and gets into the 'messy reality' behind the sanitized version of performance that is normally exchanged through company comparisons.

Lastly, **coaching** and **mentoring** methods, which focus on interaction and dialogue, can be used (Brockbank, McGill and Beech, 2002). Coaching entails a degree of directedness. The coach will typically demonstrate what is needed, get the learner to practise the tasks step by step, give feedback and gradually enable the learner to become independent. A good coach is skilled in the technique but is also able to see it from the perspective of a learner. As people become more skilled in a task it is normal for some aspects of their knowledge to become tacit. Thus, even when they are trying to explain things to a new learner, they are liable to miss out steps or small but significant aspects of the practice. Coaching skills include the ability to see the task 'as if for the first time', so that the coach can empathize with the learner. When the learning concerns complex tasks the process is likely to be one of building up several skill/knowledge areas until a composite of new skills/knowledge can be formed. This is the case, for instance, with team leadership, when the task is not merely a build-up of supervisory skills in instructing, monitoring and directing but entails a different understanding of what the interactive process is. This is an example of where coaching can merge into mentoring.

Coaching is normally a one-to-one form of learning in which the coach directs the activities of the learner and gives feedback.

Mentoring is a way of supporting reflective learning by means of questions and dialogue between the learner and a more experienced colleague.

Mentoring is concerned with dialogue and reflection and is focused on learners extracting greater insight learning from their experiences than they would otherwise do. Mentors do not instruct or teach learners directly. The process is fundamentally about enabling learners to develop insights that they would not otherwise do. Hence, this method is known as 'learner-centred'. The mentor should be someone who is senior to but who is removed from the direct management of the mentee, so that the mentee can speak freely and can explore issues of a relatively private nature. The first job of the mentor and mentee is to establish a relationship of trust. This requires not only assurances about confidentiality and the learner-centred nature of the process, but also the gradual establishment of the relationship over a period of time. The best mentors are able to work gradually with their mentees so that the mentees increasingly ask probing questions of the experiences they have had, their own roles, the impact of others and why things have gone as they have. In one sense this sounds very simple, but in reality it is very demanding. It requires a degree of emotional robustness and the ability to engage in challenge and even conflict over interpretations. The mentor may be in a counselling role to some extent, and the essential skills lie in asking the questions and providing the social environment in which the mentee can question him- or herself, and others, at a deep level without fear of recrimination. The advantages of mentoring are that the psychological contract can become very positive and increasingly fortified, mentees can reach levels of reflection and insight learning that they would not otherwise achieve and the learning is clearly focused on learners and their ability to be part of the organization and contribute to its change and development. There are costs, in that it takes the time of senior people, and it cannot be assumed that merely by dint of being senior that people will thereby be good mentors. Mentors therefore require training, and there are opportunity costs with regard to the time the mentors spend on the process. Typically mentoring, which favours reflector and theorist styles of learning, is combined with other learning processes.

The various methods of learning and development have complementary strengths and weaknesses. Some are better at the transfer of new skill-based knowledge directly to the task, others are better at lifting learners to a higher level of abstraction and enabling them to develop insights that will help them to operate more creatively and extend their career further. The crucial issues for change managers to bear in mind are the readiness of employees to learn and the development of an approach that has the appropriate blend of methods to enable the majority of learners to develop in the desired direction regardless of their preferred learning style.

Mini-Case 12.1: Boston Consulting Group

We now explore the developmental approach adopted at Boston Consulting Group (BCG), a company in which learning and development are central to its purpose and nature. BCG is a management consulting company that operates around the world and sees itself as an 'ideas boutique'. Its distinctive position comes from a track record of developing innovative ideas that have been used to help many companies grow and, as a result, become well known and part of the brand of BCG. BCG has consistently been highly ranked by *Fortune* magazine, as one of the best companies to work for and on account of its aspiration is to be 'agents of change – for our clients, our people and society more broadly' (www. bcg.com). Given that BCG has built its operation on facilitating change through its people, it is instructive to ask how it develops its staff.

Most businesses operate in climates of uncertainty, and BCG has argued that the aim of change should not be to 'turn off uncertainty' but to prepare people to thrive in uncertain times (von Oetinger, 2004). BCG takes on trainee consultants with any degree subject and so there is a considerable need for professional development. This incorporates both technique and insight learning. Technique learning includes the skills of consulting, analysing and presenting, and as consultants move on to new projects there is a need for them to become familiar with the sector and the business they are advising. Insight learning is concerned with the consultants' abilities to understand quickly how and why things are being done in a business and to find ways forward. This involves them in being creative in their own ideas and being able to facilitate creative thinking on the part of the client. These are not skills that can be learned from a manual but entail the development of a level of professionalism, judgement and innovative capacity.

BCG has a comprehensive approach to learning and development. There are two areas of activity of particular note. First, there is a continuous process of formal training. This involves classroom technique learning. New consultants take courses on analysis, project management, problem solving, strategy, finance, accounting and organizational behaviour. As they progress to higher grades, there is input on people development, value creation, project leadership and client development. At the initial level, the technical training equips the learners with the 'how to' knowledge so that they can operate effectively in a very short space of time.

Alongside this there is a focus on insight learning, which moves the consultants beyond merely implementing skills and into more creative ways of making a difference with clients. This aspect of learning is managed through a combination of on-the-job learning and mentorship. The mentorship and coaching support within BCG is seen as a core strength and is a foundation of the company's process of continuous feedback and development (Domsch and Hristozova, 2006). The on-the-job learning is seen as a form of apprenticeship in which the managers and project leaders teach the new consultants the craft of consulting. This type of interaction is akin to coaching, in which there is a degree of direction from the teacher to the learner. However, in addition, the consultants have mentors who are in a non-evaluative role. The mentors meet regularly with the consultants to discuss how they are doing, what is working and what their development needs might be. Moreover, the mentors provide a sounding board, so that the consultants can reflect with them and think through their own evaluations with trusted partners. At the end of each project the consultant receives a review of performance, which includes feedback from the project leader and clients. It is not unusual for feedback to be challenging/negative, and in order to progress consultants need to pass through the professional grades within a timescale on the 'up or out' principle that is common in top consultancies. Therefore, dealing with such feedback can be difficult. It is very important, because it impacts on their careers, and this can accentuate the emotions associated with receiving it. The mentors help with interpreting, keeping things in proportion and encouraging consultants not to be too defensive. This form of mentorship enables a dialogical approach to reflection. The consultant experiences work, has performance reviews and then has the opportunity to talk this through with an experienced person who can offer a broader perspective. Of course, unless there is also personal internalization of the learning the impact on future performance is unlikely to be sufficient, and so the process is ongoing and the mentor and mentee meet regularly during and after each project to keep the learning progressing.

Enacting practices

The BCG example is one in which the purpose and nature of the company are based around learning and innovation. The psychological contract of those who join includes an expectation of regular change and personal development. The approach the company uses fits well with the employees and the clients they have. It combines formal and class-based learning with on-the-job learning and mentoring. In this way the company covers both technique and insight learning. Those who succeed in building a career at BCG are clearly proficient at both and are willing to develop continuously. In other companies and change projects it may be that the aspiration is more modest, but the implications are useful nonetheless. When enacting learning and development strategies as part of change management, issues to consider are:

- whether the focus is on technique or insight learning;
- which methods should be used, bearing in mind their strengths and weaknesses and their fit with particular purposes;
- that a combination of methods should be used, so that learners with different preferred styles all have a good chance of learning;
- that learning incorporates personal, social and dialogical aspects, and it is important to incorporate all three in learning plans; and
- learning and development can be part of a positive psychological contract, and as such can be a foundation in the relationship of trust between the organization and the employee.

EXERCISE

Consider the approach to learning and development taken in Case 6, Power Provision plc.

(1) To what extent is the company aware of the skills and knowledge that are being retained and those that are being lost?

(2) Is the company adequately aware of the blend of technical, commercial and leadership skills that are needed for the new organization?

(3) What learning and development methods could the company use to address the problems? How would it resource these methods?

WHO TO READ

The journal *Management Learning* is a very helpful source, and articles by Russ Vince, Elena Antonacopoulou and Ann Cunliffe, amongst others, are helpful in discussing topical debates in the field. Mark Easterby-Smith and Marjorie Lyles's (2003) handbook on organizational learning is also a good entry point into the field.

USEFUL WEBSITES

- www.bcg.com is Boston Consulting Group's website. It provides information on their services and case studies of people who have established careers in BCG.
- www.cipd.co.uk/learninganddevelopment is the Chartered Institute of Personnel and Development's site for learning, training and development. It includes articles, examples and practices on workplace learning. It also includes material on e-learning and talent management.
- www.peterhoney.com is the website for the Honey and Mumford learning styles inventory. There are two versions available, and in addition there is access to books and other learning resources.
- www.learning-styles-online.com provides an alternative to the Honey and Mumford inventory. The questionnaire on this site can be completed online, and feedback is provided.

REFERENCES

Antonacopoulou, E. (2006) The relationship between individual and organizational learning: new evidence from managerial learning practices. *Management Learning*, 37(4): 455–73.

Antonacopoulou, E., and Chiva, R. (2007) The social complexity of organizational learning. *Management Learning*, 38(3): 277–95.

Antonacopoulou, E., Jarvis, P., Andersen, V., Elkajaer, B., and Høerup, S. (2006) *Learning, Working and Living: Mapping the Terrain of Working Life Learning*. London: Macmillan.

Binsted, D. S. (1980) Design for learning in management training and development.

Journal of European Industrial Training, 4(8): 1–32.

Brockbank, A., McGill, I., and Beech, N. (eds.) (2002) *Reflective Learning in Practice*. London: Gower.

Collin, A. (2007) Learning and development, in Beardwell, J., and Claydon, T. (eds.) *Human Resource Management: A Contemporary Approach*, 5th edn.: 260–306. Harlow: Pearson.

Domsch, M., and Hristozova, E. (2006) *Human Resource Management in Consulting Firms*. Berlin: Springer.

Easterby-Smith, M., and Lyles, M. A. (eds.) (2003) *The Blackwell Handbook of Organizational Learning and Knowledge Management.* Oxford: Blackwell.

Honey, P., and Mumford, A. (1992) *Manual of Learning Styles*, 3rd rev. edn. London: Peter Honey.

Kolb, D. A., Rubin, I. M., and McIntyre, J. M. (1984) *Organizational Psychology: An Experiential Approach.* New York: Prentice Hall.

Macpherson, A., Jones, O., Zhang, M., and Wilson, A. (2003) Reconceptualising learning spaces: developing capabilities in a hi-tech small firm. *Journal of Workplace Learning*, 15(6): 259–70.

Sims, D., Murray, L., Murakami, K., and Chedzey, K. (2006) Work placements as narrative learning: stories for learning and for counterpoint. *International Journal of Innovation and Learning*, 3(5): 468–87.

Von Oetinger, B. (2004) A plea for uncertainty. *Journal of Business Strategy*, 25(1): 57–9.

13 Changing through dialogue

The aims of this chapter are to:

- show how conversations and interaction fit into broader social and interactive context of organizational change;
- introduce narrative analysis and its relevance for managing change; and
- discuss transactional analysis as a way of understanding and planning interaction.

It is very common for problems and successes in change management to be traced back to communications. Many reports of failure claim that there had been insufficient or ineffective communication, with the result that people did not know what they were meant to do or felt excluded. However, communicating clearly is only part of the answer. When we are communicating about complex matters such as change, people often do a lot of sense making, in which they can understand quite different things from the same set of words (Brown, Stacey and Nandhakumar, 2008). For example, a leader might explain clearly that the changes will lead to greater customer satisfaction, but different members of the audience might interpret this as meaning, for example, that there will be less autonomy for employees because they will have to follow customer demands, that the new approach will lead to better profits or that the statement is merely rhetoric and the leader does not really care about customers (amongst many other possible interpretations) (Sims, Huxham and Beech, 2009). The interpretive process can impose quite different understandings, and hence prompt very different reactions. Therefore, it is important to understand how different interpretations are made and what might be done about this when leading change (Grant and Marshak, 2011).

Communication is an essential part of the models introduced in Part A of this book. For example, in Chapter 2 we discussed Kotter's (1996) approach, in which deciding on a vision for the change and communicating it throughout the organization is regarded as essential. Burnes (2009) develops these ideas, arguing that, in addition to planned and formal communication, much successful communication is informal. For example, it is not just within meetings that agreements can be brokered; through informal contact outside meetings, potential disagreements and problems can be worked through before they become problematic. Successful communication for Burnes includes material support, and so face-to-face interactions are enhanced by ICT systems, databases and more traditional forms, such as noticeboards and flip charts. In addition, as can be seen in the example of Oticon (see Extended Case 4), the physical arrangement of facilities can either encourage or discourage communication. When communication is successful it tends to be intensive – that is, in meetings and interactions the participants are fully engaged and there is evidence of action that flows through and out of the interaction. Communication is not merely about the one-way transmission of information. It is about gathering information and exemplifying the behaviours that are desired. Hence, listening and showing that you have listened is central to involving and engaging employees and other stakeholders; but, beyond this, sensitivity to how and why others might develop diverse interpretations is fundamental to change management practice (Grant and Oswick, 2010). In order to do this we now explore the significance of narratives in communication.

Narratives and communication

It has been argued that humans are storytelling animals, in that one crucial way that we make sense of our world is through the stories we tell each other (see, for example, Boje, 1995; and Humphries and Brown, 2002). For example, children are taught about moral behaviour through fairy tales, religions explain the nature of belief through parables, and in business success and failure stories are encapsulated both in the formality of case studies and the informality of office gossip (Gabriel, 2000). The point of such storytelling is not just to inform and/or entertain. Stories operate as carriers of culture (Currie and Brown, 2003) – ways of explaining things that might be too complicated to explain in others ways – and they are ways of learning lessons. The moral of the story has the potential to be transformed into future action, and, because stories are often memorable, such morals may carry more weight in practice than detailed procedures or policy documents, which may not be fully remembered. A short example can illustrate this, and the following is provided by Andrew Brown (1995: 15).

In the Revlon Corporation there was a story about Charles Revlon. He required staff to be on time and sign the sign-in sheet, which should not be removed. Revlon himself, however, was not normally on time. One day he arrived and took the sign-in sheet to examine. The new receptionist, not knowing who he was, told him to replace the sheet. He refused and there was a short 'debate' which was concluded when Revlon said "do you know who I am?" and the receptionist said "no sir, I don't". "Well, when you pick up your final paycheck this afternoon, ask 'em to tell ya."

This story was still being told and retold within the company many years after it had occurred. It is significant because, in a short and memorable way, it explains certain things about the company. For example, is there one rule for everyone or are the senior people treated differently? If you inadvertently break a 'rule', what will happen? Are the senior managers reasonable and open-minded? In effect, the story explains that the company is not in favour of engaged forms of change and operates in a traditional, hierarchical way. The fact that the story existed for a long time is also important. When this happens it often means that the story 'resonates' for the tellers, in that it seems to encapsulate something that is true. In this case, no one knows whether the story is true or not, but, for those who tell it, the moral of the story is true. Hence, they act as if it is true, and an 'us and them' culture in which conformity is socially enforced proliferates. Clearly, such a culture has an impact on the management of change, because, as a result, it is more difficult to get people to generate ideas, take risks and work beyond the rules that are already known.

In order to understand the potential of stories for supporting or militating against change it is useful to use narrative analysis (Vaara and Tienari, 2011). The first step is to reveal the underlying **plot summary** – in effect, who did what, to whom, and in which order. This requires us to identify the actors in the story. The actors can be individuals, groups, collective nouns (e.g. the company, the customers), impersonal or contextual 'actors' (e.g. the system) or even material objects (e.g. the product). In the Revlon story, the actors are Charles Revlon (CR), the new receptionist (NR) and '[th]'em', the people who will give the final 'paycheck'. Typically, actors are constructed in such a way as to (at least partially) establish their character. For example, the receptionist is new and naive, Charles Revlon 'needs no introduction' and the 'paycheck' people are not merely the crowd but those who know how the system works – that is, they are *not* naive. The plot summary can be expressed as follows.

(1) CR establishes the rules of sign-in.

(2) NR operates the rules.

(3) CR apparently breaks the rules.

(4) NR challenges CR.

(5) CR displays his power over NR in a humiliating way, leaving NR in ignorance.

(6) The payroll people have to carry out CR's wishes and display to NR that everyone else knows how things work around here.

The story hinges on the difference between [th]'em and NR. NR knew only the official rule and was naive in believing that this was *the* rule. In fact, there was a rule about the rule, which was that the rules apply only to normal people. Things went wrong because, instead of following the rule (which she thought she was doing), she was actually breaking a superior, but covert rule. In this way, NR played out her character, which was one of naivety, and the moral of the story is that the listener should not be naive in the same way as NR. Hence, the second step, having established the characters and the plot summary, is to unpick the moral of the story: how it relates to the characters and what it teaches the listeners.

The plot summary is a reduced version of the story, produced as a series of points that show how the characters acted and in what order.

The third step is to recognize the construction of the space to act. CR had a broad **action space** and was able to set and change official rules and the rules-about-rules. He had a distinct identity (there is only one CR) and others could not question him. NR had a narrow action space. She had to follow the rules and could not question others, particularly the elite. '[Th]'em' also had a restricted action space, as they had to follow the rule of giving NR her final 'paycheck'. Hence, some characters had considerable agency, which allowed them to enact a change, whilst others believed themselves to have very little agency and so had to wait to be instructed or permitted to do things by other (senior) people or the system (e.g. the rules) (Thomas, Hardy and Sargent, 2011).

The action space is the area of agency that actors are perceived to have in the narrative.

Change management communication often includes stories (Oswick, 2008): of the journey from A to B; of crises that need to be escaped from; of markets and business environments that have already undergone dramatic change, which needs to be accommodated. The way that the stories are constructed can have a significant impact on how people approach the change (Brown, 2006). A plot shaped around a systemic threat from the outside may stimulate either defensive (opposing the change) or radical (changing everything) responses (Vaara and

Tienari, 2011), whilst a plot that gives people more agency in developing a new process or product may lead them to assume that they have a broad action space, and hence to feel that they can and should take action. We explore a mini-case study that illustrates different assumptions about the action space, but prior to doing so we explore an approach that focuses less on the overall narrative of the situation and more on the micro-level interaction between people.

Transactional analysis

Transactional analysis (TA) was developed by Eric Berne (1964), originally for individual/personal development within a group setting, and subsequently for organizational change. From this perspective, communication is conceived as a set of transactions. The transactions happen at the simplest level between two people, but in TA a person is understood to have three 'ego states' and the transactions occur between these states. **Ego states** are sets of related behaviours, thoughts and feelings, and the three ego states are parent, adult and child. These states are learned, and early life has a strong influence, as the way children encounter the world can appear natural to them (Stewart and Joines, 1987), and subsequent learning often has to start by undoing what has become taken for granted. (This was discussed in Chapter 6, when we looked at routines, habits and unlearning.)

Transactional analysis is a way of interpreting interaction on the basis of the ego states of the actors.

Ego states are positions from which interactions occur from the perspective of TA theory.

The parent state is influenced by the parenting that one received and contains nurturing, rule giving and discipline. The parent state is divided into *controlling parent* (also referred to as critical parent) and *nurturing* parent. When acting in the parent state people make judgements, seek to get others to act in line with rules and offer support from a position of superiority. Controlling parent tends to be more judgemental, and is positive when aimed at improving things for the other (e.g. 'Do it this way, it will work') and negative when delivering a transaction that might appear to be guiding but that is mainly critical (e.g. 'I see that you've made a mistake again; do it this way'). The child state is associated with creativity, humour and happiness, but also anger and feelings of hurt and confusion. Like the parent state, the child state has two versions: the *free child* and the *adapted child*. Free, or 'natural', child is the automatic, unfiltered response of, for example, joy or despair. The adapted child relates to the adaptations that one learns as a child; for example, screaming when angry (free child) is not accepted, so the child learns to express anger in other ways, such as by sulking (adapted child). Equally, excited self-expression (free child) may be reprimanded as showing off, such that the adapted child learns to perform in socially acceptable ways. The adult state is thoughtful and exploratory. In this state one seeks information, tests out ideas, is interested in the ideas of others but not totally swayed by them, and is willing to engage in constructive criticism.

In TA everyone has all three ego states, and they are used in transactions that often become patterned. For example, an adult–adult interaction might be seeking and giving information: 'What was the customer satisfaction level?' 'It was 75 per cent.' Alternatively, a child–parent interaction might be: 'I can never find the customer stats!' 'Don't worry, they are in this file.' These transactions are complementary, because they occur between two ego states that reward each other. The adult is looking for and receives factual information. The child state is looking for and receives nurturing support.

However, transactions can also be 'crossed' – that is, when the response is not in line with the initiating action. An example of an adult–parent interaction could be: 'What was the customer satisfaction level?' 'You really should know that.' An adult–child example could be: 'Do you know what the customer satisfaction level was?' 'Oh, who cares!' Such interactions are partly about information exchange and communication, but are also about emotion and how the person feels at the end of the interaction. People seek '**strokes**', or acts of mutual recognition, in the transaction for their psychological well-being, but strokes can be negative as well as positive (as in the crossed transactions above), and in such cases the recipient can feel worse as a result of the interaction. Some forms of transaction deliberately allocate negative strokes to the other whilst having the appearance of being positive. These are called 'ulterior' transactions. For example, the transaction 'How did the customer satisfaction ratings compare for products A and B?' 'Oh, pretty much what you would expect' might look like adult–adult but, depending on the context, tone of voice and non-verbal behaviours, might carry other meanings, such as: 'My ratings (A) were better than yours (B)', or 'Anyone could sell A'. When transactions such as this occur, one or both participants can end up feeling worse, and often there is a motivation to equal things out in the future. The negative stroke is 'stored', and when the opportunity presents itself the person is likely to try to give a negative stroke to the other. In this way, patterns of transaction can become established in an organization.

A stroke, in TA, is a unit of recognition – either positive or negative.

Negative patterns of transaction can form 'games', and there are many familiar ones, such as 'If it weren't for you, I could have...'. This game is often played in the absence of the blame-worthy player; for example, workers talking together can agree that, had it not been for the manager's ill-informed instructions, they could have completed the job in a more effective way. Hence, the problem with cost is the manager's fault, and blame is transferred away from the self. Another common game is the 'Yes, but...' game, which is played in response to suggestions. For example: 'My job is impossible; I can't deal with all these important clients.' 'Why don't you pass some of them on to more junior staff?' 'Yes, but then we would lose the clients, and that would be bad.' 'Well, if you can't deal with them we might lose some anyway, so why not decide which are most important?' 'Yes, but you never know who will turn out to be the most profitable, and they all want someone at my level.' Games such as these operate not only to generate strokes (positive and negative) from the other but also to preserve the status quo (people tend to repeat games that produce a result that confirms their view of the world and themselves). Hence, their impact when managing change can be considerable.

For Berne, there are four basic **life positions**, from which people produce life scripts (Kreyenberg, 2005). Scripts such as 'I am a leader' or 'I am normally the last to be chosen' are carried by people into transactions and into their way of being in broader narratives. The four basic positions are 'I'm OK; you're OK'; 'I'm OK; you're not OK'; 'I'm not OK; you're OK'; and 'I'm not OK; you're not OK'. The first position (OK; OK) is the winning position, in which the main operation is to get on with the action. The second position (OK; not OK) may look like a winning position, but it often leads to the focal person seeking to put others down in order to maintain his or her script. Thus, game playing and the storing of negative strokes occurs. The third position (not OK; OK) is likely to result in scripts of the self as loser and possibly self as victim. The fourth position (not OK; not OK) is one of futility and sometimes despair, in which mutual rejection is the norm. In the Revlon case above, Charles Revlon is in an 'I'm OK; you're not OK' position, and, as this becomes established through repetition and the power of his position, others come to accept the futility of resisting. The aim in change management is mainly to enable transactions to occur in the 'I'm OK; you're OK' position and to maximize adult–adult interaction. However, there can often be a place for the creativity of the child state and the nurturing of the parent state. In order to explore this in a little more depth, we now consider the case of NSC Finance.

Life positions are the role and script that a person has come to find natural.

Mini-Case 13.1: NSC Finance

NSC Finance is a global finance services company that is a brand leader around the world. It has various products, but this case focuses on financial advice services in the United States. NSC Finance is very successful and has a strategy of growth. In this mini-case we explore three perspectives: senior managers, group one advisors and group two advisors.

The senior managers aimed to grow the business by doubling the number of advisors and by making them more entrepreneurial. In order to do this they created two groups. Group one would have traditional employment contracts, in which they would have office space, the organizational back-up of analysts, the brand and the range of products, and they would report through the traditional management structure. The reward structure was a base salary plus 15 per cent commission on sales above a revenue target. Group two was more entrepreneurial. In this group, advisors would be encouraged to think of themselves as 'running their own business'. They would have more freedom to develop their client base and would be rewarded in proportion to the sales they achieved. They would receive a small basic salary but make most of their money through commission (typically 80 per cent). They would pay a fee to NSC for the back-office and support services they used and for the ability to use the brand. The strategy was to increase the number of group two advisors, who would be highly motivated to grow their businesses, and NSC would minimize its costs whilst making revenue from the sales and growth of the group two advisors.

The senior managers' story of the change was that it was a rational and successful process. After doing a pilot study in two offices they rolled out the change programme across the company. They communicated the change under the slogan 'It's all about choice'. Managers held meetings with advisors in each local area, and advisors could choose which group to join. Those who joined group two moved to new offices and quickly developed a strong culture. The group one advisors progressed more slowly, and local managers spent a lot of time with them, but advisor numbers in group one and revenues overall were increasing. Talking about the success, one senior manager said: 'We are a great company, we have been around a long time and we can only get more impressive.'

However, group one advisors had a rather different perspective on the change. For them, the slogan 'It's all about choice' was just rhetoric. In order to opt for group two you had to have a client base that already produced a prescribed minimum level of revenue. The group one advisors were not making enough to move to group two. Although the local managers were meant to help group one advisors grow their client base, the advisors found that the managers who were brought in knew less than they did and were of little or no help. After six months quite a few of the group one advisors were struggling to achieve sufficient revenue, but at this time NSC changed the reward structure, decreasing the basic salary and increasing the percentage commission above a higher revenue level. However, most of the group one advisors lost out, because their revenue levels were lower than the target. Twelve months into the change many of the group one advisors were quite despondent. Their incomes had suffered, they felt they had had a 'blind-side hit' from NSC and they were holding on to their jobs as hard as they could because their colleagues who had become so disillusioned that they had left had struggled to find new jobs in the industry, where rival companies wanted to recruit only experienced advisors who could bring client contacts with them. Group one advisors defined themselves as 'peons, the lowest of the low'.

Group two advisors had a third, and different, narrative. They felt that the change had been slow in coming but were happy to be running their own businesses. They acknowledged that the change had 'hit group one hard', but the difference was that group two advisors had 'been courageous and made the move'. They were determined to succeed, and 'it is this courage and determination that will see us through'. Many of the group two advisors saw increases in personal income, and for them the change was a major success initially. However, there was a downside, and that was the amount of support being given to group one. The group two advisors believed that they delivered 80 per cent of the profit for NSC but that they were continually 'taxed' to fund group one and the support they got through local managers and back office. In the words of one advisor, 'The bank robbers [senior management] are taking too much money... [I]f I get one more haircut [fee levied on commission] I'll be bald!' As another put it, to general agreement, 'We are the saviours, getting the work done... I don't need the brand any more. People are buying the advisor... [M]y clients are with me.' Increasingly group two advisors left NSC, and, although there was growth in group one advisors, the size of group two was decreasing.

Applying narrative and transactional analyses to NSC Finance

Clearly, these are quite different narratives of what are ostensibly the same events. At the point at which we stop the story a significant blockage to the change is emerging. Because of the sense making that is created and reinforced through the narrative construction and interaction, the effort to change is becoming self-defeating. The senior managers have a heroic/epic construction of the story, in which everyone has the ability to act. Their definition of 'the problem' is that group one has not yet acted with sufficient entrepreneurial verve. Therefore, senior managements' action is to wait for group one advisors to act and, if necessary, stimulate them by reducing the base salary and increasing the commission further. Their positions in TA terms are: 'I'm OK with me, you're OK with me and I'm OK with group two but not group one. Hence, the problem and the solution are located strongly in the other.'

Conversely, for the group one advisors the story is a tragic one, in which they have little or no ability to act or make a difference. The slogan 'It's all about choice' is simply rhetoric for them. Their TA positioning is very negative: 'I'm not OK with me, you're not OK with me.' They believe others see them as the 'lowest of the low' and they internalize this, regarding themselves as relative failures. In their self-construction they are innocent, possibly victims, awaiting support and help so that they can thrive. Instead of this, what they receive (in their perception) is management that is naive and unhelpful and a 'blind-side hit' when their base salary is further reduced. Most would leave if they could, but as they cannot find alternative employment they are hanging on for all they are worth. Group one advisors also see the problem and potential solution as being in the other, but for them the next steps lie with the senior managers. They are getting nowhere with the situation.

Group two advisors have a different perspective. For them, the story started long before the senior managers piloted the new arrangements. They had been waiting for a change for a long time and were already frustrated with the slowness of development by the time the change got under way. Their construction of the story put themselves firmly in the role of hero, and their TA positioning placed themselves as the only 'OK' group. Senior managers were slow to act and were wasteful. Group one advisors were non-contributors who ought to 'shape up'. Consequently, the problem and potential solution was located in the other, and, increasingly, members of group two were being genuinely entrepreneurial and leaving NSC.

The point of this type of analysis is not to prove that one version of events is true whilst another is false. Rather, it follows the dictum 'That which is perceived to be real, is real in its effect'. Because the three groups construct the story and the TA positioning as they do, their ongoing interactions and interpretations tend to reinforce their perceptions, and so each becomes ever more embedded in its own version of the story. As a result each is waiting for the other to solve the problem, and in the meantime those who fit least well with the entrepreneurial image that the senior managers aspire to are most attached and want to stay, whilst those who are most entrepreneurial, rather than wanting to stay and expand the company, are most attracted to leaving. In this way, the change strategy has become self-confounding. Table 13.1 summarizes this analysis.

Enacting change

NSC is a very successful company that has effectively managed significant transformations over the years and has achieved longevity and dominant position in a turbulent business environment. In many ways the company is good at managing change. In this case it had taken a series of steps that would be recommended in many change manuals. It identified a clear objective (low-cost expansion) within a timescale and set of resources. It devised an approach in which the behaviours that were wanted were incentivized. The management piloted the approach in two offices before roll-out and communicated clearly and repeatedly with those who would be enacting the change. So far, so good. However, the stumbling block was the subtlety of the social processes through which people make sense of their organizational world. Managers were unaware of the way the separate stories were developing and of the embedded nature of the positioning. They also lacked the feedback processes through which the dominant story could be interrupted. This is not merely a matter of giving people an opportunity to complain or give feedback. Because of their vulnerable self-positioning, the group one advisors would be highly unlikely to be able to take advantage of such an opportunity. What is needed is a way of reframing the stories and self-positioning such that dialogue can lead to redefinition of the problems and solutions and the action space can be expanded.

The narratives and identity positions become embedded because they are not questioned, and the first actions should be to recognize and question them. In TA terms, people habitually occupy a life position, and the best one for long-term effective change is 'I'm OK; you're OK'. In this position complementary transactions such as adult–adult on a business matter or child–child when having fun are most likely to be achieved. Therefore, the intention of a change intervention is

Table 13.1 Summary analysis of NSC Finance

	Narrative	Narrative	TA	TA	TA	TA	TA
	Plot trajectory and moral	Characters' action space	Our belief about self	Our beliefs about others	Our belief about how others perceive us	Overall position
Senior managers	Heroic story. Those who exercise freedom will succeed.	All have choice and can act.	I'm OK with me.	Group one – not OK. Group two – OK.	Others see me as OK.	Get on with. Optimistic.
Group one	Tragic story. The rhetoric is that things are getting better, but we are worse off.	We have no choice. Whatever we do will not make a difference.	I'm not OK with me.	Others are not OK.	Others see me as not OK.	Get nowhere with. Pessimistic.
Group two	Heroic story, and we are the heroes.	We have choice and act. Others have choice but don't act.	I'm OK with me.	Others are not OK.	Others see me as OK.	Get rid of. Narcissistic.

normally to get people to move to 'I'm OK; you're OK' and, in general, to occupy the adult state. However, in many cases people occupy other life positions.

People who are in 'I'm OK; you're not OK' are likely to adopt defensive positions in which they stay 'one up' on others. In such cases, the aim of dialogue is to reveal the consequences of this positioning to the people involved and get them to have a more balanced perspective on their own performance. This can be done through focusing on observable behaviours and their consequences so that good performance is recognized. Their need for recognition can be addressed in part by giving them recognition, and in so doing the aim is to reduce their need to establish themselves as superior to others by attributing failure to others. The corresponding action is that they need to be made aware that, even if others are not performing at the ideal level, consistently branding them as failures has negative consequences for the performance of the team/organization. In the short term the 'I'm OK' individuals might feel better by giving a negative stroke to the others, but in the long term this is very destructive and debilitating for team working. Hence, by giving recognition, people's need to defend the self by asserting themselves over others can be reduced and in exchange they can be expected to act *as if* they are less condemnatory of others for the good of the company (even if they do not actually believe this). This also entails a moderation of their narrative. Such people hold themselves to be the hero, and to unpick this could be a very significant personal change requiring considerable intervention. However, people can change their understanding of what it is that heroes do – that is, heroes are not all about conquering, proving a point or making sure that others know how good they (the heroes) are. Heroes can also exercise nurturing leadership and tolerance and have the aim of drawing performance from others. Ultimately, if individuals in this narrative TA position are unable to reform and have a strong negative impact on others it may be necessary to remove them from the team or organization, not necessarily because of their individual performance but because of their negative impact on others.

People who are in 'I'm not OK' positions may require different kinds of change intervention. They may need to break out of script positions in which everything is futile or their ability to achieve anything is limited. Sometimes such a position occurs when people have an unrealistically perfectionist perspective – that is, 'There is a good way of doing things but I am not up to it'. The problem is that what they see as good performance may be an illusion. The response to this can be to 'embrace failure' and see 'good' performance as unachievable. A step in confronting this is to debunk the excessive construction of good performance.

The aim is to replace this notion with ideas of 'good enough' or 'fit for purpose' performance. (It should be noted that this is anathema in some TA positions and organizational cultures.) One way of achieving this is to get them to explore the reality of performances that might look perfect from the outside but are less than perfect when understood from the inside. This might be done by getting them to work more closely with others who are high achievers or by getting them to analyse the impact of 'good enough' performance, which is generally not that the whole process collapses. Sometimes, as transitions occur, individuals may inhabit a 'You're not OK' position, and it is important to keep them moving through this towards 'I'm OK; you're OK'. The 'I'm not OK' position often goes along with tragic constructions of the story. Sometimes these can be so strong that, even when things seem to be going well, the individuals can reconstruct them as a temporary bright exceptional event en route to the normal failure. The people concerned may not be able to completely revise their story of the organization or change programme, but they might be able to modify their understanding of what constitutes success. In many walks of life '70 per cent' (however it is measured) can be perceived as a great achievement if we focus on the 70 per cent and not on the 30 per cent that was not achieved. Moving up a ranking can be success even if the number one position is not achieved. As with people who are in the 'I'm OK; you're not OK' position, if people in the 'I'm not OK' position are unable to shift their perspective such that they have an ongoing negative impact on the team or organization it may be necessary to remove them.

Conclusion

Communication is central to change management and it is often asserted that clear vision and communication are required for success. Whilst this is true in so far as it goes, it underplays the complexity of communication. Interaction takes place within a context, which strongly influences the meaning making that occurs. As a vision for a change programme is introduced it does not enter a neutral 'green field' in social or psychological terms. People already have an ongoing personal narrative, into which the pronouncements of the change leader are inserted. It might be that the message is just what they have been waiting for, or, conversely, that what is being introduced as a positive change is perceived in very negative terms because it will upset the flow of the personal narrative. Equally, the nature of the interactions can serve to reinforce TA life positions that will militate towards or against change. In dealing with these matters, considerable insight and subtlety is required on the part of the change leader. There are likely to be multiple and sometimes contradictory reactions and interpretations. Therefore, understanding how the same words are reinterpreted is important so that, in feedback with the different constituencies, the message can be reformulated in a meaningful style. However, to reformulate in terms of content can lead to accusations of inconsistency and lack of clarity. Therefore, regarding communication as a dialogical process in which participants are framing each other and engaging in a mixture of activities, including transmitting facts and exchanging psychological strokes, may be a more productive way to understand communication in change management.

For the change manager, it is helpful to do the following.

- Look beyond the 'tick list' of planning change – piloting, communicating a clear vision and reinforcing through reward. These are necessary steps but on their own they may not be sufficient to make significant change in the mindset and sense making of the participants.
- Recognize entrenched scripted positions. These are often dressed up as rational explanations ('That won't work; we've tried it before' or 'The problem is those underperformers over there'). The crucial question for the change manager is what such scripted perceptions do to the perceived action space: do people believe themselves to have agency or not? Convincing participants to take action and supporting them in this even when they do not believe it will work is vital.
- Undertake the process so that dominant scripts that are unproductive are challenged – e.g., in response to a 'No one ever listens to us' script, make processes of listening overt and present the evidence of having heard people back to them. If people have (ironically) embraced failure because of unrealistic perfectionist ways of thinking, there is a need to give them evidence that a more pragmatic approach can work by focusing on outcomes that are fit for purpose.
- Intervene to get people to 'rescript' what they mean by 'hero', 'victim', 'villain' etc., so that they do not become locked in to a dysfunctional dominant script.
- If these approaches do not work then it may be necessary to remove people from the change project, the team or even the organization.

EXERCISE

Read and analyse Extended Case 3, Island Opera.

(1) What might be the TA life positions of Bella the soprano, Jeremy the artistic director and Simon the conductor?

(2) How does each character narrate the story? What is the plot line according to them? What role do the characters take? How much freedom of action do they believe that they have?

(3) If you were in the role of Jeremy what could you do to change the interactions with the cast, and Bella in particular.

(4) If you were in Simon's role how would you balance being a company director and being conductor? Which position would you use in dealing with the situation, and what would you do?

WHO TO READ

Further reading on narrative could include the work of David Boje (1995), and also authors such as Brown (2006; with Stacey and Nandhakumar, 2008), Gabriel (2000) and Sims (with Huxham and Beech, 2009). Reading on TA should start with Berne (1964), and Ian Stewart and Vann Joines (1987) provide an insightful analysis and illustration.

USEFUL WEBSITES

- www.organizational-storytelling.org.uk. On this website the work of Gabriel and other scholars of organizational storytelling is explained and there is access to resources such as a regular seminar series on storytelling.
- www.business.nmsu.edu/dboje/storytelling. This site gives an alternative perspective. There is a focus on 'anti-narrative' and access to the work of Boje, who is a leading scholar in this field.
- www.ericberne.com/transactional_analysis. This site is an introduction to the concepts of Berne, who originated transactional analysis. The use of the concepts is explained and illustrated.

REFERENCES

Berne, E. (1964) *Games People Play: The Psychology of Human Relationships*. New York: Grove Press.

Boje, D. (1995) Stories and the storytelling organization. *Academy of Management Journal*, 38(4): 997–1035.

Brown, A. D. (1995) *Organisational Culture*. London: Pitman.

Brown, A. D. (2006) A narrative approach to collective identities. *Journal of Management Studies*, 43(4): 731–53.

Brown, A. D., Stacey, P., and Nandhakumar, J. (2008) Making sense of sensemaking narratives. *Human Relations*, 61(8): 1035–62.

Burnes, B. (2009) *Managing Change*, 5th edn. Harlow: Pearson.

Currie, G., and Brown, A. D. (2003) A narratological approach to understanding processes of organizing in a UK hospital. *Human Relations*, 56(5): 563–86.

Gabriel, Y. (2000) *Storytelling in Organizations: Facts, Fictions, Fantasies*. Oxford University Press.

Grant, D., and Marshak, R. J. (2011) Toward a discourse-centered understanding of organization change. *Journal of Applied Behavioral Science*, 47(2): 204–35.

Grant, D., and Oswick, C. (2008) Actioning organization discourse to re-articulate change practice. *Practising Social Change*, 1(2): 15–20.

Humphries, M., and Brown, A. D. (2002) Narratives of organizational identity and identification: a case study of hegemony and resistance. *Organization Studies*, 23(3): 421–47.

Kotter, J. P. (1996) *Leading Change*. Boston: Harvard Business School Press.

Kreyenberg, J. (2005) Transactional analysis in organizations as a systemic constructivist approach. *Transactional Analysis Journal*, 35(4): 300–10.

Oswick, C. (2008) Narrative research, in Thorpe, R., and Hutchinson, G. (eds.) Dictionary of Qualitative Management Research: 141–2. London: Sage.

Sims, D., Huxham, C., and Beech, N. (2009) On telling stories but hearing snippets: sense-taking from presentations of practice. *Organization*, 16(3): 371–88.

Stewart, I., and Joines, V. (1987) *TA Today: A New Introduction to Transactional Analysis*. Nottingham: Lifespan Publishing.

Thomas, R., Hardy, C., and Sargent, L. (2011) Managing change: negotiating meaning and power resistance relations. *Organization Science*, 22(1): 22–41.

Vaara, E., and Tienari, J. (2011) On the narrative construction of MCNs: an antenarrative analysis of legitimation and resistance in a cross-border merger. *Organization Science*, 22(2): 370–90.

PART D
Explaining

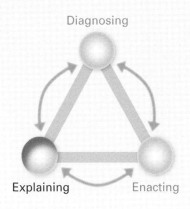

Diagnosing

Explaining   Enacting

Many scholars suggest that change is difficult because people resist change. The third focal area of the enquiry–action framework focuses on explanation, as it is highly likely that a change that cannot be understood is likely to be more problematic than one that is explicable. Of course, explanation does not imply universal agreement, since different stakeholders may be inclined to warm to some explanations whilst disputing others. In the enquiry–action model, explanation can involve establishing the need for change as well as allowing those involved in change to signal the achievement of aims or goals signalled in an earlier round of problem specification. In Part D we examine the nature and role of evidence in change processes and how feedback from change initiatives can drive a reflexive process in which the organization, the change process itself and the change agent might be reconceived. The part also considers the way in which accounts of the change process are used by focusing on two different audiences: organizational audiences (such as management teams, organizational members, suppliers and a range of other stakeholders) and academic audiences (for which change is being studied as part of a formally assessed programme of study). Being able to explain what is going on and why you think this is the case is essential. Being able to explain this to yourself is a necessary precondition for being able to engage others in that explanation.

14 Developing/interpreting evidence, reflexive learning

The aims of this chapter are to:

- introduce the concept of evidence;
- build familiarity with a range of techniques used to gather evidence; and
- identify the political and social challenges of gathering and presenting evidence in change processes.

The concept of evidence is not unproblematic. Some research traditions challenge the very idea of what it means to claim to have evidence if one is operating with a view that our experience in the world is a socially constructed and relational phenomenon (Berger and Luckmann, 1966). However, the view that reality is socially constructed does not mean that 'reality' is any less 'real' in how people experience it. In some of our own research we have discussed the ways in which those managing an organization relate to evidence about aspects of that organization, in that there are 'areas of interaction between the fantasized and the experienced' (MacIntosh and Beech, 2011: 31). Hence, what to one individual or group within the organization might be taken as straightforward and factual might be seen by others as untrue or a fantasy that is being used for political ends. Our own view is that a constructionist and dialogic perspective offers a useful means of looking at both how views come to be held (for example, that some aspect of a change process is important or unimportant) and how those views might impact on future action. On a related note, Scott Cook and John Seely Brown (1999) offer an excellent discussion of the distinction between knowledge and knowing. They use the example of riding a bicycle to suggest that there are aspects of our abilities that we nonetheless struggle to articulate. Theoretically, it would be possible for people to specify in great technical detail the mechanics of how to ride a bicycle even if they were unable to do so themselves, but most of us who know how to ride a bicycle could not offer a solid explanation of the process. As a result, the tacitness of how we know something and the social process by which we construct explicit knowledge are both problematic.

Whilst acknowledging these distinctions and problems, our purpose here is simply to accept as a starting point the observation that evidence plays an important role in change and a vital role in explaining change. Depending on the politics and epistemology of the world view that dominates in the organization, evidence (in whatever way it is meaningful to those in the situation) is vital precisely because its currency and credibility are negotiated amongst the stakeholders in the situation (Nutley, Walter and Davies, 2007; Briner, Denyer and Rousseau, 2009), as discussed in Chapter 5.

Establishing the need for change may require a case to be made, and in the first instance this could be as simple as identifying a problem and demonstrating that it exists. If the problem relates to delays and customer deadlines, it may be helpful to look at last year's figures to establish the percentage of cases that were delayed. If the perceived problem is staff turnover, gathering evidence to show the proportion of people leaving the organization and the consequences of this may help focus attention on what can be done about the issue.

Equally, evidence can play a key role in drawing change processes to a close. In Chapter 2 we reviewed Kotter's framework for organizational change (1996). In Kotter's model the final three steps (delivering quick wins; consolidating and assessing progress; linking change activities to outcomes and achievements) all require some grounding in evidence. It may be that a new training programme has reduced staff turnover, but being able to substantiate and calibrate the claim is critical to the perception of the change process as having 'worked' and perhaps now concluded. Marking the beginning and end of change episodes allows those in the organization to deal with the relationship between ongoing organizational life and change processes (Hendry and Seidl, 2003).

In the examples given thus far, evidence usually takes the form of **data**, which can be sourced in a number of ways. Data may already exist in the form of reports, performance figures or similar materials that are produced as part of the ongoing conduct of organizational life. If so, this can save time, so long as you are sure that the data are accurate enough to serve your purpose. In some industries, tracking certain key data are mandatory, but such freely available data must fit your intended purpose. You may want to break customer retention down by product or service categories, but find instead that the data that are readily available are broken down on geographical grounds. Similarly, if you are introducing a new process and want to be able to compare the existing process to the new process, you must ensure that the data you are using will be comparable. Inevitably there are occasions when it would be quicker and more reliable to gather new data that meet your exact requirements. In this chapter we begin with a brief review of the more common methods used to gather and present evidence and conclude by returning to the relationship between the data gatherer and the data.

The term 'data' is derived from Latin and is the plural form of 'datum', which means 'something given'. This is typically assumed to result from direct observation or measurement.

Gathering evidence

Evidence can be classified in relation to a number of dimensions, as set out in Table 14.1.

The type of evidence required will be heavily influenced by the characteristics of the change process. Training Co. is a provider of web-based training to a range of large corporate clients. The firm wanted to change the way in which training materials were developed, piloted and updated. The change meant relinquishing some editorial control of the content to users of the service, and this in turn made some staff nervous. A pilot scheme was initiated in which one subset of training materials was handled in this more participative and collaborative way, and evidence was gathered about the new approach. This included some quantitative data (e.g. the number of hits on particular web resources and the number of users who elected to update the materials). These data were readily available through reports, which flagged and monitored **key performance indicators** for Training Co.'s senior managers. However, some modifications were required to keep track of users updating materials, since this had not been done historically. In addition to this quantitative data, Training Co. decided to ask customers what they

Table 14.1 Classifying evidence

Qualitative	Quantitative
Longitudinal	Snapshot
Based on sample	Based on whole population
Gathered specifically for the purpose	Already available
Sourced and analysed internally	Sourced and analysed externally

thought of the new materials and give them the opportunity to participate in updating them. This meant thinking of searching questions to ask, then holding a series of interviews with those customers who had used the new site. Interviews offer a useful way of getting detailed insights into the way customers think and react. However, fifteen one-hour interviews produced a mass of transcripts, which Training Co. then struggled to analyse.

Key performance indicators are those subsets of organizational performance measures that have been identified as critical to the overall success of the organization. Often referred to as KPIs, these may form the basis both for contractual arrangements with customers and suppliers and for incentives and rewards.

We now review the most commonly used approaches to gathering evidence, to try to avoid the problems that Training Co. encountered.

Questionnaires

We are regularly asked to complete questionnaires for customer surveys and academic projects, but you may never have designed a questionnaire yourself. The single most important design issue is to be clear about the purpose and intended audience of your questionnaire. There are specialist resources on questionnaire design both online and in book form (see, for example, Graham, 2008), so we do not attempt a comprehensive summary here. However, there are three helpful pieces of advice to bear in mind.

First, think about the people who you hope will complete the questionnaire. It is important to be honest with yourself about your ability to access respondents and to ask yourself how long is it realistic to expect them to spend filling it out. Starbuck, the former editor of one of the world's top academic journals, *Administrative Science Quarterly*, uses the example of a lengthy questionnaire sent to the chief executives of major US corporations to suggest that the intended recipients are unlikely to make the time to complete the questionnaire. Indeed, any completed returns may actually have been completed by someone else in the organization (Starbuck, 2006). Access to a mailing list or similar contact details may also be challenging, as well as keeping the questionnaire short enough that it may be completed in a reasonable time. Some questionnaires appeal to the greater good of mankind, some offer incentives or prizes for completion, others carry some threat or fine as completion is mandatory. Finally, look at the response rate to your questionnaire in terms of both representativeness and statistical validity. A typical response rate may be in the region of 5 to 15 per cent. If your response rate is very low the fear is that you may not be getting a representative view from those completing the questionnaire. It could be that only the very aggrieved or the most loyal supporters are filling the questionnaire in, raising the issue of how representative these respondents are and how to present such 'evidence' to your intended audience. Relatedly, some forms of analysis require a minimum number of respondents for the particular statistical tests involved to be seen as valid.

The second piece of advice is to think about the nature of the questions that you want to ask. First, think about the difference between open and closed question formats. Closed questions are typically easier and quicker to answer, which helps with completion rates but limits the richness of what you might discover. Open questions can allow you to access unexpected insights and surprises but can be more difficult to answer, more challenging to analyse and more likely to produce misinterpretation from your respondents. It is best to avoid leading questions, jargon and vague descriptors such as 'regularly' or 'often'. Proofreading and pilot-testing of your questionnaire might also help eliminate phrasings that create so-called 'double negatives', when disagreeing with the statement has complex consequences (e.g. 'Prices should not be raised at more than the rate of inflation'). Other common errors in questionnaire design include combined questions ('I believe in being able to edit the training content and in lower pricing') or overly long, complex questions.

The third piece of advice is to think about how you will analyse and present the findings from your questionnaire *before* you send it out. Simple spreadsheet functions make it relatively straightforward to carry out basic collation and analysis of data. This may be exactly what you need if you are hoping to explain simple patterns in the data. Often this is enough to get your point across. Figure 14.1 is drawn from a questionnaire that Training Co. used to ascertain the likelihood of existing customers making increased usage of their site given the new approach to co-created content. Such descriptive statistics offer a powerful way of summarizing large quantities of data. However, more sophisticated analysis typically requires expert input from those with sufficient statistical training.

Interviews

The second common approach to gathering evidence is to use interviews. This is much more time-consuming than issuing a questionnaire but the trade-off is the opportunity to interact with the interviewee(s) and to try and understand the ways in which they make sense of the world (Kvale, 1996). Interviews can be structured (the interviewer follows a detailed schedule of specific topics and questions), semi-structured (the interviewer works from a broad outline of topics

Training Co. customer survey

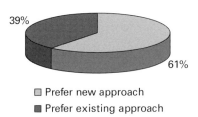

39%

61%

☐ Prefer new approach
■ Prefer existing approach

Figure 14.1 Customer reactions to Training Co.'s new material

to be covered) or unstructured. Each approach is appropriate for different circumstances but more structured approaches are generally thought to be easier for novice interviewers. The very nature of what is going on in an interview is itself challenging, with Alvesson (2003) suggesting that interviews constitute a setting in which a complex social performance occurs. Whilst it may be tempting to assume that interviewees are 'competent and moral truth tellers' (2003:14), Alvesson argues that multiple agendas may be played out in the interview. These may include power hierarchies (e.g. 'I'll tell you what I think my boss wants you to hear'), identity dynamics (e.g. 'I'll tell you how it is in this organization, since you're only visiting') and interpersonal dynamics (e.g. 'I like/don't like you [the interviewer] as a person so I'll try to impress/outsmart you'). Whilst acknowledging the complexity that this brings to an interview, we would suggest that interviews may offer rich insights regardless of whether they are positioned as opportunities for moral truth telling or social performance.

Issues to consider include the location and duration of the interviews and whether to record them. Audio and/or visual recording of the interview takes the pressure off the interviewer, in terms of taking notes, but can increase the pressure on the interviewee. If you do record the interview, transcription is both time-consuming and costly. Once the interview has been transcribed there remain significant challenges in terms of analysing its contents. Typically interview transcripts are analysed by looking for patterns in the responses of individual respondents. A **grounded theory** (Strauss and Corbin, 1998) approach would involve coding the interview transcripts to allow some comparison between respondents. For example, each individual interviewee may use his or her own terminology to describe the opportunity to co-create training materials (e.g. 'editing', 'changing', 'shaping', 'correcting', etc.). In a grounded analysis of the interview transcripts, one introduces a category and checks for instances of that category. As new transcripts are reviewed, subcategories may become necessary, and the process continues until saturation has been achieved – i.e. new interview transcripts do not require you to add new categories.

Grounded theory refers to an approach to research in which categories and classifications are built directly from the data rather than from some prior theory. This is contentious, since some argue that it is impossible in practical terms to exclude all theoretical biases when coding the data.

Focus groups

Another way of gathering evidence is to use a focus group (see Morgan, 1997, for detailed advice), which some describe as a form of group interview. The group of participants that comes together is selected and assembled with the express intention of getting them to share their views and comment on the topic in hand. Focus groups allow more people to be involved than is the case with one-to-one interviews, and therefore they are more efficient in this regard. Perhaps more importantly, focus groups create opportunities for participants to interact, build on each other's comments, disagree, etc. The dynamics of the conversation in a focus group can be insightful, but there is also the risk that one or two voices may dominate the proceedings, and skilled facilitation is needed to ensure that the research process does not get stuck on a single issue.

Typically focus groups have some structure, in that there is at least a series of prompts or questions to which the group will react. Sometimes it is helpful to have more than one host for the focus group, with one observing whilst the other chairs the session. Again, there is a trade-off between the richness and complexity of the conversation and the ability to capture, structure and analyse the outcomes. Transcribing a focus group is a major challenge, as voices often cut across each other, and a high-quality recording device is essential. As with interviews and questionnaires, focus groups require you to have thought carefully about what you hope to discover. Some sensitive issues may be less likely to be raised in a focus group than in a one-to-one interaction such as an interview, since participants may be unwilling to voice their opinion in front of their peers.

Issues such as your opinion of co-workers, superiors or customers may well be sensitive, particularly when a critical view is being offered. Such sensitivities can occur in questionnaires, interviews or focus groups, and they are one of the reasons that Alvesson is suspicious of the performative aspect of any evidence gathering (2003). In the animated children's film *Robots*, the chief executive introduces a controversial new set of proposals that makes many of the management team uncomfortable, and he closes his presentation by saying: 'I have to say

I think it [the idea] is fantastic, but I'd love to hear what you *employees* think.' On the surface, an effort is being made to assess the suitability of a new idea, but the power dynamics of the situation are made visible here for comic effect. In reality, such dynamics may be much more subtle, but they do raise a number of issues relating to ethics in your evidence gathering.

Ethics

When you are gathering evidence in any change process there are several ethical considerations. Many organizations have policy statements about the ethical conduct of research, and most universities require ethical approval to be secured before any data can be collected. Participants should know what they are committing themselves to, what is involved and how their contribution will be treated. This is sometimes called informed consent, and it can involve interviewees or respondents providing written confirmation of their willingness to participate. Informed consent often involves making explicit the way in which confidentiality will be handled, how the security of the evidence will be ensured and who will have sight of the findings of the research. These are obviously significant questions, since they help provide a basis for establishing trust in advance of the research process.

Using evidence in Her Majesty's Revenue and Customs

Taxation is collected by the UK government through an organization called Her Majesty's Revenue and Customs. The organization employs almost 100,000 people and brings in the revenue that pays for the delivery of government policy in areas such as health, education, enterprise, the environment and social welfare (Extended Case 8 offers a more detailed overview of HMRC). Tax is collected from individual employees and whole corporations using a variety of processes. The complexity of the task is enormous and the organization is organized into units that focus on particular aspects of taxation policy. One such unit is concerned with the taxation of charities, assets and residence (CAR), and it employs over 1,500 staff. As part of an on-going change process to improve efficiency, the CAR unit introduced a new helpline service to handle enquiries from customers. The helpline combined several different areas of work, and there were differing opinions about the feasibility of having a single member of staff capable of dealing with the technical complexities of tax enquiries across what had historically been different areas of activity within the organization. We were involved with those inside the organization as evidence was gathered about both the effectiveness of the new service and how staff felt about the new approach. A questionnaire was developed and issued to those working in the helpline service. The questions ranged from simple 'Yes'/'No' formats to establish whether individuals had completed training modules in a range of specialist tax regulation to more open questions that sought to understand what people liked and disliked about the helpline service (e.g. 'Rank the following areas for improvement in terms of their importance to you: further training for multi-skilling, flexibility of working patterns, better communication amongst staff, availability of cover/relief').

The questionnaire produced a range of evidence that was crucial in shaping the change process that unfolded within the organization. First, it highlighted confusion amongst those working in the helpline service about the thinking behind the new approach. Senior management hoped to improve service levels and be helpful to customers, who often called with a related set of queries. Staff thought that it had been introduced to cut costs. These mismatched explanations created the potential for difficulties and tensions. Second, it highlighted problems with performance data. Many of the staff working in the new service felt that service levels had slipped, yet data gathered in the first few months of the helpline's operation showed that targets were being exceeded. Given the mismatched explanations at play, some staff were therefore fearful that further headcount reduction would focus on those parts of the service that were 'failing'. The stated intention was to have 90 per cent of calls completed with 'full and accurate' information fed directly back to the customer, and in questionnaires and interviews staff reported feeling unable to meet these targets. In fact, separate performance data showed that the actual levels being achieved were in the range 95.1 per cent to 100 per cent. Third, the questionnaire helped shape training programmes designed to support new staff joining the helpline service. The service covered five areas of taxation activity, and the questionnaire highlighted serious concerns amongst staff as to how long it would take to achieve competence in each of these areas, and what form of training would best achieve this. A rethink of the training process followed and included greater emphasis on job shadowing and mentoring rather than classroom-based activities. Senior managers within the CAR unit felt that the evidence gathered from those involved had helped enormously in shaping the way in which a new service was developed, with some describing it as 'central to turning round what could have been a difficult change process'.

Reflexivity and change

So far we have focused our attention on the practicalities of gathering evidence using appropriate techniques such as interviews or questionnaires. Indeed, Steve McKenna (2007) suggests that the use of 'acceptable apparatus' in gathering such evidence might be more important than the actual findings themselves. Our research work has given us the opportunity to study a large number of change projects, and the use of evidence in such projects is commonplace. However, one of our main interests in researching the ways in which organizations change is the reflexive process experienced by change agents. Just as the organization changes, our experience is that change agents themselves emerge from change processes with new insights into what worked and why, as well as new perceptions of their own areas of strength and weakness in executing change.

In reviewing change processes, it is helpful to separate out the related terms: reflection and reflexivity (Hibbert, MacIntosh and Coupland, 2010). First, reflection is often thought of as some mirror-like process in which we can examine our own way of doing things. Reflexivity, then, is more than this simple reflection. When thinking reflexively, we complexify our thinking by questioning our ways of doing things. The critical thinking involved means that reflexivity is related to reflection but is qualitatively different from it. Shotter's view that managers are 'practical authors' (1993) suggests that reflexivity has a crucial role, as managers create the organizational realities that they then experience. Cunliffe goes further, suggesting that this process of authorship may relate to how managers construct a sense of who they are and how they may influence others to talk or act in different ways through their own dialogical practices (2001). In her own research, Cunliffe is fascinated by the role of reflexivity and the relationship between the researcher and the research phenomenon. In the practice that she describes as social poetics, she tends to revisit the research process: 'I began to videotape my conversations with managers. I then videotaped a second conversation where I, and the manager, watched the first video and commented on what "struck" us, how we connected and created meaning' (Cunliffe, 2002: 142).

In a similar sense, we believe that it is immensely valuable to consider the extent to which your own practice as a change agent merits further consideration. The enquiry–action model we have presented in this book suggests that change involves elements of diagnosing, enacting and explaining. Central to your ability to deliver change is the quality of the explanation that you can build of your own role in the change process. Of course, no two changeful situations are likely to be identical. Therefore, before we enter new change settings, we need to engage in a process of abstraction in order to be able to conclude that 'situation A is quite like situation B but different in the following ways...'. This ability to reflect and think reflexively helps ensure that we learn from our experiences, both positive and negative, and continue to develop as skilled practitioners of change.

EXERCISE

ITS Canada attempted a major cultural change when the organization broke away from its parent company and moved to new premises (see Extended Case 2). From the point of view of the senior managers at ITS Canada, answer the following questions.

- What evidence might they have gathered to support and inform the change process?
- Which techniques might they have used to gather that evidence?
- What difficulties or sensitivities might the gathering and the analysis of such evidence have thrown up?

WHO TO READ

It is worth reading the work of three people. John Shotter, now Emeritus Professor at the University of New Hampshire, has written extensively on the social conditions that are conducive to people having voice and being heard in conversations. Ann Cunliffe is now based at the University of New Mexico and writes about both critical thinking and reflexive practice. Finally, Mats Alvesson, from Lund University in Sweden, is known for his work on both reflexivity and identity.

USEFUL WEBSITES

- www.surveymonkey.com: a web-based service that helps create and analyse questionnaires.

REFERENCES

Alvesson, M. (2003) Beyond neopositivists, romantics and localists: a reflexive approach to interviews in organizational research. *Academy of Management Review*, 28(1): 13–33.

Berger, P., and Luckmann, T. (1966) *The Social Construction of Reality: A Treatise in the Sociology of Knowledge.* London: Penguin Books.

Briner, R., Denyer, D. and Rousseau, D. (2009) Evidence-based management: concept clean-up time? *Academy of Management Perspectives*, 23(4): 19–32.

Cook, S., and Seely Brown, J. (1999) Bridging epistemologies: the generative dance between organizational knowledge and organizational knowing. *Organization Science*, 10(4): 381–400.

Cunliffe, A. (2001) Managers as practical authors: reconstructing our understanding of management practice. *Journal of Management Studies*, 38(3): 351–71.

Cunliffe, A. (2002). Social poetics and management inquiry: a dialogic approach. *Journal of Management Inquiry*, 11(2): 128–46.

Graham, W. (2008) *Developing a Questionnaire*, 2nd edn. London: Continuum International Publishing.

Hibbert, P., MacIntosh, R., and Coupland, C. (2010) Reflexivity, recursion and relationality in organizational research processes. *Qualitative Research in Organizations and Management*, 5(1): 47–62.

Hendry, J., and Seidl, D. (2003) The structure and significance of strategic episodes: social systems theory and the routine practices of strategic change. *Journal of Management Studies*, 40(1): 175–96.

Kotter, J. P. (1996) *Leading Change.* Boston: Harvard Business School Press.

Kvale, S. (1996) *Interviews: An Introduction to Qualitative Research Interviewing.* London: Sage.

McKenna, S. (2007) Deconstructing a personal 'academic'/'practitioner' narrative through self reflexivity. *Qualitative Research in Organizations and Management*, 2(2): 144–60.

MacIntosh, R., and Beech, N. (2011) Strategy, strategists and fantasy: a dialogic constructionist perspective. *Accounting, Auditing and Accountability Journal*, 24(1): 15–37.

Morgan, D. L. (1997 *Focus Groups as Qualitative Research*, 2nd edn. London: Sage.

Nutley, S. M., Walter, I., and Davies, H. T. O. (2007) *Using Evidence: How Research Can Inform Public Services.* Bristol: Policy Press.

Shotter, J. (1993) *Conversational Realities: Constructing Life through Language.* London: Sage.

Starbuck, W. H. (2006) *The Production of Knowledge: The Challenge of Social Science Research.* New York: Oxford University Press.

Strauss, A., and Corbin, J. (1998) *Basics of Qualitative Research: Techniques and Procedures for Developing Grounded Theory*, 2nd edn. London: Sage.

15 Accounting for change

The aims of this chapter are to:

- introduce the challenges of writing for organizational and academic audiences;
- focus the production of accounts of change by examining critical questions that help frame the account; and
- prepare those studying change in the context of assessed courses to produce academically grounded accounts of change.

The role of accounts in organizational life has been studied extensively, and such accounts are obviously related to the narrative view of organizations discussed in Chapter 13. Accounts are defined as a linguistic device employed whenever an action is subject to a process of enquiry (Scott and Lymann, 1968). Scholars have considered the contents of such accounts, the conditions under which people present accounts and – perhaps most interestingly for our purposes – the conditions under which people accept the accounts of others (see Orburch, 1997). Erving Goffman argues that narrative accounts are created for existing audiences in order to help maintain social identities (1959; 1971). In this chapter we consider both the rationale for providing an account and the audiences to which these accounts are presented. In terms of rationale or impetus, we would highlight two related but distinct reasons for giving an account of change. First, organizational members must often give an account of the change process in which they are involved. This could be to signify that the change has drawn to a conclusion or it could be to assess progress in an ongoing process. In either case, there is a need to report an account of the change to a particular set of audiences.

A second form of account is often required when studying change in the context of an academic programme as part of an assessed qualification, such as a certificate, diploma or degree. Both types of account are subject to some scrutiny and assessed. One type of account may be used to inform the other, but both merit consideration in their own right.

Accounting for change with organizational audiences

In the enquiry–action model, explaining can occur either at the beginning or at the end of the change process, since the explanation may be to establish that change is required or that a set of change-related activities have now reached a point at which it is helpful to signal that they are complete. In either case, the explanation is likely to be strengthened by the use of evidence that is seen as credible to the audience(s) you are addressing.

As discussed in Chapter 14, it is important to understand what forms of evidence are likely to work for which audiences. One way of thinking about this would be to consider the relative power and influence of audience members (using a stakeholder approach, as discussed in Chapter 5). A first step might be to think about the plot summary (see Chapter 13) that will form the basis of the account you wish to give. For example, the change introduced at Oticon (see Extended Case 4) is summarized in Figure 15.1.

An account such as this may help those embedded in the situation to make sense of their experience, and as such it may be considered a sense-making narrative (Brown, Stacey and Nandhakumar, 2008). This particular account suggests a change process that has drawn to a successful conclusion. Particular forms of evidence would be important, in that the change process was initiated as a response to deterioration in both financial performance and product development. Measurement of these factors in a 'before and after' sense

(1) Oticon's performance deteriorates.
(2) Cost-cutting measures help but do not resolve the problem.
(3) A radical new approach (the spaghetti organization) is introduced.
(4) Performance improves significantly.
(5) Oticon is congratulated for its organizational innovation.

Figure 15.1 Accounting for change at Oticon

further reinforces the view that the change process has delivered against its intended objectives. In particular, the change project at Oticon was described as aiming to deliver 30 per cent greater efficiency within three years. Here, then, is an account of change in which some early diagnosis of a problem led to a radical set of changes within the organization, and these changes led, in turn, to the resolution of the problem.

However, there is always a problematic relationship between the lived reality of organizational life and the before/after mentality associated with an account of the organization. In particular, the difficulty lies in delineating the beginning and end of the account. John Hendry and David Seidl signal the importance of recognizing the start and end of such accounts, since they argue that these start and end points signify the transition from what they call 'episodes' and ongoing organizational activities (2003). In selecting the start and end points for the account given in Figure 15.1, the reactions of particular audiences are interesting. Lars Kolind, the CEO who introduced the spaghetti organization, may be delighted with this account, as his intervention appears to have successfully dealt with the problem of poor performance. Oticon's employees may prefer an account that starts somewhat earlier and acknowledges the heritage of the firm as an innovator and market leader. Choosing an earlier starting point for the account places the more recent difficulties in a new light. Here, the recent challenges might be seen as a short-term aberration in an otherwise long and successful organizational story. Such an account might reinforce the need to go back to former practices as a means of resolving current difficulties.

Likewise, moving the end of the plot line further forward highlights an unexpected twist in the tale. In the period after the introduction of the spaghetti organization, performance does improve but falls away again. Subsequent changes in Oticon reintroduce some elements of structure to the so-called structureless organization. In this expanded account, it is possible to question the success or failure of the spaghetti organization. No longer a straightforward success story, the account may shift emphasis to highlight the role that the more radical solution played in introducing more conventional changes. As this short example shows, accounts of change that are produced are often politicized, in that they must speak to more than one audience. These audiences might be characterized by any number of groupings, such as internal/external, new staff/long-serving staff, shareholders/employees, etc., and different forms of evidence will be seen as credible in these various contexts. Figure 15.2 suggests a set of questions that are helpful in framing an account of the change process.

(Q1) Is it possible to establish the objectives of the change process?
(Q2) Which stakeholders will form the audience for the account that you will produce?
(Q3) How will these stakeholders frame the episode that you are accounting for (i.e. where will they place the start and end points)?
(Q4) What forms of evidence will appear compelling to the audience that you most hope to influence?

Figure 15.2 Critical questions in accounting for change

Reports on change processes and outcomes are usually directed towards senior management audiences, who can either continue to support an ongoing change project or accept the successful/unsuccessful conclusion of such an initiative. In larger organizations such change projects are often undertaken in phases, and interim reports form the basis for access to continued support in both financial and political terms.

Accounting for change with academic audiences

A related but different problem faces anyone who must give an account of change for some academic purpose (e.g. writing an assignment that will be assessed as part of a formal qualification). Here the kinds of accounts discussed so far are an excellent starting point but are in fact insufficient for the particular academic audience(s) that will read an assignment.

Many business or management-related qualifications feature a change-related module or course, and a common form of assignment requires you to choose an example of organizational change that you then explain using one or more models, theories or concepts. Faced with such an assignment, the details of the plot line described in Figure 15.1 would help create an account of the change process, but for academic purposes the task typically includes the need to build an explanation of *why* the change process occurred in the way that it appears to have. The need to build a theoretical explanation adds another level of complexity. We continue to explore the Oticon case, but the same basic premise would hold for any other case study. Figure 15.3 illustrates three ways in which academically oriented explanations of the account might be developed.

Hence, for academic purposes, it is important to be clear about the explanatory device that you plan to employ. In addition, for an academic audience the questions in Figure 15.2 remain valid but are interpreted differently. The

Explanatory device	Consequences
Models (e.g. Kotter's eight-step model)	There are many models that describe how change can be understood and/or executed. One example of the use of models would be to explain the success or failure of a case study [say Oticon] by considering whether the advice of the model was followed or not. Hence, the involvement of large numbers of staff in the planning process might be seen as evidence that Kotter's requirement to build a coalition to deliver the change (step 2) was enacted.
Tools (e.g. the cultural web or market segmentation)	There are also many analytical tools that can be used to shed light on some aspect of the change process. A tool-oriented explanation would focus on the particular phenomenon that a tool highlights. For example, in building a cultural web for Oticon one might highlight the symbolic importance of the shredded paper passing through a perspex pipe in the staff canteen, or the ways in which power structures and organizational structures relate to one another in the pre- and post-spaghetti phases of the organization.
Theories e.g. Learning or dialogue	Many tools and models draw from broader bodies of theory. A third type of academic explanation might draw on such theories. For example, in the Oticon case one might argue that there are habitualized behaviours which occur (such as the creation of new project teams) or that the informality of the Spaghetti approach encouraged greater diversity in dialogic terms.

Figure 15.3 Three types of academic explanation

assessment of your explanation will rest on the quality of the argument that you build in academic terms. This introduces a new type of evidence – i.e. evidence of familiarity with appropriate academic material. Imagine a series of assignments that offer an account of the changes taking place at Oticon. The more successful submissions are likely to be factually accurate in relation to the firm, its markets and its performance outcomes. However, it is also important to be accurate in terms of the theoretical explanation that you build. Common mistakes that are seen in the marking process include:

- cherry-picking aspects of a model (e.g. Kotter's) in order to skip over the parts that do not fit with your case data;
- failing to locate tools and models in broader theoretical debates; and
- placing theoretical material alongside empirical material without making explicit connections between the two.

Since case material is rarely pre-packaged, the job of building a compelling explanation falls to you, the author of the account. It is important to be clear, concise and precise. If you think that a particular aspect of the change process you are describing fits with a model, tool or theory then make clear why you think this to be the case. In academic accounts, one form of evidence that is likely to find favour with the audience is referencing. By citing not only the source of the model, tool or theory that you are working with you make clear to the reader that you have acknowledged the work of those who originated the material you are using. In this book, the chapters conclude with a 'Who to read' section, which offer clues as to the names of significant voices in the academic community.

It is worth noting that an informal hierarchy exists in the academic world. Journal papers are judged at least in part on the basis of where they are published. Major journals, such as the *Academy of Management Journal, Academy of Management Review, Administrative Science Quarterly* and *Organization Science* (in the United States) and *Human Relations, Journal of Management Studies* and *Organization Studies* (in the European Union), are held in high regard because the review process tends to screen out all but the most carefully crafted work. Interesting work appears in many other places too, but one of the ways of gaining credibility in academic accounts is to demonstrate that you have been looking for work in prestigious peer-reviewed outlets such as these. If you are lucky enough to have access to academic databases it is relatively easy to find articles as well as where those articles have been cited in the literature. A search process of this sort helps narrow the focus of your reading. If you do not have access to e-journal type facilities, Google Scholar offers a powerful alternative that is free. Going back to source material, searching beyond core texts and researching those who have been critical of the work you are using all point towards good scholarship. Accordingly, consider counter-arguments, set out limitations to your analysis and – perhaps most important of all – remember to turn your critical attention to the assumptions built into the theory that you are working with.

All theory frames problems in particular ways, foregrounding some issues whilst downplaying others. High-quality academic explanations of change take the reader behind some of these tacit and messy issues. Most institutions operate with a marking scheme that suggests that the highest grades are reserved for submissions that are academically well grounded and theoretically insightful and from which the tutor learns something new. If you are undertaking an assignment as part of an academic course, look for the assignment instructions or brief. Be clear about issues such as word count, primary data and structure and pay at least as much attention to researching the academic material you plan to use as the empirical case that you select.

EXERCISE

Choose one of the cases from the book and undertake the following tasks.

(1) Construct a short plot summary (no more than seven steps) that summarizes the case.

(2) If you worked for the organization concerned, which organizational audiences might require an account of the change to be constructed?

(3) Consider at least one model, tool and theory that you could use to give an account of the change contained in your plot summary.

WHO TO READ

In thinking about the role that accounts of change play in the way that we make decisions, there are three people it might be worth reading more from. First, Steven Kerr's 'The folly of rewarding A, while hoping for B' makes thought-provoking reading (1975). Second, Karl Weick is most well known for his work on sense making, but his views on the role of theory and theorizing are relevant to the discussion in this chapter (see Weick, 1995). Finally, Andrew Brown's extensive work on narrative, identity and sense making offer a more contemporary take on the issues discussed in this chapter.

USEFUL WEBSITE

- www.scholar.google.com provides an excellent service that can help you find academic articles. More recent material is often copyright-protected by the publisher but a surprising amount of material is available to read at no cost.

REFERENCES

Brown, A. D., Stacey, P., and Nandhakumar, J. (2008) Making sense of sense-making narratives. *Human Relations*, 61(8): 1035–62.

Goffman, E. (1959) *The Presentation of Self in Everyday Life.* Garden City, NY: Doubleday Anchor.

Goffman, E. (1971) *Relations in Public: Microstudies of the Public Order.* New York: Basic Books.

Hendry, J., and Seidl, D. (2003) The structure and significance of strategic episodes: social systems theory and the routine practices of strategic change. *Journal of Management Studies,* 40(1): 175–96.

Kerr, S. (1975) The folly of rewarding A, while hoping for B. *Academy of Management Journal,* 18(4): 769–83.

Orburch, T. L. (1997) People's accounts count: the sociology of accounts. *Annual Review of Sociology,* 23: 455–78.

Scott, M. B., and Lymann, S. (1968) Accounts. *American Sociological Review,* 33(1): 46–62.

Weick, K. E. (1995) What theory is not, theorizing is. *Administrative Science Quarterly,* 40(3): 385–90.

16 The enquiry–action framework in practice

Introduction

In this concluding chapter we revisit the enquiry–action framework in the light of the ideas, techniques and cases that have been discussed. We explore how the framework can be used in leading and managing change and we consider how the separate practices of the framework can be integrated. The aims of the chapter are to:

- elucidate the practicalities of the enquiry–action framework;
- discuss the integration of practices;
- identify connections between the enquiry–action framework and the theories of change introduced earlier in the book; and
- explore implications for the nature of leading and managing change.

Fineman, Sims and Gabriel (2005) introduce the metaphor of a river as a way of thinking about organizations, or, rather, the set of practices that constitute organizing. This relates to a perspective on organizations as being in flux (Chia, 1995) as actors act, interact and react within a socio-economic climate that is typically changeable. In some senses, this may appear to be unsettling. In this way of thinking we never reach the 'refreezing' part of Kurt Lewin's (1947) model of change (unfreeze, change, refreeze), and hence there is never a finished conclusion or a point at which we can objectively say that a change was a success or a failure. Although this might be disconcerting, we see it as being of more practical help than a traditional way of thinking of organizations as objects, machines or closed systems (Marshak, 2009). There is constant motion but at the same time an identity and a set of meanings that are conserved over time. Viewed by a swimmer in the river, it is a place of constant change. Viewed by a cartographer on a series of maps drawn over time, it is an incrementally changing feature of the landscape. Hence, it is not only that there is a core of organizing practices that remain the same over time and a periphery that changes. Rather, what changes, what is core and how these ideas are interpreted will vary from different perspectives (Tsoukas and Chia, 2002). For example, in the Oticon case one can ask whether manufacturing hearing aids is the company's core or if the core as experienced by designers is a combination of innovation, speed and hearing aids – that is, the core might reflect the values introduced by the CEO Lars Kolind. However, one might equally argue that part of the reason for Kolind's success is that he did not introduce new values but recognized and 'gave flight' to values that already existed in the company. What might be significant 'big scale' change for some (Burnes, 2009) might be relatively modest re-emphasizing for others. The questions for a change manager are to be able to judge where and when to intervene and how to do so in a way that is productive.

As will be recognized from the cases we have explored, 'managing' change does not imply 'controlling' it. Rather, there is a set of practices that need to be reflexively balanced. Practices include:

- directing;
- coaching;
- stimulating; and
- enabling.

Directing

If we thought of directing as a form of autocratic leadership then its use in change management would be limited. There are times when autocratic instruction from the top of the organization can work. Sometimes it is thought that such an approach works in times of crisis, although it can fail even then if people are not sufficiently coordinated to respond effectively to instruction. Wendell French and Cecil Bell (1984) identify three strategies for change: empirical-rational strategies, in which it is thought that people will change what they do if the desired behaviours are associated with rewards they desire; normative-re-educative strategies, in which it is assumed that people will give up their old ways of thinking and acting once they are educated in the benefits of the new way of doing things; and power-coercive strategies, in which legitimate authority, or another form of power, is used to get those with less power to comply. Proponents of organization development such as French and Bell regard the power-coercive approach as problematic and as, at best, a last resort. However, all these strategies entail direction, in the sense that the plan for change is devised at a senior level and these intentions are then put into action. Ian Palmer, Richard Dunford and Gib Akin (2006) point out a significant problem with this, which is the issue of unintended outcomes. Unintended outcomes can occur internally due to politics, the 'drag' of past practices that people are attached to or a conflict of values. These can result in people complying with instructions but carrying them out in such a way as to lead to a different outcome. For example, customer service staff who are given a new script to encourage customers to purchase more might deliver it in such a way that customers feel less inclined to buy. External influences that lead to unintended outcomes include the full variety of factors that impinge on performance. For instance, competitors could react to a reduction in price by reducing theirs even further, thus producing a 'pricing war' and an unprofitable situation for everyone. Achieving too much dominance in a market can lead to macro political pressure or even legislation (for example, by monopolies controls), or customers deserting the brand for other niche brands that are perceived to be 'cooler'. Such internal and external forces can be more powerful than the influence that change managers wield, and hence even the best of intentions can go awry. At best, a controlling form of direction may produce conformity, but it is less associated with positive psychological contracts and employees being committed to a change.

However, there is a form of direction that can still be useful in managing change. Its uses include confidence giving, coordination and conflict resolution. Directing may not dictate exactly what will be done but, especially when goals have been agreed through involvement or dialogue, the setting of boundaries from a position of authority can be very functional. This means that, once the orientation of change has been agreed, direction can be used to make sure that people consciously remember what has been agreed, that the message is consistent enough to enable action and that actions that are destructive for the community trying to build change are recognized and checked. Such actions can be deliberate, but it is a common experience that people with good intentions can produce unintended outcomes and not realize until it is too late. Equally, when people do not follow through with agreements it is important to have an authority source that will give others confidence that the agreement will be reinforced and enforced where necessary. Trying to achieve this through the issuing of orders may be problematic, but asking 'How does that take us towards our agreed goal?' in a setting in which people can change their behaviour without losing face can enable them to re-enter the change process in a more positive way. This form of intervention can help with conflict resolution, but, ultimately, if someone is behaving unreasonably and destructively towards others, it may be necessary to remove him or her so that others are not disadvantaged by his or her behaviour.

Coaching

Coaching entails a combination of task (Whitmore, 2009) and person (Mearns and Thorne, 2007) foci. The task focus can entail elements of instruction, demonstra-tion and guidance in getting the person or group carrying the change forward to see how to do things differently. Depending on the task, demonstration can take different forms. For example, in a hands-on task it can entail the change manager or another skilled person doing the task whilst others observe, then gradually taking a back seat as the others try it out and gain skill and confidence. This can have the effect of the role modelling that was discussed as an important part of culture change in Chapter 6. For example, in the Island Opera case, Simon the conductor could have role-modelled for Jeremy the director to help improve his assertiveness and interaction skills by acting assertively in the difficult meetings but then subtly handing back authority to Jeremy and supporting him when necessary. Instead, Simon took over from Jeremy, and the effect was to usurp what authority he had. Hence, Jeremy's learning is negative and his confidence to take a leadership role next time is reduced. This can be contrasted with the action of the leaders in the ITS Canada case. Although they failed to role-model the change initially, after feedback they very visibly acted as they wanted others to do.

An alternative is to use a case study or external benchmark as a model. This can work effectively when the task is less hands-on and more cognitive or symbolic. In such cases, the intention is almost never merely to copy the example. In part this is because, however similar the focal organization and the benchmark case may appear to be, there will always be differences that need to be taken into account, even if it is only the fact that someone else who has already carried out the change is considered, and so the focal organization will not be the 'prime mover'. Cases and examples are better used to facilitate reflection and enable people to develop their own solutions. This has the advantage of greater buy-in, because, even when people's innovations are rather derivative, if they feel they have invented it themselves they are likely to be more motivated towards implementation. For instance, the Oticon case could be used not as a prescription of best practice when it comes to restructuring the organization but as a way of thinking that can be challenged and adapted. The essence of good coaching is that the people who are carrying out the change are active in this way and that they therefore become independent of the coach. Task-focused coaching goes beyond demonstration and entails feedback and reinforcement so that the learners know how they are doing and are motivated to keep changing.

Coaching also involves the ability to understand the social and psychological position of the person carrying out the change. What people hear relates to their psychological readiness to hear the message. For example, whilst in coaching mode a change manager may demonstrate a skill or an idea that comes across to one person as a useful example and to another as a criticism of what he or she has been doing. In Chapter 13 we considered the roles of narrative (Gabriel, 2000) and interaction (Berne, 1964) analysis in understanding how others can interpret the words and action of the change manager. In the NSC Finance mini-case, discussed in Chapter 13, it can be seen that the peons are in a tragic narrative and that any implied criticism is likely to be over-internalized and to stymie action (MacIntosh and Beech, 2011). However, for the self-styled 'saviours', criticism is likely to be dismissed from a superior, critical parent position, from which they portray themselves as blameless. Indeed, a criticism by managers would probably be taken by the 'saviours' as (further) evidence that the managers did not know what they were talking about, which has the effect of transferring the criticism away from the self and thereby preserving their sense of identity (Coupland, 2001). Therefore, the change manager has to make a judgement about when and where to introduce coaching demonstration and advice that fits in with people's self-identity, narrative position and transactional script position, and when to disrupt or gently challenge their self-positioning. As was discussed in Chapters 8 and 13, not only is this cognitive but it can have significant emotional content too, and this can have the effect of amplifying reactions, interpretations and (mis) readings of intentions.

Stimulating

Stimulating is about actively encouraging and motivating those who will change but exercising some restraint concerning the precise direction of the change. Unlike directing and coaching, for which there are clearer goals and stronger views on what would constitute a successful outcome, the practices of stimulating change give greater freedom of self-direction to those who change. This style of intervention can be based on what David Cooperrider, Diana Whitney and Jacqueline Stavros (2007) term 'appreciative inquiry'. Appreciative inquiry is seen as being part of a new paradigm of organizational change (Fuller, Griffin and Ludema, 2000). The old paradigm is seen as being focused on problem solving. In this perspective, changes are responses to problems, threats or gaps that need to be confronted. Analysis is concerned with understanding the causes of the problem, and action is aimed at eliminating it. Appreciative inquiry seeks to take a more positive alternative. The first step for Connie Fuller, Thomas Griffin and James Ludema is discovering the best of current practice. The next stage is to envisage how the future could be if this practice was generalized, and to build up the positive knowledge. Third comes the step of designing what changes should take place, and this is often carried out through collective dialogue. Lastly, the practices are spread to new areas of application and sustained. Whether or not this is a genuinely different paradigm is a moot point, but the process of stimulating change by seeking positive examples within the organization, giving them public recognition and overtly building action on this basis is a good way of either keeping or turning the psychological contract on a generative track (Conway and Briner, 2005).

Stimulation can also work in quite a different way in change management. Sometimes it can be a process of providing a catalyst rather than discovering a practice that can be rolled out. Rick Delbridge, Lynda Gratton and Gerry Johnson (2007) develop the idea of 'best' practices, recognizing that, empirically, the idea of imitating what a successful organization has done is highly problematic. In many cases, if not the majority, such efforts do not result in the duplication of success, and in some instances the adoption of best practices can make things worse. This can be because of a lack of fit with the new organizational context or because of a diminished psychological contract whereby workers feel that their best efforts have been ignored or supplanted from the top down. Delbridge, Gratton and Johnson argue that it might be better to think of 'promising practices' rather than best practice. The idea is that what has worked in one organization might not transfer unadulterated into new settings, but that, by examining it and adapting it, it is possible to redevelop the promise of the practice into a new form of implemented practice.

This approach can be linked to 'practical authorship' (Cunliffe, 2001), which was introduced in Chapter 14. The idea of practical authorship is that, through reflexivity, managers can 'rewrite the text' of practice, partly by retrospective sense making and partly by prospective acting into a new way of doing things. Recognizing the alternative interpretations of what has happened is, for Cunliffe, key to being able to recognize change in the self and hence to act differently. Therefore, with promising practices, the process can be one of treating them as a way of stimulating retrospection on one's own practice and enactment of new practice. In some cases the new practices might be a close approximation of the promising practice. In others the new practice might be quite different, either deliberately, when the manager-as-author seeks to write a new version of the practice, or unintentionally, when the manager seeks to emulate the promising practice but does so in an inaccurate way that can nonetheless be productive. For example, in the ITS Canada case there are some benefits from the inaccurate imitation of Silicon Valley operations, which, if they had been done at 'full strength', would have resulted in a high degree of discomfort and poor cultural fit. By contrast, the adapted version they ended up with worked better for their own circumstances.

Enabling

Palmer, Dunford and Akin (2006) suggest that some change management practices entail being an interpreter. This idea draws on the work of Weick (2000), who developed the sense-making approach to organizing. Weick, like Haridimos Tsoukas and Robert Chia (2002) and Fineman, Sims and Gabriel (2005), sees change as the normal condition of organizing practices. Given this perspective, he argues that the Lewin (1947) model of unfreeze, change, refreeze has a built-in assumption of inertia that is inappropriate in many situations. (To be fair to Lewin, we should note that his own understanding of the flows and processes of change was rather more nuanced and developed than the simple statement of the model might suggest.) However, Weick's concept is helpful when we are considering change practices of enabling. If we see organizations as flows of changeful activities then the first thing to do is *freeze*, not unfreeze. This allows people in the situation to see what is occurring and how things are adapting and changing incrementally. The second action is to *rebalance*, which is concerned with spotting and removing blockages that get in the way of the ongoing adaptive processes. The last stage is to *unfreeze*, so that further emergent and improvisational change is enabled.

As ways of enabling change to be enacted by others, either Lewin's model or Weick's can work depending on the culture and circumstances. For people who feel that they have been stuck in a way of doing things that they want to change, Lewin might be particularly helpful. Thus, for example, in the Oticon and ITS Canada cases the change managers could enable the process by getting people to unfreeze the old way of doing things, encouraging them to work through the changes and then reinforce or refreeze new behaviours that were devised. On the other hand, the constancy of change that is evident in the Admiral Insurance case might mean that, at some points as they grow, there would be value in the change managers enabling reflective change by adopting Weick's *freeze, rebalance, unfreeze* approach. Jean Helms Mills (2003) studied Nova Scotia Power in Canada and found that extensive sense making was carried out in the company as it went through a protracted sequence of changes (including privatization, downsizing, re-engineering and the creation of strategic business units). The sense making related to Weick's model and was crucial for allowing competing voices to be heard and for multiple interpretations to be explored as large-scale programmed change ran alongside (and through) emergent and incremental change.

Mentoring was discussed in Chapter 12, and this is an appropriate way to think about enabling practices. Mentoring is much less directive than coaching, as it does not entail giving direction or demonstrating. Rather, it is a process of helping mentees develop their practice by supporting them in reflecting upon it. This is commensurate with Cunliffe's (2001) dialogical approach, in which mentees come to understand themselves differently through questioning who they were being when they were acting and how they were seen by others. For example, they might see themselves as skilled speakers who can gave a motivational talk, and others might or might not agree. Either way, critical reflexivity can help, as understanding divergent views can help improve self-presentation or alter self-image, and understanding convergent views can help in seeing *why* a practice has worked and how it might be applied in the future. When managing others going through change a mentorship attitude can help, as it focuses on the person and supports him or her in developing a way forward. Weick's model can be helpful in this regard, as it is a way of pausing in the midst of the change and considering how things are going and how to progress. In some cases this might be done literally, and the change manager acts as a mentor. In other cases, particularly when there are a large number of people, it might be that processes such as question and review sessions are planned to enable people to reflect. Alternatively, the change manager might train others to become mentors and so support a broader population.

Enabling can also mean the change manager (typically in a senior position) helping to set the context, giving clear backing so that the need for change is less disputed, providing resources and removing barriers or blockages to change. In addition, there will often be a need to have resources allocated, and it is desirable to be able to reward the outcomes of efforts to change. These aspects of enabling relate to positioning, the skills of influencing and the use of authority/power that were discussed in Chapter 5 on stakeholders and positioning. Quite often the role

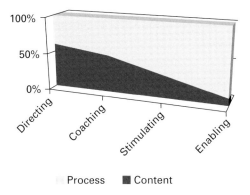

Process   ■ Content

Figure 16.1 The process/content balance in change management practices

of senior managers who are supporting a change process is to 'clear the space' for the change to happen, and this form of enabling can involve them in keeping other priorities and pressures away from those enacting the change.

These four practices can be seen as varying along a scale of the balance between content and process intervention. Content is what the change is meant to be – for example a change in structure, culture, relationships with customers or competitors and so on. Process covers the forms of engagement that are designed to produce change, including styles of interaction and dialogue, learning, aligning people and tasks and developing evidence to persuade others. The balance between content and process is illustrated in Figure 16.1. As the job is managing change rather than doing it, even directing is only about 60 per cent content and 40 per cent process. This is because, whilst it is important that when directing is used it moves in the right direction (content), a significant part of directing is the way that conflicts are resolved and confidence is inspired (process). Coaching as a style of managing change involves a fair amount of content because there is an idea of how things should be done differently, but process is equally important, because it only really works if the person doing the change understands and is confident and inspired. Hence, in coaching, content and process might be roughly 50/50. When stimulating change, the change manager has less content in mind and there is active awareness that innovation can and should happen by the actions and thoughts of others. Therefore, there is a bigger focus on process than content, but content should still meet the agreed objectives. Enabling is principally about process and minimally about content (90/10 in the illustration), because the aspiration is that the managerial activity is mainly about inspiring content production by others and supporting it. The balances are notional and all the practices involve both content and process, and, ultimately, the proportion is down to the judgement of the change manager.

The enquiry–action framework

In this book we have set out to develop and explore the enquiry–action framework for change. It has three focal activity areas, as illustrated in Figure 16.2. These are diagnosing, enacting and explaining.

Diagnosing activities include judging the balance between ambiguity and clarity. There is a need for sufficient clarity, so as to enable people to interpret symbols and make sense of what they should be doing. However, it is neither possible nor desirable to entirely eliminate ambiguity. Even the most carefully expressed vision is susceptible to reinterpretation, and what is needed is for those who are enacting change to be able to have a vision that works for them locally. As a result, the ability to fit within an overall agenda but allow local variation that renders the change plan meaningful is the desirable situation. Change is normally preferable when it produces vitality in the organization on the basis of an engaged process. Chapter 4 provided a diagnostic on these dimensions of the organization and suggested implications for change. It is unusual for change not to have a political dimension, and in Chapter 5 we explored how to map stakeholders, think through their dynamics and understand the organization's position. Lastly, in order

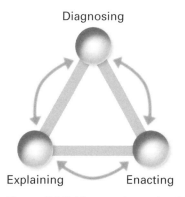

Figure 16.2 The enquiry–action framework

to understand the internal context of change, it is necessary to understand the culture and its degree of fit with the purpose of change. Changing culture is a complex and longitudinal process and so it is important to judge whether or not this should be embarked upon or whether it would be sensible to work with the current culture, seeking to make only minor modifications.

Enacting change entails the building up of a repertoire of options for action. A common approach is to change structure (see, for example, the ABB and Oticon cases). The structure of an organization performs various functions, and we discussed the balances that need to be struck to achieve flexibility, the management of interconnections, levels of diversity and processes of coordination. It is rarely worth changing the structure in the belief that this will produce a shift in performance. It is far better to understand what the structure is doing and how it could be reorganized in order to allow the organization to achieve something different. Change often impacts on people's identities. Work provides an important aspect of meaning in people's lives and hence they undertake identity work in order to preserve a sense of self. Introducing change can either support a positive sense of self or be an attack upon it. Therefore, when managing change, we should expect strong and emotional reactions (both positive and negative) when there are implications for what people see themselves as being. Enacting change can focus upon external relations with customers and competitors. There are consequences to the customers one chooses, and this has an impact not only on marketing but also on operations and strategy. Changing processes is central to many organizational changes. These changes can focus on increasing efficiency, cutting costs or increasing quality, and process change was discussed in Chapter 10. In order to achieve these changes it is necessary to have the right workforce oriented in the right direction, and this is the topic addressed in Chapter 11 on aligning people and tasks. Most change entails people doing things differently, and quite often thinking differently. These changes mean that learning and development are necessary, and we discussed how these can be achieved for matters of insight and technique in Chapter 12. Lastly, in this section we have discussed the implications of interaction, narration and dialogue in order to understand how people communicate and make sense of change, and what the change manager's role might be in this set of processes.

Managing change entails being able to explain it effectively. There is a need to communicate with different stakeholders, often at short notice and in a compelling fashion. We discussed how this might be done for internal and external stakeholders, and for students we explored what assignments might demand, and why.

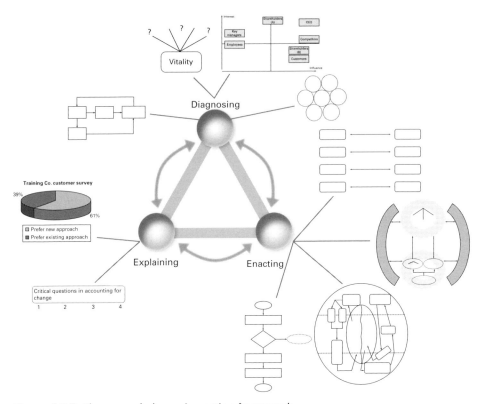

Figure 16.3 The expanded enquiry–action framework

Accordingly, the enquiry–action framework incorporates a number of options for each of the focal activities, as illustrated in Figure 16.3. The focal activities are strongly interconnected, and the four practices of change managers discussed above – directing, coaching, stimulating and enabling – occur in each of the activity foci. Diagnosing by setting goals, mapping stakeholders or analysing the culture can either be carried out with a degree of direction on the content from the managers or be achieved through an enabled process in which the managers are supporting others to do the analysis. Similarly, enacting the change through structure, identity work, competitive and market positioning, process change, personnel alignment, learning and development and dialogue can be achieved through the coordination and support of direction or the processsual facilitation of enablement. Equally, explaining can be a one-way reporting process or a dialogue and polyphonic account of what has and should happen. It is not that there is a single right way of proceeding. Rather, there are a series of professional choices as to how these activities are conducted. The choices are cumulative, and the change manager will be judged, in part, by his or her consistency and transparency in decision making. Such choices ultimately become the style of the manager, and the style can be developed through reflexive dialogue and the practices of practical authorship discussed in Chapter 14.

The focal activities are also linked in that practice in one area can also constitute practice in another. When choosing which form of diagnosis to use and which questions to ask, one is thereby forming the basis for explanation. In addition, the way that diagnoses are performed can be part of the enactment of the change. For example, vitality can be explored in a way that enhances it through open involvement and dialogue. Similarly, a stakeholder analysis can be performed in such a way as to increase competitive feelings or to develop collaboration between the parties.

Enacting change is an act of symbolism. The way that one acts in a culture is as important as what one says, and therefore one way of explaining the change is to enact it. This allows people to interpret the evidence as they see it, and this can have a long-lasting impact (see, for example, ITS Canada and Admiral Insurance). Similarly, through enacting a change one comes to realize even more effectively what the situation is like and what it would mean to achieve a changed outcome. Hence, enactment can be both part of the explanation and the diagnosis.

Explaining change is not just a communication of results; it is a process of sense making. To paraphrase Weick (1995), 'How do I know what I think until I hear myself say it?' At a minimal level, as people explain their position to others they are forced to think it through, and this can be very helpful in clarifying their own thoughts. In addition, dialogue and feedback can lead to the understanding expanding to incorporate multiple perspectives. Recognizing how others respond can be enhanced by a conceptualization of interaction and narrative analysis. Hence, explaining can be part of diagnosis, and it is also central to enactment by achieving understanding and commitment, and in being open to changing oneself as a result of feedback.

For many managers, change can present both telling opportunities and all-consuming challenges. Personal change, programmed and incremental change and ad hoc change often all occur simultaneously. Rarely is there the luxury of generous time and resource to manage the change, and therefore there is a need for an approach that incorporates reflexivity and complexity as part of taking timely action. Following a 'recipe' for change is unlikely to be satisfactory, because it will not be sufficiently innovative. We believe that being equipped with a set of useful questions, alternative ways of answering them and a framework to aid professional judgement is a more productive approach, and it is our hope that the enquiry–action framework will be helpful in this regard.

USEFUL WEBSITES

- www.aimresearch.org provides reports and podcasts on the latest management research.
- www.aimpractice.com provides management tools and techniques derived from research findings.

REFERENCES

Berne, E. (1964) *Games People Play: The Psychology of Human Relationships*. New York: Grove Press.

Burnes, B. (2009) *Managing Change*, 5th edn. Harlow: Pearson.

Chia, R. (1995) From modern to postmodern organizational analysis. *Organization Studies*, 16(4): 579–604.

Conway, N., and Briner, R. B. (2005) *Understanding Psychological Contracts at Work: A Critical Evaluation of Theory and Research*. Oxford University Press.

Cooperrider, D., Whitney, D., and Stavros, J. (2007) *Appreciative Inquiry Handbook*. San Francisco: Berrett-Koehler.

Coupland, C. (2001) Accounting for change: a discourse analysis of graduate trainees' talk of adjustment. *Journal of Management Studies*, 38(8): 1103–19.

Cunliffe, A. (2001) Managers as practical authors: reconstructing our understanding of management practice. *Journal of Management Studies*, 38(3): 351–71.

Delbridge, R., Gratton, L., and Johnson, G. (eds.) (2007) *The Exceptional Manager: Making the Difference*. Oxford University Press.

Fineman, S., Sims, D., and Gabriel, Y. (2005) *Organizing and Organizations*, 3rd edn. London: Sage.

Gabriel, Y. (2000) *Storytelling in Organizations: Facts, Fictions, Fantasies*. Oxford University Press.

French, W. L., and Bell, C. H. (1984) *Organization Development: Behavioral Science Interventions for Organizational Improvement*. Englewood Cliffs, NJ: Prentice Hall.

Fuller, C., Griffin, T., and Ludema, J. D. (2000) Appreciative future search: involving the whole system in positive organization change. *Organization Development Journal*, 18(2): 29–41.

Helms Mills, J. M. (2003) *Making Sense of Organizational Change*. London: Routledge.

Lewin, K. (1947) Frontiers in group dynamics. *Human Relations*, 1(1): 5–41.

MacIntosh, R., and Beech, N. (2011) Strategy, strategists and fantasy: a dialogic constructionist perspective. *Accounting, Auditing and Accountability Journal*, 24(1): 15–37.

Marshak, R. (2009) *Organizational Change: Views from the Edge*. Bethel, ME: Lewin Center.

Mearns, D., and Thorne, B. (2007) *Person-Centred Counselling in Action*, 3rd edn. London: Sage.

Palmer, I., Dunford, R., and Akin, G. (2006) *Managing Organizational Change: A Multiple Perspectives Approach*. Boston: McGraw-Hill/Irwin.

Tsoukas, H., and Chia, R. (2002) On organizational becoming: rethinking organizational change. *Organization Science*, 13(5): 567–82.

Weick, K. E. (1995) *Sensemaking in Organizations*. Thousand Oaks, CA: Sage.

Weick, K. E. (2000) Emergent change as a universal in organizations, in Beer, M., and Nohria, N. (eds.) *Breaking the Code of Change*: 223–41. Boston: Harvard Business School Press.

Whitmore, J. (2009) *Coaching for Performance: Growing Human Potential and Purpose – the Principles and Practice of Coaching and Leadership*, 4th edn. London: Nicholas Brealey Publishing.

PART E
Extended Cases

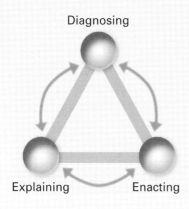

Diagnosing

Explaining   Enacting

In this part we present nine extended cases. As noted in Chapter 1, these extended cases cover a range of public and private sector settings as well as varying sectors, technologies and time frames. Some of the cases are anonymized accounts drawn from our own research with those organizations. The data in these anonymized cases are typically drawn from a wealth of material gathered over longitudinal research engagements. We have also worked closely with a number of the named organizations, but we have drawn only on publicly available sources in order to make it easier to gather further details if desired. Some of the cases (e.g. ABB, Admiral and Oticon) present an overview of the organization from foundation to the present day, and, again, this was a deliberate choice to offset the tendency in some cases to focus on isolated episodes. Viewing change against a longer time frame helps ground any analysis in a sense of where the organization is coming from and heading towards.

The extended cases are included for a number of reasons. First, they offer opportunities to use the various tools, techniques and frameworks presented earlier in the book. We have used each of these extended cases ourselves in various classroom settings, and each has been developed and refined for use with the analytical approach we have set out. Second, the extended cases might offer a useful starting point for group work or coursework when there is a need to choose an organization and offer an analysis of the change process within that organization. In particular, there is a wealth of further data available on each of the named organizations, which means that they all offer ideal candidates for further analysis. Finally, the extended cases present an opportunity to provoke a reflexively oriented conversation based around how you would have handled similar circumstances and choices, and the similarities/differences from your own organizational settings or experiences.

1 ABB

In the late 1980s Percy Barnevik was CEO of Swedish firm ASEA, an engineering firm employing some 71,000 staff globally. He had overseen a dramatic improvement in ASEA's performance, quadrupling sales and increasing profits by a factor of ten. By 1988 he was looking for ways to continue the growth of the firm, and he led ASEA into a merger with a larger Swiss firm, Brown Boveri, which employed around 97,000 staff. At the age of forty-six Barnevik became the first CEO of the newly merged firm ASEA Brown Boveri, or simply ABB, with a combined staff of some 160,000 people operating in 140 countries and combined sales of $15 billion. From the moment it was formed, ABB became a major player in the global engineering and technology sector.

Barnevik had big plans for the new firm, and within months of taking office as ABB's CEO he held a gathering of a few hundred senior ABB managers to set out his vision for the future. He introduced what he called the 'corporate policy bible', which included details of the firm's approach to change. He described the firm's strategy at that point as being 'a two-stage rocket: restructuring then growth' (Barham and Heimer, 1998). Over the next few years he delivered both restructuring and spectacular growth. Although he was not a native English speaker, Barnevik insisted that English had to be ABB's corporate language, and he created a new corporate identity for ABB to deliver his strategy. He focused hard on making a huge corporate organization feel like a much smaller one, citing his early experiences in his father's small business, which had employed only fifteen people. His mantra was to create small, customer-facing business units in which the entrepreneurial flair of staff could be released. Decentralizing and individual accountability through distinct and separate profit centres were the order of the day. What followed was a period of tremendous change in the organization.

ABB undertook 150 acquisitions in the six years that followed its formation, with forty in 1988 alone. In the year that two large, complex and independent firms were merged, new organizational elements were added at a rate of almost one per week. This pace did not let up, and ABB grew to employ some 215,000 staff worldwide. These staff were employed in almost 5,000 separate profit centres[1] as ABB tried to find ways of being both a global player and a localized, entrepreneurial firm. This was not entirely pain-free, with 90 per cent of all staff above the level of the operating companies being removed. This meant that ABB had a relatively small corporate centre running a vast network of firms. Barnevik described the change process as operating on what he called a 30 per cent rule. When a new firm was added to the ABB portfolio, 30 per cent of the headquarters staff left the business, another 30 per cent were moved on to new roles in other ABB companies and a further 30 per cent were 'spun out' to create new profit centres. In breaking up the organization using his 30 per cent rule, Barnevik felt that the 10 per cent who were left would get on with the business of running what was left of the acquired business. The growth strategy took ABB into new territories, notably the United States, China and India, as well as new areas of work, including contracting, financial services and reinsurance.

Barnevik was aware that he was managing a very complex organization but he used a global matrix structure to resolve three key contradictions. First, the firm was trying to be both global and local. Second, the firm felt both big and small, with well over 200,000 staff operating in semi-autonomous groups of thirty to fifty individuals. Third, ABB was decentralized, with decision making happening at local levels, yet operated a highly centralized approach to strategy, integration, standardization, etc. ABB was heralded by many commentators and scholars for its approach to the management and development of its organization. Tom Peters, the American author and management guru, often cited ABB as a great example precisely because it was not an advertising agency or a software firm. Rather, he argued, ABB showed that new ways of managing were possible in old industries, with longer culture histories.

In 1997, after eight years as CEO, Barnevik moved to become chairman and handed executive responsibility to Goran Lindahl, who had worked alongside

---

[1] A profit centre would employ between thirty and fifty staff. The 5,000 profit centres were spread across 1,300 operating companies. Despite this complexity, ABB's headquarters employed only 150 people.

ABB   221

Barnevik since the formation of ABB. The transition did not go smoothly, with net income falling by 54 per cent in 1997 (see Table C1.1). ABB was hit hard by the Asian financial crisis, which occurred around that time, and the order book suffered, with profits decreasing. Lindahl cut 13,000 jobs in an effort to secure ABB's future stability, and he was eventually replaced by Jörgen Centreman, then head of ABB's automation business. Centreman had a vision of ABB as a solutions-oriented business with a greater emphasis on information technology (IT) and services. He created 200 strategic accounts to try and manage key customers in an integrated way, as many operating companies might interface with the same customers. During his tenure Centreman faced major liabilities from asbestos claims that could be traced back to the acquisition of a US power generation firm (CE) in 1989. These liabilities led ABB to report its first ever loss, of $691 million, in 2001.

In 2002 Centreman was replaced as CEO by Jürgen Dormann, who was ABB's chairman at the time. Dormann led a series of initiatives to simplify ABB's structure. These included divesting a number of businesses that he perceived did not fit with ABB's core business. Financial services, reinsurance and petro-chemicals were removed and ABB was reconfigured around two new divisions: power technologies and automation. R&D investments in these core business areas were reprioritized, yet the firm still faced difficulties. Barnevik and Lindahl were both widely criticized when it became public knowledge that they had left with a combined retirement pot of $136 million. Further difficul-ties emerged in the form of fines for bribery in some operating companies that had been doing business in Angola, Kazakhstan and Nigeria between 1998 and 2003. ABB had a total debt of $4.4 billion and reported a net loss of $767 million in 2003, caused partly by weak industrial demand. Dormann reduced the work-force to some 100,000 globally as part of a cost-cutting drive that he hoped would stabilize the firm.

In 2005 Fred Kindle, a former McKinsey consultant, was appointed as ABB's fifth CEO. One of his first moves was to settle ongoing asbestos claims that were a source of continuing uncertainty for ABB and its key stakeholders. The settlement figure ($1.4 billion) was a significant sum, but it allowed the firm to move forward. He focused attention on reducing annual corporate costs from $507 million to $450 million by the end of the year and continued the process of divesting non-core businesses. He argued that all firms needed to deal with strategy, execution and people but that ABB had not been paying sufficient attention to execution, which 'cannot be delegated, takes diligence, patience, persistence and hard work' (Zalan, 2007: 12). Kindle started to change the culture of ABB, trying to ensure that

Table C1.1 ABB's financial performance, 1988–2010

Year	Orders received ($ millions)	Net income ($ millions)	Return on equity (%)	Employees
1988	17,822	386	12.5	169,459
1989	21,640	589	16.8	189,493
1990	29,281	590	14.5	215,154
1991	29,621	609	13.9	214,399
1992	31,634	505	11.8	213,407
1993	29,406	68	1.8	206,490
1994	31,794	760	20.2	207,557
1995	36,224	1,315	28.4	209,637
1996	36,349	1,233	22.2	214,894
1997	34,803	572	10.3	213,057
1998	31,462	1,305	23.2	199,232
1999	25,379	1,614	27.9	164,154
2000	25,440	1,443	30.6	160,818
2001	23,726	-691	-19.2	156,865
2002	18,112	-783	-52.4	139,051
2003	18,703	-767	-38.0	116,464
2004	21,689	-35	-1.2	102,537
2005	23,194	735	21.1	104,000
2006	28,401	1,390	24.2	108,000
2007	34,348	3,757	34.6	112,000
2008	38,282	3,118	28.7	120,000
2009	30,969	2,901	21.7	116,000
2010	32,681	2,561	17.2	116,500

Notes: All figures are sourced from ABB annual reports. However, from 2006 onwards ABB's annual reports do not specify return on equity, so from 2006 to 2010 these figures are taken from the Amadeus database.

ABB   223

decisions were no longer made at headquarters in Switzerland. Instead, he stressed the importance of teamwork and the need for active participation from all those involved. New structures were introduced that set clearer job responsibilities, and a share participation programme began to boost the morale of the workforce. Kindle was credited with turning ABB around, and the firm began to report its best quarterly results for many years. However, he was clear that he did not foresee any major acquisitions in the near future. 'Any larger deals will have to wait at least 18 months, for we are in stabilization mode right now' (*The Hindu*, 2004). Kindle continued to focus efforts on organic growth and driving profitability from the order book through to ABB's bottom line.

Kindle continued on an upward trajectory until, in February 2008, he left the business unexpectedly. Commentators at the time suggested that he had clashed with other board members over strategy. These 'irreconcilable differences' (Buckley, 2008) were said to have created substantial uncertainty over the ABB group of companies. The disagreement centred on ABB's strategy for mergers and acquisitions. One stock market analyst commented that 'Fred Kindle [was] probably the most successful CEO in ABB's history and for him to resign during ABB's most successful trading period will be a shock to the markets' (Buckley, 2008). The organization had a history of growth by acquisition, bringing significant gains. However, the acquisition spree had also been the root of two significant problems that had plagued successive CEOs. First, the acquisitions had led to challenges when defining ABB's core business, and therefore its corporate identity. Second, the asbestos liabilities that had threatened the firm's viability began in acquired businesses. Shares fell sharply on Kindle's departure.

Michel Demare, the then chief financial officer (CFO), became interim CEO, and he was quoted saying that 'we don't have to buy something because we are not growing enough. We are growing at 20% per year organically. It is simply a question of how best to make use of our cash' (Buckley, 2008). Kindle's permanent replacement, Joe Hogan, undertook a major acquisition when ABB bought Ventyx, which he described as 'an acquisition [that is] in line with ABB's strategy to pursue growth opportunities that complement the company's product, technology and geographical portfolio' (ABB, 2010).

The firm that Barnevik had created might be regarded as having come full circle, back to a strategy, culture and mode of operating that had restructuring and growth at its heart.

USEFUL WEBSITES

- www.abb.com: ABB's website.
- www.ft.com: *Financial Times*.

REFERENCES

ABB (2010) ABB acquires Ventyx to strengthen its network management business. ABB press release, 5 May (available at www.abb.com).

Barham, K., and Heimer, C. (1998) *ABB, the Dancing Giant: Creating the Globally Connected Corporation*. London: Financial Times/Pitman Publishing.

Buckley, C. (2008) ABB chief Fred Kindle exits over strategy clash. *The Times*, 13 February.

The Hindu (2004) ABB sees India in the thick of 'Asian century'. www.thehindu.com, 23 November.

Zalan, T. (2007) Rebuilding ABB, Case Study no. 3-1797. International Institute for Management Development, Lausanne.

2   ITS Canada

ITS Canada was formed as a spin-off from a major international bank. It was formed with a group of forty-three bank employees who transferred to the new company. ITS Canada was wholly owned by the bank but operated separately. At the outset the aim of those who transferred to the new organization was to create a different way of working. In the bank they had been providers of information technology and communications systems dealing with both installation and support. The initial plan was to continue to provide this service whilst developing new revenue streams by offering similar services to other external clients. In the geographical region where ITS Canada was situated there was a preponderance of small and medium-sized enterprises (SMEs), many of which lacked internal IT departments, and the business plan included targeting SMEs as potential clients.

ITS Canada was founded with a senior management team of three, whose responsibilities included strategic leadership, business development and client relations. The rest of the staff worked in a relatively flat structure in which work groups were to be arranged around specific projects. The staff were highly trained, with most being graduates, and the more senior staff had considerable professional experience. In addition, most staff had spent the majority of their career to date in the IT department of the bank.

The senior management team of ITS Canada aspired to develop a company with a 'creative buzz' and an 'egalitarian, can-do approach'. This was in stark contrast to the bank culture in the parent organization they had come from, in which formality was recognizable in symbols ranging from committee structures to clear hierarchies and dress codes. Car parking was also a significant symbol. The bank had a large headquarters building, which was a noticeable distance from the nearest train station. Most employees chose to drive to work, and whilst there were only a small number of reserved parking places (for board members and visitors) people parked in an observably regimented way. The more senior you were, the closer you parked to the entrance to the building. This hierarchy was also recognizable in the size and style of company cars – and in the dress of staff as well. The area was subject to considerable rain- and snowfall, and it was possible on some days to see some (senior) people arriving in reception dressed for business and other (less senior) people arriving in waterproof coats looking as if they were coming in from a hard trek. These symbols were indicative of a particular style of culture that was concerned with security of operations and accountability. Hierarchy was important as a way of controlling what went on. Many middle and senior managers at the bank had worked at lower levels and progressed up and there was therefore a respect for managerial experience and the structure. The bank had highly developed protocols for its operations with internal audit and quality assurance departments that regularly reviewed the work of operational departments. The bank had gained a reputation for its solidity and caution and occupied a comfortable position in its market. However, the downside of this culture was that it was slow to change.

Although this formal, careful and hierarchical way of working had been effective for the bank, ITS Canada aspired to being different, and in particular the desire was to achieve a more entrepreneurial culture and organic way of working. The reason for this was that, in order to survive in the longer term, ITS Canada would need to adopt more of a market orientation and be able to satisfy the requirements of different clients if it was to gain a share in the SME market. In order to create a different way of being the senior managers deliberately made certain symbolic changes. They were impressed by the reputation of relatively young companies such as Google and Cisco, whose cultures seemed far removed from that of the bank. In these cultures, it seemed to the ITS Canada leaders, 'ideas, innovation and customer orientation were the core values'. This vision was attractive because it implied the possibility of dispensing with formality, excessive rules and bureaucracy in favour of team working, a more flexible approach and a focus on the task. They also aspired to putting people at the top of the agenda. In the bank it was the role that was important, not the individual. In ITS Canada they wanted to relate to each other as human beings and, ideally, have some fun at work.

ITS Canada moved into the ground floor of a new building in a business park. The space was open, with windows on three walls, meaning that it received plenty of natural light. A section of the area was enclosed for storage and

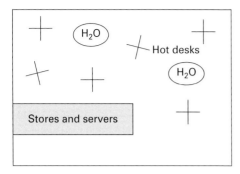

Figure C2.1 ITS Canada's initial floor plan

servers, but the rest of the floor area was deliberately left open-plan. This was a contrast to the bank, where junior staff had worked in communal offices and more senior officers had individual offices, the size of which increased with promotion. In their new building ITS Canada staff would all work in the same open area. The thinking behind this decision was that everyone would work in project teams, which would form and re-form as new projects were tackled. Furniture for the new office was chosen so that desks were movable and could be used for 'hot-desking'; when a team was working on a particular project, the team members could sit together with their laptops and work on the task at hand; as some or all of that team moved on to new or parallel projects, they could physically move to make team working easy (Figure C2.1 gives an impression of the floor plan of the new building). Hierarchy was de-emphasized and teams could be led by relatively junior people if they were the most skilled in critical aspects of a specific project. The matrix structure meant that people would report to project leaders on their projects but would also be accountable to the senior managers who were responsible for hiring, work allocation and appraisals. At the outset there was a lot of enthusiasm for the new culture, and the informal, flexible way of working created an energetic atmosphere. Water coolers were spaced out around the floor to encourage people to move around and teams were expected to draw others informally into conversation, then feedback, when their expertise was helpful. The members of ITS Canada had been chosen by the three leaders but all were also volunteers, and in general they shared the aspirations of the leaders.

Over time, evolutionary change took place in ITS Canada. The researchers were not physically present during this time but were in regular contact with the leaders. The early months of ITS Canada's existence featured a strong task focus, and, as most of the operations were still with the bank, there was a need for confidential working. In addition, the managers needed to meet potential

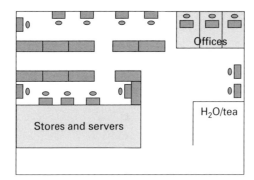

Figure C2.2 ITS Canada's subsequent floor plan

clients in a suitable setting. There were performance pressures but the leaders consciously tried to maintain a human, personal approach. People were allowed to personalize their workstations with pictures and plants. Many had cartoons pinned up. Staff also found that they needed greater filing capacity than had originally been designed into the office, and additional storage was bought to deal with this problem.

Eighteen months after the set-up, things had moved on. ITS Canada was still mainly reliant on the bank as its main customer but had made some inroads into the SME market and was diversifying its client base. It had expanded its range of offering and been able to purchase, install and support a greater variety of products than the company had been skilled in at the outset. The leaders invited the researchers back to see how things had progressed. Figure C2.2 gives an indication of what the office now looked like. When entering the office, the researchers were struck by how quiet it was. The furniture and storage had been rearranged, a little at a time. Glass offices had been constructed for occasions when confidential work needed to be carried out, and these offices also offered spaces in which the leaders could meet clients. Each person now had his or her own workspace, most of which had been personalized. Behind most workstations sat a row of high filing cabinets, in which individual staff members kept their own paperwork. On top of the cabinets were piles of paper and plants. Since this meant that it was not possible to see who was at each desk, the staff had suggested putting nameplates on the filing cabinets that led into workstations. These nameplates featured in/out sliders, so that colleagues would know who was in before walking round to speak to someone as they sought ideas or input to a project in an unplanned way. The water coolers and tea/coffee station had been moved to a new site, which made it easier to maintain, clean, store and refill bottles, milk, sugar, etc.

The three leaders were quietly pleased with the progress that had been made. In business terms, new customers were being brought on board and performance was improving. Moreover, the leaders were proud to report that they had kept people at the heart of the agenda, citing the series of individual requests that had been approved to allow more storage, personalization of workstations, the use of in/out boards, etc. However, to the researchers the difference in the physical structure of the office seemed dramatically different. The energy and buzz from earlier visits had been replaced by a quiet atmosphere of hushed conversations more reminiscent of a library than a Google or Cisco. The changes were not obvious to the leaders, since each change had been incremental and had been initiated for good rational reasons, such as the need for confidentiality and a place to meet clients, or people's desire to personalize their workspace and need for filing. The crucial thing was not the questions that they were seeking to answer but that the way they answered them reflected their actual culture, rather than the one they aspired to. For example, client meeting rooms could have been constructed in ways that did not create offices for the senior officers, but making offices for the leaders that could be used for meeting clients was the 'obvious' answer. Similarly, over time, people had started to work individually on their own subsections of projects, and this was encouraged by the reward system, which included basic pay calculated on the basis of experience and skills and an individual bonus based on the senior managers' assessment of contributions to project performance. As with many cultures, what seemed striking to outsiders who walked into the environment was just the taken-for-granted normality of the insiders. In a sense, the whole story could be seen as one of rationality and individuality, in which the old banking culture retained its grip on the thinking and behaviour of the staff.

Perhaps unwisely, the researchers chose to give feedback along these lines to the ITS Canada leaders. It may be a reflection of the researchers' culture that this seemed a normal and appropriate thing to do. However, to the ITS Canada leaders, who saw themselves as being on a change journey, the feedback was disappointing and felt very critical. Despite this they reacted positively, and a couple of months later they invited the researchers back to see what they were now doing. Rather than trying to replace the bank culture completely with a 'buzzy' culture, they were now adapting their existing culture to maximize its strengths, minimize its weaknesses and introduce new incremental steps in culture change. Three examples will serve as an illustration of their new approach. First, they knew that they did not want to be as bureaucratic as the bank but accepted that they needed certain protocols and secure ways of working. Therefore, they adopted a 'light touch rules' approach, in which rules were kept to a minimum, protocols and meeting minutes were kept to a minimum (the aim being to never have more than two pages) and filing would be for essential documents only. The light touch rules became joke-worthy in the company, and those who accidentally became 'rule-heavy' were gently mocked by their peers. Secondly, the leaders recognized that they were not going to have a work setting in which there was lots of noise and continuous multi-way communications, and, in fact, such an environment would probably be counterproductive for work. Instead, they agreed to have an open agenda meeting at 8:30 every day. People would update each other on projects, problems, ideas and also just chat about sport and other topics. The leaders could give updates on company news, and as a result it was possible for people to ask others for help on projects when they needed particular skills, or just a 'critical friend' to help review development. Finally, and perhaps most importantly, the leaders were very careful to exemplify the behaviour they wanted to see. They came out of the offices, which became bookable spaces for use by anyone who needed them to meet a client, and worked in the office space with everyone else. They tried to encourage others to raise questions and debate ideas with them and they took on support roles in projects that were led by more junior staff.

The result was that the change was less radical than the original intention, but the people who worked in ITS Canada found it realistic and comfortable. They experienced it as being quite different from the bank, and staff turnover and absence rates were very low. The reward system was modified. It retained an element of individual bonus awards, but in addition team bonuses were awarded equally to all members of a team to reflect the successful completion of projects. This culture suited them well for maintaining their relationship with the bank, and after three years this was still their main source of revenue. However, they had grown their client base during this period, and had achieved a cultural evolution, if not a revolution.

3   Island Opera

The Island Opera Company operates on a project basis. There is a senior management board that oversees the company, and it appoints what is in effect a project team to run each production. This case concerns the final rehearsal phase for the opera *The Marriage of Figaro*. The artistic director, Jeremy, was a relative novice director but was appointed to the position because the board was impressed by his talent. Previously he had been a singer, and he only recently finished his successful performing career. The board put one of its own members, Simon, into the project as conductor in order to support Jeremy. Although on the project Simon would 'report' to Jeremy, outside the project Jeremy was junior in Island Opera compared to Simon's position. The other central character in this case is Bella, who was the lead soprano. She was relatively young and this was her first major role, and she was generally regarded as an up-and-coming talent.

The soloists have been in preparation for a considerable period of time, but we focus on the last six weeks of rehearsals, when the chorus and then the orchestra arrived. Bella's ambition was to become a singer with the Metropolitan Opera House in New York:

[I]f you have a talent like this and you have the abilities and you've had the training to … express yourself and let it develop, then – why not? If that's what you were made to do then that's what you should try and do. I was born to sing in some way, and if I can do that and if I can make myself and other people happy from doing it …

Bella was relatively young in her peer group, and she was 'excited beyond belief' because of 'the magnitude of the role' and 'the size of opera', and for her this was 'the culmination of seven years of work'. Indeed, she was aware of the opportunity *The Marriage of Figaro* presented in terms of raising her profile and advancing her career. For Bella, this role was a vehicle to attract the attention of artistic directors, to gain legitimacy as an opera singer. However, Bella was not superficial about the opera: 'The thing about this character – I see so much of me in her . . . It's more natural for me to become [name of character]; for me it *is* my wedding day.' Bella said that she did not 'want to sound like a diva' but did naturally enjoy people fussing around her and looking after her: 'The guy . . . in charge of props – he's always asking "How are you doing? Are you feeling OK? Are you all set?"' Bella recognized the importance of what she was doing and did not want to be distracted. She kept a little distance from the 'kids' in the chorus, referring to them as singers who were 'not people at my level – not up at the top'.

Jeremy came to the production in a somewhat different way. Having previously been a singer, he felt he was 'aware of the singers' personalities and performance abilities'. He thought his knowledge allowed him to get 'into the heads of the cast', which would help him to 'best manage their temperaments to get the best performance out of them'. He ran an open rehearsal process and invited ideas from the performers, regarding himself as 'more of a carrot than a stick man'. He allowed them to interpret their parts and gave them what he termed 'freedom to fail'. For Jeremy, mistakes were learning opportunities, and the greatest singers were those able to learn and develop. Jeremy tried to work in a non-hierarchical way. For example, he rescheduled rehearsals around singers' requests and requirements and he 'mucked in' with the crew, helping with props and sorting the staging out.

Initially the singers liked Jeremy's informal style, but after a while some thought that there was not enough actual direction. Disagreements occurred and did not seem to be resolved, so that singers had different interpretations of what they were doing. It was also felt by some soloists that some of the chorus were not seriously enough engaged and that the production needed to be 'taken in hand'.

Jeremy started to have some problems with Bella. She seemed to have very strong preferences for how the role should be performed, and Jeremy was having difficulties in getting his ideas through. After each rehearsal he would prepare detailed notes for each soloist, including Bella, but even written feedback did not seem to make a sufficient impact on her understanding of what he wanted from the role. Jeremy was concerned that 'some of it's a bit hit and miss', but he was willing to continue to try to develop the performance in a consultative way.

By week three of the rehearsals there was something of a gulf between Jeremy's interpretation of what should have been happening and some of what was actually going on onstage. Jeremy provided even more voluminous and detailed notes, which the singers found time-consuming and rather irritating. On occasion Jeremy would become frustrated, and sometimes this was obvious to the cast. One chorus member explained that Jeremy was too strict sometimes and that frustrations were vented backstage. This was not helped by an increasing divergence with the lead male, Wilf. In Wilf's view, Jeremy was very 'honest and deep' in his interpretation of the opera, trying to get to the bottom of the characters and their motivation for acting as they did. However, for Wilf, there was a strong comedic strand: '*Figaro* is a comedy, and it's a farce, and I thought the moments of farce could have been jacked up.'

As time moved on, Simon joined the rehearsals and the orchestra became involved. The orchestra was run in a rather different way. Simon said very little to them, and did not explain the drama or the characterization that Jeremy was working so hard on. He simply took them through the score with very little fuss. If and when there was something he did not like he corrected the player(s), but in a relaxed way. Although Simon was not consultative, by this stage an orchestral player noted that Simon was 'inscrutable' but 'relaxed', while Jeremy had become 'pedantic in his direction and stressed'.

In the last two weeks the atmosphere in the rehearsal rooms was tense and difficult. Jeremy had tried to create a safe place for experiencing the roles, but things were becoming fractured. Ultimately there was an incident, when Jeremy shouted at Bella when she persisted in playing the role in her own way and ignoring his suggestions and direction. Bella immediately became very upset and could not sing. She felt that she was being criticized unfairly and treated harshly when so much of the production already rested on her shoulders.

Jeremy tried to rescue the situation, but there was almost an 'us and them' situation by now. The singers knew that Bella had difficult personal circumstances at this time and were sympathetic to her. There was little 'life' in the performances, and Jeremy could not seem to inspire them. At this point another major difficulty arose. Wilf suffered a major problem with his voice and, after discussing the situation with Simon, agreed that he would stand down and the understudy would step into the role. Wilf did not discuss this with Jeremy, although Simon did tell him later. In the last week there were more orchestral rehearsals and Simon appeared to have taken over the direction. Jeremy was still present but would sit at the back of the room, taking notes. After rehearsals he would put notes in the pigeonholes of performers, but he had little input during rehearsals. Early in the last week he put a note in Bella's pigeonhole, apologizing and saying that he thought that she had captured the role. It was rumoured that Simon had told him to do this.

In the event, the performances went well, the critics approved and audience numbers were good. However, Wilf had left the company by then, Bella felt vindicated but was mainly interested in moving on to a higher-profile company, Jeremy had had a mixed experience of directing and Simon remained inscrutable.

4 Oticon

When Hans Demant founded Oticon in 1904 he could not have foreseen that the firm would become almost as famous for its approach to organizing as it was to be for its hearing aids. Inspired by a desire to help his wife to cope with her hearing loss, Hans began by importing devices from the United States. During the Second World War it proved impossible to import hearing aids, and the son of the founder (William Demant) began manufacturing under licence. By the 1960s Oticon had moved into international markets, and during the 1970s dedicated research and development facilities helped place Oticon at the forefront of hearing aid technologies. When the firm celebrated its centenary in 2004 it was the world's second largest hearing aid manufacturer, and today the company has a turnover of around Dkr 5billion (£600 million) with sales offices in twenty-three countries. However, there have been difficult periods in Oticon's evolution, and this case study explores the changes that took place as a response to one of those difficult periods.

From its founding through to the early 1970s, Oticon gained a reputation for excellence that centred on the company's ability to miniaturize the electronic components for sound amplification and filtering. The mainstay of the business were so called 'behind-the-ear' (BTE) products, which used analogue components. However, as digital technology began to make its way into the hearing aid industry, Oticon suffered from a competence trap (Foss, 2003). The organization had developed a view that digitization and the switch to 'in-the-ear' (ITE) products were not commercially viable. Despite having developed the world's first ITE product in 1977, Oticon managers considered that the costs of digital technology would probably be prohibitive for most customers. This uncertainty

Table C4.1 Oticon's financial performance, 1988–99

Year	1988	1989	1990	1991	1992	1993	1994	1995	1996	1997	1998	1999
Revenue (Dkr)	423	449	455	476	538	661	750	940	1,087	1,413	1,613	1,884
Profit margin (%)	1.6	8.0	3.7	1.8	5.8	13.1	17.9	12.4	12.8	13.8	15.4	17.9

about the use of digital technology was set alongside obvious and existing competences in existing analogue devices, leading to a period when Oticon was trapped by its own skill set. The net result was that Oticon's position in the marketplace was eroded, and by 1988 the firm faced a number of challenges. These included fierce competition from larger multinational competitors and low profit margins (see Table C4.1).

In 1988 Lars Kolind was appointed as chief executive officer, and he focused his attention on improving the financial performance of the firm. He introduced a round of cost-cutting measures that were intended to boost profitability, and these produced significant improvements in the short term (see 1988 versus 1989 in the table). However, these benefits were transient, and by 1990/1 Kolind felt that he was no further forward. The early hesitation over digital technology meant that Oticon's competitors had now developed significant advantages, and the industry view at that time was that conditions favoured larger corporations such as Siemens and Philips, as these large firms had large R&D budgets to exploit the rapidly changing technology, which would eventually lead from in-the-ear to in-the-canal (ITC) products.

Oticon faced tough choices. Rather than focus on further cost cutting, Kolind and his fellow directors initiated a change process that would revolutionize organizing processes within Oticon. He issued a six-page memo that set out an ambitious change programme and encouraged staff to 'Think the unthinkable'. Kolind was concerned that the prevailing culture in Oticon focused on the gradual refinement of existing products whilst placing little emphasis on breakthrough innovations. Moreover, Kolind wanted to change perceptions of Oticon and to move away from a view of Oticon as a mass production company. Instead, he wanted Oticon to be seen as a service firm that offered first-class service experiences to customers, with the focus on individual fitting and tailored products. He coined the term 'spaghetti organization' to capture the far-reaching implications of this new approach.

Table C4.2 Four dimensions of change at Oticon

Pre-1991 Oticon	Post-1991 Oticon
Mono-job culture	Multi-job culture
Traditional/hierarchical	Spaghetti organization
Hardwood-panelled offices	Open-plan/mobile offices
Communication by memo	Dialogue and action

In the spaghetti organization there would be no more functional departments or hierarchical reporting. Kolind wanted to 'take away the entire organization structure' and replace it with a project-driven approach. The project offered a grand vision of a company that would be 30 percent more efficient within three years, and it was referred to internally as 'Project 330'. The aim was to make breakthroughs in three key areas: creativity, speed and productivity. This meant the introduction of four main dimensions of change; these are set out in Table C4.2.

In removing the formal organizational structure, Oticon was pushing the boundaries of what it meant to organize and to be an organization. Every member of staff was expected to work on at least one project that was outside his or her normal sphere of activities and expertise. This would occur as new project teams were formed and individuals were recruited onto the teams to fill particular roles. Anyone could instigate a new project, and there was a simple project approval process that could be signed off by Kolind or a few other senior managers. Once approved, the project sponsor was responsible for recruiting colleagues to work on the project, and everything worked on a voluntary basis. A project leader might want to recruit an excellent chip designer, but the chip designer could be looking for opportunities to work outside his or her core skill set and might lobby for the chance to work on marketing or logistics. The resulting web of projects and individuals created the image of spaghetti rather than the formal pyramid structure of a hierarchy or the rigidities of a more recognizable matrix arrangement. In Kolind's words, it would be 'able to change quickly, yet still maintain coherence'.

To make these changes possible, several other things had to change. Oticon became one of the first paperless offices, scanning important documents and logging them on a central database. To reinforce this shift, Kolind had a Perspex pipe run from the mailroom down through the canteen, so that shredded paper would tumble past staff whilst they ate their lunch. Further, the organization became much more transparent, making almost every document available to any member of staff. Finally, as part of a move to new premises, Oticon also shifted from a tradition of having individual offices for management staff to having a completely open-plan layout, with mobile workstations and hot-desking. The thinking behind this move was that it would facilitate the formation and re-formation of flexible work teams during the day. Since everyone was expected to work on multiple projects it was important to be able to gather staff together, then allow them to disperse again. Finally, much greater emphasis was placed on face-to-face communication. Kolind was clear that he wanted a shift 'from writing memos to speaking to people and getting things done'. His hope was that this would effect a dramatic shift, from a culture in which staff expected to be told what to do to one in which there were only minimal direct controls and staff were free to express themselves and be creative.

In planning the changes, Kolind was careful to involve as many people as he could. The initial 'Think the unthinkable' memo was issued in 1990, and it generated mixed reactions internally. Planning for the change began in March 1990 with the formation of working groups that included staff and external experts. The new structureless approach was launched in October 1991, and it produced significant improvements in performance, with turnover doubling and profit margins growing to more acceptable levels (see 1991 to 1995 in Table C4.1). In the same time frame product development lead times were reduced by 50 per cent. These radical changes were not restricted to a single site. Documents from a product development team based in Copenhagen would be accessible to colleagues in the United States or elsewhere, meaning that there was much more direct feedback from local markets.

The new spaghetti organization minimized central administration, since project sponsors and leaders held a devolved responsibility for all aspects of the project. The multi-job culture meant that individuals could influence their own training and development, by seeking opportunities to build the skills that they wanted in new projects. However, by 1996 the firm began to feel the need to reintroduce some structure. Marketing and product development was rationalized into three segments – mass-market, mid-price and high-performance – and a competence centre (CC) was established to deal with the financial aspects of all projects. The CC was headed up by the chief HR manager. Another team was created to manage administration, logistics and IT as critical infrastructures that enabled business to be executed. However, the intention was not to revert to a traditional hierarchical or functional model, and these central resources were intended to enable project teams to focus on the creativity of their work rather than getting bogged down in housekeeping issues. These adjustments helped sustain and support the improvements that the original spaghetti organization had produced (see 1996 to 1999 in Table C4.1).

Since Kolind's original transformation project Oticon has continued to thrive. Despite a slow start with digital technology, Oticon launched the world's first fully digital hearing aid (the DigiFocus) in 1995 and followed this with the MultiFocus, which was the world's first fully automatic digital hearing aid. The firm has also incorporated artificial intelligence into its product range and continues to innovate by creating time for staff to network with each other, with customers and with the therapists who act as a critical interface to users of Oticon's devices. The firm doubled its investment in research and development in the period 2001 to 2005 (from Dkr 253 million to Dkr 505 million) and now holds a global market share of around 20 per cent. The firm relocated again in 2006, and the new headquarters building features fewer walls but more seated areas for informal gathering and conversation. Employees now report to a named supervisor but the emphasis remains firmly on informality and individual freedom. In the period from 2003 to 2007 revenue grew from Dkr 3.6 billion to Dkr 5.4 billion, whilst profit margins remained steady in the range 23 to 25 per cent. Soren Neilsen was appointed as CEO in 2008, and the continuing emphasis on competitiveness through innovation has helped cement Oticon's position in the hearing aid industry.

USEFUL WEBSITES

- www.oticon.com: Oticon.
- http://kolindkuren.dk: Kolind Kuren.

REFERENCES

Foss, N. J. (2003) Selective intervention and internal hybrids: interpreting and learning from the rise and decline of the Oticon spaghetti organization. *Organization Science*, 14(3): 331–49.

5   Admiral Insurance

Admiral Group plc was launched in 1993 by a start-up team of five people with prior experience in financial services. Most of the group had completed MBAs, and they saw a gap in the market for a new insurer. From an insurer's point of view, those who presented the lowest risks were viewed as the most attractive customers. Those with a long and unblemished history of driving, living in the suburbs and – preferably – driving a modest but safe car were seen as the best kinds of customers, because they were statistically less likely to make a claim. Admiral was keen to offer insurance to those who were not traditionally seen as safe drivers. This meant that they targeted younger drivers, owners of faster and more powerful cars, those living in inner cities or people with combinations of these characteristics. The logic was simple. The most important thing was finding an appropriate premium for an appropriate level of risk. By targeting customers that other insurers often ignored, Admiral was able to exploit a space in what was a mature and problematic industry in which many of the incumbent firms made losses on a regular basis.

Based in the Welsh capital, Cardiff, Admiral is now a highly profitable group of companies operating in the United Kingdom and in several international markets. Henry Engelhardt, the CEO and one of the original founders of the business, believes that senior managers should be accessible to staff. In the company's own words, Admiral feels: 'People who like what they do, do it better.' Hence, the firm places a heavy emphasis on staff engagement. Regular staff surveys allow senior managers to get a sense of whether people enjoy working for the business, and they are very proud of the fact that Admiral regularly appears in the 'Best places to work' lists generated by both *The Sunday Times* and the *Financial Times*. The

Ministry of Fun which Admiral runs is one way that the firm encourages staff to celebrate success by organizing a range of events and activities to build a sense of belonging within the business.

Engelhardt says 'We go out of our way to make this a nice place to be' (Davies, 2011). It is striking that everyone who works for the firm owns shares in the business, with Engelhardt arguing that the best way to ensure that all employees feel as if they own a piece of the business is to make this a reality. When the business floated, the average payout to employees was £39,000, and almost everyone benefited financially at that point. The net result is a committed and loyal workforce, reinforced by strenuous efforts to avoid the trappings of status and seniority. The dress code tends towards casual and informal and the firm deliberately avoids the use of company cars or luxurious office furniture. The founding team's experience of life in other financial service firms means that they understand the significance of small details, such as senior managers being given chairs with arms. 'At Admiral, we all have the same chairs,' says Engelhardt (Treanor, 2005), and it means that the focus stays firmly on the business. In fact, the only two employees who do not benefit from bonuses or shares are Engelhardt (the CEO) and one of the other co-founders, David Stevens (the chief operating officer), both of whom draw relatively modest salaries given the scale and profitability of the business. Neither is on any long-term incentive package, and, indeed, in 2007 Stevens donated Admiral shares valued then at around £100 million to the Waterloo Foundation to support its charitable activities (Cohen, O'Doherty and Shelley, 2007).

This creates an unusual mix, with high performance and profitability sitting alongside corporate frugality and informality. Since 1996 an annual staff survey has been collated and analysed, and the results have been fed back to all staff. Unusually for a staff survey, response rates are high, typically over 80 per cent, and the figures presented in Table C5.1 highlight how positively disposed staff are towards their organization. By making information about how the firm is doing available to all staff, Admiral has managed to create a virtuous cycle. The results are broken down internally and fed back at department level, with awards going to the best departments within the firm.

The growth of Admiral has been staggering. From a start-up team of five people, the business launched in 1993 with fifty-seven staff and just the Admiral brand. Since then the business has grown to cover a range of household brands in the United Kingdom, including Diamond, Bell and Elephant. They now employ over 4,700 staff and have offices in the United Kingdom, Canada, Spain, Italy, Germany, France and the United States. The growth has been entirely

Table C5.1 Extract from Admiral staff survey results

Survey question	2006	2007	2008	2009	2010
I am proud to be associated with Admiral	91%	91%	94%	96%	95%
I would recommend Admiral as a good place to work	90%	90%	94%	95%	94%
Admiral is truly customer-oriented	90%	88%	90%	90%	86%
Every effort is made to understand the opinions and thinking of employees	74%	73%	86%	87%	88%

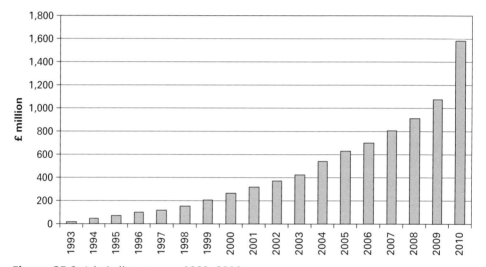

Figure C5.1 Admiral's turnover, 1993–2010

organic, in part so that the business can protect its entrepreneurial culture. When the firm posted its first quarter results in 2011 it reported that turnover had grown 56 per cent year on year (Figure C5.1 shows annual turnover growth from 1993 to 2010), and Admiral now holds around 10 per cent of the UK car insurance market. When asked whether this meant that Admiral's growth rate might be expected to slow down, Engelhardt replied: 'Ten down, ninety to go.' He was firm in his view that there was no natural ceiling to Admiral's market share and his focus was on making sure that the business 'got better as it got bigger'.

With revenues now exceeding £1.5 billion the firm has experienced a number of significant changes, including the adoption of internet sales and the introduction of the aggregator business model with the launch of Confused.com in 2002. Confused was Admiral's sixth brand but, unlike the other brands, Confused did not sell insurance. Rather, it acted as an intermediary between customers and providers in the increasingly confusing marketplace, where the number of providers had grown rapidly. By capturing customers' details and searching on their behalf, Confused was able to offer an overview of the best deals that were available. Admiral's own insurance products would be available on the price comparison site but so too would their competitors' products. By switching to a price comparison or aggregator model, the relationship between Admiral and its competitors had to shift. This was a revolutionary breakthrough for the industry, and, following its launch in 2002, Confused.com was joined by a range of competitors. Admiral is now bringing the aggregator model to international markets with offerings such as Chiarezza.it (Italy) and Rastreator.com (Spain). International markets represent one of the main sources of future growth for the business, but this has not all been straightforward. The board's decision to exit the German market after three years demonstrates that 'young and immature does not give a new business [Admiral] carte blanche to underperform' ('Chief executive's statement', *2010 Annual Report*). Andrew Probert, another of the founders and the former finance director, came back from retirement to oversee the sale of the German business.

The firm has a clear strategy of taking 'relatively small and inexpensive steps to test different approaches and identify the way forward' (Group chairman, 2011). This was the logic that underpinned the creation of Confused.com within the Admiral Group. A start-up team left the main company headquarters and moved into low-cost office space elsewhere in Cardiff. Despite having a wealthy and powerful parent company, Confused.com launched with minimal resources and, initially, spent little on advertising. The arrival of other competitors meant that advertising spend eventually became a significant cost to the business but Confused avoided spending money until it was sensible to do so. Here, again, we see a corporate sense of frugality and a preference for growing organically rather than by acquisition. The Confused start-up team was drawn from within the Admiral Group. At each stage of its development from a single-brand phone and postal direct insurer to a multi-brand, multi-platform business operating in several international markets, the one constant for Admiral has been its culture. The focus on employee as well as customer satisfaction has engendered a loyal, productive and innovative culture within the business and may help explain how the organization has managed to move from one set of technologies and business models to another whilst maintaining growth in revenues and profits year on year.

At some point in the future the business will face the challenge of succession planning. As the founders move on and are replaced, it will be interesting to see whether the particular culture that they fostered will survive. This is a challenge that the founders acknowledge, but Engelhardt is clear that eventually 'you need fresh blood, new ideas, new ways of doing things'.

USEFUL WEBSITE

- www.admiralgroup.co.uk contains information on the company's history and culture as well as holding copies of annual reports.

REFERENCES

Cohen, N., O'Doherty, J., and Shelley, T. (2007) Companies UK: Admiral founder donates £100m in shares to charity. *Financial Times*, 7 March.

Davies, P. J. (2011) View from the top: an interview with Henry Engelhardt. *Financial Times*, 27 January (available at ft.com/video).

Treanor, J. (2005) Full steam ahead: an interview with Henry Engelhardt. *Guardian*, 21 May.

6   Power Provision plc

Power Provision plc is one of the main generators and providers of electrical and gas power in Europe. It has extensive distribution networks and over 10 million customers. In addition to domestic and business supply, services include municipal activities such as street lighting supply. Power Provision has a long history of generation and had an interest in renewables before most of its competitors. During the last ten years this area of activity has been emphasized, and Power Provision is regarded as a leader in renewable energy, although a considerable proportion of its generation is still produced in conventional ways (fossil fuel power stations). Although the branding and publicity tend to focus on renewables, the strategic aim is concerned with delivering dividends and share price performance to its shareholders by having highly efficient operations. Power Provision has been successful in doing this, and over the last five years it has delivered returns that are above those of almost all of its main competitors. Hence, Power Provision can tell a success story, but the changes along the way have entailed challenges and problematic phases.

Power Provision plc was formed by a merger of two companies in the late 1990s. At the time the industry was seeing a lot of merger and acquisition activity. In the case of Power Provision, the integration of two successful companies was portrayed as a merger in which agreement was formed through collaboration. To some extent this was true. The two pre-merger companies operated in different geographical areas, had largely different modes of power generation and served different customer bases. Therefore, there was a clear logic to the merger strategy. However, the two companies were not the same size and were not in the same financial states. The smaller company was more successful financially and had a brand that was more conducive to a market in which customers were becoming more interested in environmental matters. The larger company had more extensive infrastructure and a bigger customer base but was less successful financially. Following the merger the new CEO and finance director came from the smaller company. Although the initial rhetoric was about sharing best practice in both directions and maximizing the synergies of the two businesses, over time it became clear that the culture and mode of operating of the smaller company was regarded as the 'default position', and this caused some difficulties in efficient working across what used to be organizational boundaries.

The CEO had a macho management style. He claimed affinity with the operators who were doing skilled manual jobs but behaved in an antagonistic way towards office-based and professional staff. He was famous for marching into offices and removing any mobile phones he saw, saying that people 'clearly didn't need them if they left them lying around'. He would do this even with people's personal phones. He was equally famous for shouting and swearing in the office, giving the staff the impression that they were not doing anything of any value. People were fearful of the CEO and few would argue with him. The stories about his behaviour were rife and his pugnacious image was well established internally. He had a close team around him and decisions were taken at the top of the organization. The company was highly unionized, and therefore certain aspects of the changes had to be negotiated, but the CEO adopted an autocratic approach to leadership whenever he could. Although this style did not win the CEO many friends internally, he was seen as having a clear direction and purpose by investors, and this certainly helped the position of the company.

The CEO believed that costs needed to be stripped out of Power Provision plc. After the merger there were some duplications and a range of systems that did not fit together well. For example, the IT systems of the two pre-merger companies were not easily compatible, and so that of the larger company was replaced with the one from the smaller company. Part of the envisaged advantage of the merger was that shared services could be delivered more economically. An early change, therefore, was a reduction in the headcount in support and professional services. However, although the CEO wanted to make cuts overnight, the unions objected, and so the process became longer and was not carried out by management diktat. The two pre-merger companies did not have similar performance management systems, and in the smaller company bonuses were awarded on the basis of line managers' judgement, rather than having a developed appraisal system with performance being measured against objectives or competences. This meant that it was difficult to make redundancies on the grounds of performance. Therefore, areas of 'overstaffing' were identified. These areas were ones in which both pre-merger companies had similar departments, and the CEO and his team believed that the work could be done by fewer people. Areas identified included legal and compliance work, finance and marketing. Line managers were expected to have informal talks with their staff and make people aware of the overstaffing problem and see if there were any potential volunteers for redundancy. In some areas pressure was exerted on staff, and a fair amount of disquiet developed. In some cases this was expressed as an anti-management feeling and in other cases there was some internal conflict in teams as people 'jostled for position'. This process was all informal, and it cannot be said with certainty that this was a deliberate tactic, but the rumours and stories that circulated reinforced the idea that it was purposeful. At this time relations between the staff of the two former companies were very poor, as people believed that there would be a process of centralization in which one or other of the legal, finance and marketing departments would be closed. Hence, cooperation was at an all-time low.

After a couple of months a voluntary redundancy scheme was announced. The voluntary scheme had been agreed with the trades unions and, in effect, favoured early retirement. People over the age of fifty-five could receive a financial package, including an enhanced pension, that was designed to be attractive. There was an initial surge of interest and the numbers going through the scheme appeared to be hitting the target. Leaving parties became regular occurrences, and they were largely celebratory affairs. However, the number of volunteers then dried up, and the scheme had to be extended as sufficient savings had not yet been made. Managers had meetings with staff in order to encourage people to apply and this led to some more applications to the scheme from younger people. However, these people did not receive quite the same financial advantages, as they were not able to access pensions, and some felt pressured into leaving. At this point morale was relatively low, because the people who were leaving were not happy to be doing so while those who stayed often feared for the future.

The downsizing (or 'right-sizing', depending on whose terminology you accepted) led to significant headcount reductions. Considerable savings were made, and further savings were made by significant reductions in the training budget. Power Provision, unlike its predecessors, did not fund any degree study, including MBAs or in engineering, and when training was retained it was substantially less than what had been done beforehand. Travel expenses were cut and in general there was a culture of austerity. The external perception, particularly amongst shareholders and analysts, was largely positive and the share price increased. Internally there were mixed views. Many people believed that some cuts were warranted, but the general view was that it was not just the 'fat' that had been cut but that the CEO had 'cut into the bone'. The critical voices were bolstered by what appeared to be some contradictions. Although many redundancies had been made, Power Provision was making increasing use of consultants. In the initial phase of redundancies many highly skilled and experienced people had left. In fact, many of the managers who had left had been regarded as the good leaders by those working under them. It became apparent over the next few months that many projects had been left without sufficient knowledge, and leadership and consultants were brought in to supplement teams. These people were not counted as part of the staff, but they were relatively expensive to employ, on short-term contracts that were often renewed. In quite a few cases these consultants were former senior employees who had taken redundancy, and in one department there was a story of three people leaving one Friday and returning a fortnight later after a holiday as highly paid consultants. This did little to enhance staff morale. It also added to the cost of the operation. In some areas, such as the design capability, a shrinking number of professional staff struggled to maintain the same workload, and there were signs of stress in the company. There was no redundancy scheme for operators and manual workers, but as people left the general principle was that they would not be replaced. Hence, teams contracted and were then merged. This meant that maintenance and operations teams were stretched, and some indicators, such as reconnections of power after an outage, were deteriorating. There were also some health and safety issues, with an increase in accidents even though the reporting of near-misses (instances when an accident did not occur but the possibility of such an occurrence had been heightened) had shrunk to almost zero.

These internal concerns remained internal, and the CEO retired with the share price high and his personal reputation as an effective manager of strategic change intact. However, his successor thought that there were significant problems, and set about changing the culture and style of working. It was still important to keep costs low and to maintain the share price and dividend, but in order to develop and grow over time the new CEO believed that the whole approach should change. He started with the health and safety culture. Considerable investment in training and equipment was undertaken and a stress was put on the reporting and early detection of potential problems. Managers received additional training, health and safety matters were now emphasized as part of their job and a board member was given the responsibility for development in this area. Initially, the reporting of problems increased dramatically, but this was seen not as a negative sign but a positive development, in that the company was becoming aware of the real extent of its problems, putting it in a position to deal with them accordingly. This change gave the new CEO a positive image in the company. He was regarded as someone who got things done, but who was concerned about his workforce. This was in contrast to the state of the psychological contract in the previous regime, when many people were fearful of management and anxious as to what cuts might be implemented next.

The new CEO also took a very different approach to line management. In the first phase of redundancies many line managers who did not agree with the macho approach had left, and when they were replaced the new management population was relatively inexperienced. The new CEO invested in a series of training courses to develop the managerial population. They were to become coaches and problem solvers rather than instruction givers. At the same time a performance management system was introduced that removed the old-style subjective decision about who got what size of bonus. The new system included the competences of team leadership and review input from internal customers as well as measurement against objectives.

The next stage of development was a series of company acquisitions. Unlike the initial merger that had formed Power Provision plc, these were overtly acquisitions of smaller companies, on the basis that Power Provision would develop the business but was quite clearly the senior partner. Three significant acquisitions were made over eight years, leading to a significant growth in the size and coverage of the company. As the new companies were taken over their management population went through the same training programme, and there were no large-scale redundancy programmes. Some redundancies were made on an individual basis, but in the main the cost base was controlled through natural staff turnover, increased purchasing power and some systems efficiencies.

The culture at this point has come to be much more positive. The new CEO is seen as a 'good bloke' who is accessible to the operators and spends much of his time out and about. His style is informal and he has retained a lean approach to administration. He has introduced a more organic approach to hierarchy and decision making, with little bureaucracy and a view that well-trained professionals should be trusted to get on with the job so long as the costs and performance are managed. By now almost no external consultants are employed and there is a process of succession planning related to the performance management system.

Power Provision plc has grown in noticeably different ways under its two CEOs. In the first case there was radical change and a centralized direction of how the change should take place. In the second case there has been more incremental change, and growth. Cost control and consistency of supply are the core capabilities of the company, with the external purpose of boosting shareholder value. This is still being achieved, with above-average growth continuing to be recorded, but in the history of the company it has been achieved in rather different ways.

7   Nokia

Nokia originated in 1865 as a wood pulp mill in Finland, its name deriving from the river Nokia, which ran next to the original mill. Its roots are in paper manufacturing, then rubber and cable production. The company has gone through many changes to become the mobile technology company it is today. Its headquarters are still in Finland and it is listed on the Helsinki, Frankfurt and New York stock exchanges. By 2010 Nokia employed over 123,500 people in fifteen manufacturing sites around the world. The company's mission is stated as follows (www.nokia.com):

Nokia's mission is simple, Connecting People. Our strategic intent is to build great mobile products. Our job is to enable billions of people everywhere to get more of life's opportunities through mobile.

By the mid- to late 2000s Nokia was one of the most successful mobile technology firms in the world. However, if we compare its position in the Fortune Global 500 in 2007 and 2010, although the rankings are almost the same, the direction of travel is quite different.[1] In July 2007 the rank was 119, up from 131, and it was number one in the networks and communication equipment industry. Revenue stood at $51,593 million in 2006 and profit was $5,402 million. These figures were up 21 per cent and 20 per cent, respectively, from the 2005 position. In 2010 the rank was 120, down from 85. The revenue was $56,966 million and profit was $1,238 million in 2009. These figures were down 23 per cent and 79 per cent, respectively, from 2008. Hence, the direction of change was negative, with decreasing profits and concerns for the future.

[1] Fortune Global 500: http://money.cnn.com/magazines/fortune/global500.

The problems continued into 2011. The share price slid to 1998 levels and profits became non-existent, with profit warnings being issued to the markets. Lee Simpson, an analyst with Jefferies and Co., put it like this (Arthur, 2011a):

What does strike us as quite surprising is the level to which the markets have dropped, we're talking about breakeven now which is quite a slide. I think this level of shareholder destruction is now starting to look dangerous: what can these guys do to reverse this? Our stance is that it's very difficult to value this business right now, because it has to be a different animal if and when it gets into recovery.

What was the problem? Nokia was still the biggest producer of mobile phones and smartphones, selling about 400 million and 100 million each year, respectively. However, the company's position had been eroded. At the top end of the market the Apple iPhone, Research in Motion's Blackberry and phones using Google's Android operating system had taken market share. In 2009 Nokia had had a 40 per cent share of the smartphone market, but by 2011 this had decreased to 24 per cent, in comparison to Android's 32 per cent. In addition, Nokia faced stiff cost competition from Chinese 'white box' manufacturers, which could undercut the price for standard mobile handsets. Nokia had previously led innovation in the industry but the innovative pre-eminence had now shifted to North America, and the Nokia operating system, Symbian, was acknowledged to be 'a bit crufty' (Arthur, 2011b), meaning that, in programmers' terms, it was outdated and hence had problems in terms of operation and maintenance.

If, in Simpson's terms, it was necessary for Nokia to be 'a different animal' in order to recover, what would this change entail? Stephen Elop replaced the previous CEO, Olli-Pekka Kallasvuo, in September 2010. This occurred at the point at which the problems were having a significant impact, and Elop's view was that the company's managers were 'standing on a burning platform and not even fighting with the right weapons'. Elop led the development of a new strategy, which was aimed at accelerating change and regaining leadership in the smartphone sector, developing the company's mobile device platform and investing in a profitable way for the future. Key changes included:

- forming a broad strategic partnership with Microsoft to build jointly a new mobile 'ecosystem';
- aiming to gain volume and value growth by connecting 'the next billion' to the internet in developing markets;
- making focused investments in next-generation technologies; and
- putting in place a new leadership team and organizational structure with a clear focus on speed, results and accountability.

Nokia had experienced problems with its Symbian operating system, which had fallen behind the rival systems of the new competitors by the late 2000s. Speaking at the D9 conference near Los Angeles on 1 June 2011, Elop said (Arthur, 2011b): 'Symbian was at a deficit in some markets [compared to the iPhone and Android]. Our assessment of the speed with which we could catch up [was that it] would not be enough.'

The proposed solution to this problem was the collaboration with Microsoft. Sales of smartphones now outnumber sales of personal computers (PCs), and analysts predict that this will be the pattern going forward. Microsoft faces its own challenges, since its revenues have largely been driven by its dominance of software and operating systems in the PC market, and the US giant needs to find a stronger foothold in the emerging smartphone market. Microsoft's Windows Phone software has been adopted in Nokia smartphones. This is seen as a technical solution to the need to innovate and as providing a way forward for the business. The collaboration means that innovation will be driven by combining expertise from Microsoft on the software platform side and from Nokia on the hardware side. The aim is not just to create new products (a new high-speed Windows phone, developed through this collaboration, was launched in 2012) but also to develop the system to a point at which completely innovative services, not as yet even envisaged, can be invented and delivered. The collaboration means that there will be a brand identity advantage, and this is thought to be important particularly as competition comes from the highly branded Google and Apple. In addition, Nokia Maps will be used in Microsoft's Bing and Ad Centre, and Nokia's content store will be integrated into the Microsoft Marketplace. The new feature phones will seek to get 'the next billion people to their first internet and application experience'. The aim is to achieve this by providing affordable mobiles in emerging markets that will incorporate QWERTY touch and type, a dual subscriber identity module (SIM) facility, Nokia Maps, a browser, 'life tools', web applications and money. The intention is also to provide business opportunities for developers. These investments will be aimed principally at growth economies. Hence, the intention is to rival the growth of the iPhone and other smartphone options.

As well as collaboration and greater innovation, the change includes cost cutting. Reportedly, there are plans to cut €1 billion by 2013. This will include job cuts; estimates vary from 4,000 (Goodley, 2011) to 6,000 (Ward, 2011). Redundancies will be involved, as will transferring employees to Accenture, which will take a role in the development of the Symbian platform. Although a significant plank of the strategic change is the collaboration with Microsoft, there will also be investment in the Symbian platform, which will be used for some of the Nokia products (the others will be Microsoft systems). The aim is to increase its speed of processing and make graphics and software improvements.

There are also some political issues potentially. Elop worked for Microsoft previously, and one view that has become widespread is that Microsoft plan to take Nokia over. Although this has been vociferously denied, there have been rumours of Elop being a player in a takeover move and that he would be a 'Trojan horse', who, having entered Nokia at the top level, would engineer the move from the inside. However, Elop denies this (Arthur, 2011b): 'The Trojan horse theory has been well overplayed. I refer you to the grassy knoll [the mythical source of a second killer of John F. Kennedy in Dallas] for that one. With a situation such as this there is a difficult balance to be struck between focusing on the medium and long term and 'taking care of business', which has a short-term focus. Market pressures require a narrative from Nokia that has a believable future but also a degree of confidence in what will happen tomorrow. The news of the cost and job cuts led to share price increases, but these may be short-lived. Speaking at the D9 conference, Elop said (Arthur, 2011b): 'My principal focus and the focus of the team is to take care of the short term but make sure that the execution is flawless.' However, this could be a case of an overemphasis on the short term being a problem, when the market has changed so significantly because of radical changes by competitors.

Nokia has been a very impressive company. It has survived for nearly 150 years by being good at change. In its latest iteration it has been a world leader, but competitive pressures, technological innovation and shifts in the market have resulted in a highly pressured situation. The new leadership has a strategy consisting of collaboration, cuts, innovation and the preservation of some products/operations. It remains to be seen how successful this change strategy will be.

REFERENCES

Arthur, C. (2011a) Nokia shares dive after sales warning. *Guardian*, 31 May (available at www.guardian.co.uk).

Arthur, C. (2011b) Nokia chief denies Microsoft takeover. *Guardian*, 2 June (available at www.guardian.co.uk).

Goodley, S. (2011) Nokia to axe 4,000 jobs. *Guardian*, 27 April (available at www.guardian.co.uk).

Ward, A. (2011) Threat to 6,000 jobs following Nokia deal. *Financial Times*, 14 February (available at www.ft.com).

8 Her Majesty's Revenue and Customs

The UK government relies on Her Majesty's Revenue and Customs to fund many of the policies it initiates. Monies raised through taxation are used to fund the welfare state, the health service, the armed services and many other aspects of government activity. Taxation has been a feature of virtually all civilizations, from the Egyptians and Romans to modern democracies, to the extent that Benjamin Franklin is reported to have said that there is nothing so certain as death and taxes. However, although it is central to civilized life, taxation is neither straightforward nor popular.

When the UK government decided to merge the Inland Revenue with Her Majesty's Customs and Excise, it was simply the latest in a series of organizational changes. The resulting organization, HMRC, faced the challenge of integrating two previously independent organizations, each of which had a long history. The last chairman of the Inland Revenue, Sir Nicholas Montagu, speaking at the 2005 Scotland plc Awards ceremony, commented on the difficulty in changing the mindset of the organization:

[T]he biggest shift was a cultural one. I began to use language that seemed alien to people inside the Revenue. I would talk about customers and I'd point out that we were supposed to be there to make it easy for our customers to pay the taxes that they owed. That meant challenging the idea that most tax payers are crooks who were trying to avoid paying.

The latest version of HMRC's value statements (see Figure C8.1) suggest that Montagu made progress on this front.

If one challenge was changing the mindset of tax professionals inside the then Inland Revenue, another was merging the culture of two separate organizations

We understand our customers and their needs.

We make it easy for our customers to get things right.

We believe that most of our customers are honest and we treat everyone with respect.

We are passionate in helping those who need it and relentless in pursuing those who bend or break the rules.

We recognise that we have privileged access to information and we will protect it.

We behave professionally and with integrity.

We do our own jobs well and take pride in helping our colleagues to succeed.

We develop the skills and tools we need to do our jobs well.

We drive continuous improvement in everything we do.

Figure C8.1 HMRC's 'Our way'
Source: HMRC (2010: 3).

to form HMRC. The new organization was established in April 2005 employing some 105,000 staff in total, making it one of the largest non-ministerial government departments. HMRC is accountable to the Chancellor of the Exchequer in the UK government and provides policy advice to the government in partnership with HM Treasury.

HMRC's vision is to close what they call the tax gap – i.e. the difference between the tax collected and that which should be. To do so, the organization intends to make customers feel that the tax system is simple to interact with and that they are treated fairly by a highly professional and efficient organization. The revenues collected by HMRC come in varying forms, and this means that it is a large and complex organization dealing with a diverse set of customers. Tax is collected from individuals and organizations. Some tax collection, such as the pay as you earn system used to collect tax from employees, is relatively simple. Other forms of tax collection involve complex regulations and negotiations with customers, in the corporate, non UK resident and charitable sectors. Running a highly efficient tax collection system that is nonetheless sensitive to the needs of very different customers is highly challenging. Figure C8.2 shows the remit of HMRC.

Further complicating HMRC's ability to deliver on its mission is the harsh reality that public sector organizations remain under pressure to do more with less. A series of downsizing activities meant that, in 2008/9 alone, HMRC made value-for-money savings of around £200 million and reduced its staffing by almost 3,000 full-time equivalent posts. The organization currently employs around 80,000 staff in over 450 offices throughout the United Kingdom. The use of 'lean' technologies to reduce waste and make processes efficient has played

Direct taxes – paid by individuals and businesses on
 money earned or capital gained:
 Capital Gains Tax
 Corporation Tax
 Income Tax
 Inheritance Tax
 National Insurance contributions

Indirect taxes – paid by individuals and businesses on
  money spent on goods or services:
 Excise duties
 Insurance Premium Tax
 Petroleum Revenue Tax
 Stamp Duty
 Stamp Duty Land Tax
 Stamp Duty Reserve Tax
 VAT

Payments administered for:
 Child Benefit
 Child Trust Fund
 tax credits

Enforcement of:
 border and frontier protection
 environmental taxes
 national minimum wage
 Recovery of student loans

Figure C8.2 HMRC's remit

a significant role in helping HMRC reduce operating costs. However, there are some concerns that the standardization of tasks and processes might be stripping autonomy and job satisfaction from the organization. In recognition of this, HMRC also has a strategic goal of creating a working environment that motivates and develops its people and encourages them to take pride in working for the organization.

This latter goal has become significant in response to an external audit of HMRC by the UK government's civil service. To assess the performance of government departments, the civil service uses 'capability reviews' to identify areas of strength and weakness in each department. The capability review system has been used since 2006, and it covers three areas: leadership, strategy and delivery. Each review is carried out by a team of externally appointed assessors drawn from public, private and voluntary sector organizations, to ensure that the review team has an appropriate blend of skills to judge performance in the department under review. HMRC was first subject to a capability review in 2007, and at that point it received clear feedback that it needed to work on improving staff engagement. The capability review was intended to identify the specific measures needed to ensure that government departments were equipped to meet its future challenges and to 'develop a culture of excellence and continuous improvement' (O'Donnell, 2009: 2). The project described in Chapter 14 was one part of HMRC's response to the issues raised in the 2007 review.

Two years later the organization was subjected to a follow-up review to assess progress on the issues raised in the first review. Only one area was flagged as an urgent development area. This related to the organization's ability to ignite passion, pace and drive (part of the leadership dimension of the capability review). This aspect of HMRC was described as needing urgent action because the organization was not well placed to address the problem of poor engagement in the medium term. Staff morale and engagement were found to be very low, and, in some cases, the results in 2009 were lower than those in the 2007 review, indicating that the organization was going backwards. The 2009 staff survey showed that only 25 per cent of HMRC staff were proud to work for the organization, compared with 61 per cent of its senior civil servants. The report claimed that 'efforts by the senior leadership team to tackle poor staff engagement and improve visibility and communications are not working' (O'Donnell, 2009: 8). HMRC had articulated and communicated a vision to its staff; 93 per cent of those surveyed said they were aware of the vision but only 66 per cent felt that they understood it. A series of structural and leadership changes had compounded the effects of process improvements and lean thinking. Many staff within HMRC pointed to examples of change within the organization that had not been carried out well, with only 11 per cent of all staff believing that change was well managed within HMRC.

The 2009 capability review was obviously a difficult experience for senior management within HMRC. The organization responded by developing a new 'people' strategy and bringing in a new leadership behaviours framework. These were seen as long-term solutions to the wider employee engagement challenge. Whilst there are encouraging signs that the organization is working hard to engage staff (such as the project described in Chapter 14), HMRC continues to experience real challenges, in terms of headcount reduction and unforeseen problems, such as the loss of data relating to the Child Benefit system. Resignations followed the loss of personal details for 15 million UK citizens. The details included home and banking details, which could have been used for identity fraud. The loss of data further eroded public perceptions of HMRC, and made it harder for those managing the organization to tell success stories internally about the changes being made to improve the organization.

USEFUL WEBSITES

- www.hmrc.gov.uk: provides details on HMRC, its purpose, mission, structure, etc.
- www.civilservice.gov.uk contains details of the capability review programme.

REFERENCES

HMRC (2010) *Delivering Our Vision: Business Plan 2010–11.* London: HMRC.

O'Donnell, G. (2009) *HM Revenue and Customs: Progress and Next Steps.* London: Cabinet Office.

9   Apple

Today, Apple is one of the most successful firms in the world, with a string of hit products and a loyal group of customers. Indeed, in August 2011 Apple was cited as the most valuable company in the world when measured by market capitalization (Rushe, 2011). Apple's current success follows periods of real turbulence, and co-founder Steve Jobs was ousted from the firm in 1985 during an earlier period of poor performance. In 1997 Michael Dell (of Dell Computers) was asked how he would deal with the significant problems that Apple was facing at that time, and he replied: 'I'd shut it down and give the money back to shareholders.' With the benefit of hindsight, Apple's shareholders will be glad that Dell's advice was not taken.

Steve Jobs and Steve Wozniak founded Apple Computer in 1976 and launched their first product, the Apple I, from the Jobs family garage. The launch of their second product, the Apple II in 1977, was a major success, and helped shape the emerging market for personal computers. Apple quickly became a market leader, selling more than 100,000 Apple IIs by the end of 1980. When IBM entered the PC market in 1981 and a new software firm, Microsoft, began selling the DOS operating system, Apple faced a new competitive landscape. The now familiar tale was that IBM created a template that other manufacturers could clone with third-party software able to run on any compatible computer. In contrast, Apple cherished its proprietary hardware and was reluctant to enter into licence agreements. IBM's approach helped the company establish a new industry standard and drove up market share. Apple's products were seen as easier to use, and the firm was the first to introduce the use of a mouse and a graphical user interface, which we now see as the default way of interacting with most computers. Although Apple was seen as the more elegant product offering, the lack of compatible software inhibited sales, and the firm's net income deteriorated significantly during the early 1980s. Eventually the board forced Jobs to leave.

With Jobs gone, Apple continued to introduce new products and technologies. However, not all were successful. The Apple Newton, which was launched in 1993, claimed to redefine the personal digital assistant (PDA) category by introducing handwriting recognition and other new features. However, the technology was not sufficiently reliable, and other firms, such as Psion and Palm Computing, went on to dominate the PDA market.

Despite changes in senior management, Apple continued to struggle, and in 1997 Jobs returned – to lead one of the most remarkable turnaround stories in corporate history. He focused on a dramatic simplification of the product catalogue and applied Apple's historical tendency to 'think different'[1] by raising research and development spending. The result, in 1998, was the iMac, with its distinctive eggshell design. Jonathan Ive, Apple's senior vice president of industrial design, believed that design held the key to Apple's reputation, and his award-winning design for the iMac range highlighted the renewed focus on the look and feel of Apple products as well as their functionality. In Ive's view, 'Innovating is in Apple's DNA,' and core to the Apple brand is the idea that the technology works so well that you do not really need an instruction manual. With Ive and Jobs leading the way, Apple fought back from the brink and began to grow at a rate above the industry average. In the year that the iMac launched, Apple posted a profit and was seen as an important player in the personal computer industry again.

However, the computer industry itself was beginning to experience systemic problems. Product performance was improving dramatically but prices were falling, margins were shrinking and the market was maturing. Jobs began to look for new customers and to think carefully about areas in which Apple could engage with a new set of competitors. In 2001 Apple revealed the results of this search. The first iPod changed the music business for ever. At the press launch, Jobs was very clear that Apple was changing the rules of the game. He argued that music was a great arena for Apple to use its particular skills. He declared that there were 'a few niche players, like Creative, and a few larger companies which haven't had a hit yet with digital music, like Sony'. However, Jobs figured that

---

[1] 'Think different' was a slogan used in a range of Apple advertising campaigns following the return of Jobs.

Apple could not only 'find the recipe in digital music' but that 'the Apple brand is going to be fantastic' in this new territory, because people trusted Apple for new technology that worked well. He had found a way to reposition Apple from being a computer firm to being a consumer electronics firm. Indeed, in 2007 Apple dropped the 'Computers' from its name and became 'Apple Inc.', to reflect more accurately the firm's position as a significant player in hardware, software, mobile telephony and online retailing.

The iPod was not the first portable, digital media player but it has been by far the most successful, capturing over 70 per cent of the market, according to Apple's own market analysis. The iPod outsells its rivals despite higher purchase prices partly because it has been described as the 'most beautiful invention in music since the guitar' by U2's Bono. Management writer Gary Hamel goes so far as to describe Apple as being 'in the beauty business' (Hamel, 2010).

Apple's technology brought a new dimension to music consumption. Looking back to the launch of the iPod, the claim that you could carry 1,000 songs in your pocket seems less impressive now than it did in 2001. Today it is possible to carry your entire music library around in your pocket, and later generations of iPods meant that you were soon able to carry photos and movies too. Indeed, as Figure C9.1 shows, iPods have comfortably outstripped Moore's law,[2] with selling prices reducing whilst storage capacity increases. The slick and desirable physical product was matched by a clever tie-in to the iTunes store, which, if anything, has been more successful than the iPod itself. There are now over 100 million iTunes accounts registered, and the site sold its 10 billionth tune in February 2010. Again, iTunes was not the first digital distributor of music on the internet, but it was the first to gain significant scale, and, unlike Napster, it provided a legal means of distributing music and collecting royalty payments over the internet. Compare the process of recording, distributing and retailing music in the pre- and post-iTunes eras. Apple introduced a whole new business model that eliminated a number of expensive and frustrating steps. Even the largest high street retailer can cover only a small portion of the online library that iTunes offers, and no longer is there any need to buy the physical product then convert it into digital form for transfer to a computer, then a digital music player. In terms of the music business, Apple now controls

[2] Gordon Moore's prediction that the number of components placed on in integrated circuits would grow exponentially – Moore's law – is now used as shorthand when referring to a number of product categories for which miniaturization, reduced prices and increased performance go hand in hand.

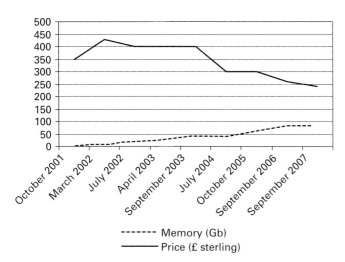

Figure C9.1 iPod sales price and capacity, October 2001–September 2007
Note: Based on UK data.

not only the hardware but the distribution channel, spawning 'the iPod economy' for a range of complementary products including cases, speaker docks,
chargers and car kits. Apple had made itself visible when others were invisible.
When listening to music on the move, most people do not see the player, so
Apple's choice of distinctive white earphones was another indication of thinking the design process through from product conception to end users. The white
headphones became associated with the iPod, and Apple used them in a series of
TV and billboard adverts to promote the product. Apple's move into new
strategic space was impressive for a firm with no history in the music business –
but Jobs did not rest there.

Apple continued to look for opportunities to exploit. The iPhone represents an
excellent example of the opportunities created by the convergence of previously
separate industries. Succeeding where the Apple Newton had failed, the iPhone
combines a personal organizer, phone, e-mail, music player, games and much
more. In contrast, the iPad demonstrates Apple's ability to create whole new
markets with the introduction of the tablet computer category. At its launch,
some industry experts described the iPad as 'a wheeled horse', but consumers
liked the product, and Apple sold 3 million units in the first eighty days from
launch in 2010.[3] Both the iPhone and the iPad have gone on to dominate the
market, commanding high prices and sustaining loyal post-purchase revenue

---

[3] Blackberry's PlayBook, which was intended to compete with the iPad, shipped some 200,000 units in its
first three months of sales. This is less than 10 per cent of what Apple achieved.

streams via iTunes. Having started in the computing industry, Apple has found itself engaged in competition with record labels, online retailers, consumer electronics firms and mobile handset manufacturers, and, with the introduction of tablet computing, Apple is back to computing.

Of course, the next stage in Apple's development will be particularly telling. Jobs left the company for a second time, this time prompted by health issues. In an open resignation letter to all Apple employees he made it clear that he felt that Apple's best days were ahead of it, not behind it (Jobs, 2011). His death in October 2011 may well be seen as a watershed for both Apple and the technology sector as a whole, with many commentators arguing that no one would be able to match his ability to bring ideas to market before anyone realized that they might need or want the product. The release of the next-generation iPhone a few days before his death met with lukewarm reviews, whilst the launch of the Kindle Fire, by Amazon, made it clear that a new competitor had arrived on the scene.

REFERENCES

Hamel,G. (2010) The hole in the soul of business. *Wall Street Journal*, 13 January.

Jobs, S. (2011) Letter from Steve Jobs. Apple website, 24 August.

Rushe, D. (2011) Apple pips Exxon as world's biggest company. *Guardian*, 9 August.

INDEX